SEPECAT Jaguar

SEPECAT
Jaguar

Andy Evans

The Crowood Press

First published in 1998 by
The Crowood Press Ltd
Ramsbury, Marlborough
Wiltshire SN8 2HR

British Library Cataloguing-in-Publication Data
A catalogue record for this book is available from
the British Library.

ISBN 1 86126 144 6

Dedication
To Vicki, Michael, Olivia and
William

Photograph previous page: Hit hard, hit fast. via
Tony Thornborough

Typefaces used: Goudy (*text*),
Cheltenham (*headings*).

Typeset and designed by
D & N Publishing
Membury Business Park, Lambourn Woodlands
Hungerford, Berkshire.

Printed and bound by Butler & Tanner, Frome.

Acknowledgements

A project of this nature would not have
been possible without superb support and
aid from a range of sources. I would like to
take the opportunity to give special thanks
to three specific people: firstly, to Gordon
Bartley of British Aerospace for his considerable patience and enthusiastic support, especially in dealing with requests for
help, information and numerous archive
searches; secondly, to my good friend Tony
Thornborough for his generous assistance;
and thirdly, to Gary Parsons of the f4 Aviation Photobank for allowing me access to
his excellent pictures.

Thanks are also due to the following
people – in no order of preference!
Paul Jackson; John Oliver, Press Officer
at Rolls-Royce; Gary Madgwick of the
Aviation Workshop; Bob Kemp, GEC
Marconi; Matt Taylor, BAe; Luc Berger,
Communications Director at Dassault;
Shirley Grainger and Reg Harris at W.
Vinten; Capitaine J. Montel, Division
Presse du SIRPA AIR; Aerospatiale; Gen-
eral Patrick Henin (Ret'd), Assistant
Director of Communications at Thomson-
CSF; Graham Causer; Sqn Ldr Alex Mus-
kett; Sqn Ldr Peter Birch; Wg Cdr Chris
Harper; Flt Lt Jim Anderson (Ret'd),
Community Relations Officer at RAF
Lossiemouth; Flt Lt Jack Love, Communi-
ty Relations Officer at RAF Coltishall;
Dale Donovan at Headquarters Strike
Command PR; Sqn Ldr Andy Cubin; Sgt
Rick Brewell, DPR Photographic; Flt Lt
Guy Walker, Intelligence Officer at RAF
Coltishall; Cpl John Cassidy; and Flt Lt
Chris Carder.

Contents

Introduction

Someone once said that the Jaguar was '... a Hunter put together by a committee'.

In the early 1960s, international collaboration was the buzzword of the aviation industry. Many countries appreciated the long-term benefits of sharing costs, workloads and technology to achieve a common aim. From one such enterprise was born the SEPECAT Jaguar, product of an Anglo-French programme to produce a single aircraft type tailored to suit the needs of their respective air forces. Undoubtedly the Jaguar was one of the best equipped, most powerful and flexible strike aircraft of its age, yet for political reasons, and the machinations of one of the Anglo-French partner companies, it has not, until more recent times, achieved its full potential.

In France the Jaguar has been, and continues to be, involved in out-of-area combat operations, and although reductions in its strength as a result of the ending of the Cold War have been inevitable, its future as a part of France's arsenal has been well, if not quietly, established. Moreover, with no possibility of any future upgrading, the Jaguar will now see out its operational life condensed into three squadrons within one wing. In the overseas market, and to the constant frustration of the British side of SEPECAT – BAe, and previously BAC – the Jaguar achieved only 'restrained' export success, notably in the Middle East, South America and India, albeit in the constant shadow of direct competition from Dassault – the French half of SEPECAT.

In the UK, overshadowed by the more 'glamorous' Harrier and Tornado, the Jaguar was fast becoming the 'poor relation' of the Royal Air Force in the 1990s, destined to remain in service, as some

observed, merely to keep pilots occupied until the much-vaunted Eurofighter 2000 comes into service during the next century. Therefore, after nearly two decades of steady yet unspectacular duty, the RAF's Jaguar force seemed to be approaching an honourable and quiet retirement from front-line service. Having regularly played second fiddle to the already battle-proven Harrier, which gained immortality in the eyes of the public during the 1982 Falklands War, the Jaguar seemed now to be in the shadow of the new and highly capable Harrier GR.7. Indeed, many observers were looking to this latest incarnation of 'jump-jet' to form a new 'Rapid Reaction Wing' at Coltishall to supersede the Jaguar in its NATO commitments. Already replaced in the overland attack role in Germany by the Tornado GR.1 and removed from its Central European reconnaissance duties by the Tornado GR.1A, it seemed that time had finally come for the RAF's 'Big Cats'. Then the fickle finger of fate threw the Jaguar an unexpected lifeline. Saddam Hussein invaded Kuwait...

On 11 August 1990, the Jaguar suddenly began a new lease of life. Within forty-eight hours of the British Government's announcement that forces would be sent to the Middle East, a detachment of twelve aircraft left RAF Coltishall, bound for the Gulf. The Jaguar force's achievements in the ensuing conflict were astonishing, and not only were they one of the major success stories of the war, but they prompted the Jaguar's deployment for further Gulf-related policing operations following the cease-fire, policing the 'Safe Havens' set up by the United Nations to protect the Iraqi Marsh Arabs from Saddam Hussein.

No sooner were they relived of that duty than they were again thrust into the limelight in the skies above war-torn Bosnia-Hercegovina. Operating in two completely different conflicts, the Jaguar proved itself a formidable and flexible warplane; above and beyond the expectations of the commanders, competently undertaking any task given, and returning high rates of both serviceability and accuracy; all this from an aircraft that had already been written off in the minds of many. These statistics were not lost on the cost-conscious decision-makers at the Ministry of Defence, who now saw the aircraft in a new and different light. With further delays in the Eurofighter 2000 programme, and the RAF's lack of a 'rapid response' autonomous laser designation capability, the Air Staff turned to its attentions to the Jaguar, and by utilizing 'slippage money' from the Eurofighter programme, the aircraft has been given a new, updated and vital role within the UK's strike force.

1998 will see the 25th anniversary of the Jaguar in RAF service, and what more fitting tribute to the aircraft and those who fly her than this long overdue history of this vitally important, yet relatively unsung combat machine? The Jaguar is the last single-seat non-VSTOL fast jet in the Royal Air Force's inventory, and is therefore a much prized posting for the ambitious pilot. The story of the Jaguar is one of international co-operation, of intrigue, of triumph in the face of adversity; and yet it is one that has until now been largely overlooked. In this Crowood volume comes the real story of the 'Big Cat' – the SEPECAT Jaguar.

Andy Evans 1998

CHAPTER ONE

Accord – Discord

The origins of the SEPECAT Jaguar can be traced back to the early 1960s, and a truly unique joint project between Britain and France that was destined to produce the world's first joint-venture front-line combat aircraft. The unique nature of the project came by virtue of the two countries involved, who had traditionally distrusted each others' intentions and shared some deep political differences, culminating in the historic *Non* by President Charles de Gaulle on the question of Britain's entry into the Common Market.

At the beginning of the decade, however, both in the UK and in France, the various Government procurement agencies were examining their future aviation requirements, mostly with regard to a high-performance advanced training aircraft. In France, such an aircraft was needed to bridge the gap between the *Armée de l'Air*'s simple Fouga Magister trainer and advanced Dassault Mirage III fighter, and was required to enter service in 1970. In the UK, a replacement for the Folland Gnat and Hawker Hunter was also being sought, to enter service in around 1975. Both countries expressed an interest in the possibility of the aircraft also having a secondary strike role.

The French accordingly issued an internal requirement, commonly known as the ECAT (*École de Combat et Appui Tactique* – Tactical Combat Support Trainer) which was for a small, relatively simple, inexpensive, subsonic operational training aircraft, with an additional light strike role and able to operate not only from runways, but also from unprepared grass strips. Five companies were invited to submit designs to meet the requirement. On 30 June 1964, Breguet, then under the control of General Henri Ziegler, offered their Br.121, using the Br.1001 Taon as its base; a short time later Dassault came in with their Cavalier proposal (which bears more than a passing resemblance to the 1990s Rafale) as well as Nord with their 3600 Harpoon, Potez with their P.92 and Sud-Aviation and their SA-12.

As an aside to this, on 9 March 1964, when Benno Claude Vallieres launched the Dassault Cavalier, the first flight was planned for April 1965, so it could be presented at that year's Paris Air Show; probably as the 'successful' candidate. Furthermore, in May 1964, Dassault and Nord signed a confidential common accord, declaring that whichever company won the ECAT, the other would be brought in as a partner.

The ECAT designs were carefully considered and the winner announced as the Breguet Br.121, a decision which infuriated Marcel Dassault, who believed his design to be far superior. One of the main reasons cited for choosing the Breguet design over the others by the French Government was their decision that Dassault should not hold a monopoly on combat aircraft. However, this flew in the face of the fact that Breguet had designed fewer than 200 aircraft in twenty years and was ill-prepared for such a major industrial operation, a fact that the French Government needed to address a little later in the project's development. Under their winning ECAT submission, Breguet proposed five models of the Br.121: the Br.121A tactical fighter-bomber; the Br.121B two-seat fighter-bomber; the Br.121C interceptor; the Br.121D advanced trainer; and the Br.121P for tactical reconnaissance.

On the other side of the Channel the British requirements, which called for a supersonic advanced trainer for the RAF, and to a lesser degree the Royal Navy, had been drawn up under the Ministry of Defence's Air Staff Target AST 362. Several famous British companies were invited to make proposals: Hunting duly offered their H.155; Folland their Fo.147; English Electric (later BAC) their P.45; and the big new aerospace group, Hawker Siddeley, their P.1173. Not perhaps by virtue of a 'bolt from the blue' – the Governments of the two countries realized it might be a good idea to join forces and jointly develop a single aircraft type, tailored to meet the needs of their individual air forces – an 'accord' was reached following a meeting between Government Ministers Peter Thorneycroft and Pierre Messmer.

This was 1964, and international co-operation was already a buzzword around the aviation industry; after all, the Anglo-French Concorde civil project was already in existence, and in the corridors of Whitehall the idea of another Anglo-French partnership was being hailed as an excellent way of furthering Britain's chances of joining the Common Market. After much negotiation, most notably between the French Defence Minister Pierre Messmer and his British opposite number, Denis Healey, the respective administrations confirmed their interest in a common operational requirement for a single aircraft type, with both the *Armée de l'Air* and RAF being instructed to look at ways of harmonizing the two requirements.

Various submissions were received from both sides of the Channel (some ten were on the final list) and again it was the Breguet Br.121 that was eventually selected as the basis for the joint venture. As a result, a Memorandum of Understanding was signed by both Governments on 17 May 1965, with Breguet nominated as the French partner company and BAC as the British 'half'. The new forms of international co-operation that were explored with the aircraft would lead directly to future collaborative projects, such as Tornado and the Eurofighter 2000. In order to pour oil on the troubled waters of the British design teams, due mainly to the French predominance in the Br.121 project, another new aircraft type was also launched, based on the English Electric P.45 submission, this being a swing-wing supersonic fighter, to be known as the AFVG (Anglo-French Variable Geometry) to which BAC would be given the lead, in partnership with Breguet and Dassault.

Under the MoU, a new company was formed to administer the manufacture of both aircraft, and in May 1966 it was registered in France as SEPECAT (*Société Européenne de Production de L'Avion d'École*

Combat et d'Appui Tactique). It was to be supervised by a management committee, whose chairmanship would be equally shared between M B.C. Vallieres of Breguet and Sir Fredrick W. Page of BAC Preston, with officials from the Ministry of Defence, Ministry of Technology, the *Delegation Ministerelle pour l'Armament* and the *Etat-Major de l'Armée de l'Air et Aéronavale*. The airframe contracts for both parties was issued

In the same manner as the airframe, so was the engine to be a collaborative effort, with Rolls-Royce teaming up with French manufacturer Turbomeca to produce an all-new powerplant common to both the Br.121 and AFVG aircraft.

Despite the *Armée de l'Air*'s requirement for a relatively simple aircraft, the RAF wanted a more sophisticated machine with what they saw as the all-important

by the French, and the resultant increase in weight, along with a ferry range of 2,600 miles (4,200km) meant that the engine power had to be re-thought on a number of occasions.

Around the same time, however, many of the RAF's future combat aircraft aspirations began falling by the wayside. On 2 February 1965 the Labour Government of the day began taking a hard look at its

The first of the many, Jaguar B E-01. Of note are the undernose strakes, the air-intake splitter plates and the short nosewheel door, all items subsequently deleted from the production programme. BAe

by the DTCA (*Direction Technique de Construction Aéronautique*), and each country was committed to purchase 150 aircraft. The French had opted for seventy-five single seat 'A' (*appui* – support) strike versions and seventy-five two-seat 'E'(*école* – school) trainers, whereas the British preference was solely for 150 'B' (British) trainers, with no provision for any tactical variant.

supersonic performance, and this necessitated considerable re-design work on the original Br.121 proposal, resulting in a thinner wing, an area-ruled fuselage cross-section, an increased weapon load, and the sightline for the rear seat instructor's view improved – which meant re-shaping the forward fuselage. The RAF also wanted a far superior avionics fit than was required

future aircraft projects, and as a result cancelled the promising TSR.2 programme and also the supersonic P.1154/P.1173 VSTOL fighters. As if to add insult to injury, the French withdrew their support for the AFVG, citing lack of funds, which angered the British side as these funds were then seen to be diverted to their own swing-wing design! Interestingly enough, the UK Government had turned to the United States and ordered to replace TSR.2 the swing-wing General Dynamics F-111K, which was then cancelled in favour of the AFVG, which was also subsequently cancelled!

The story goes that following the May 1965 MoU concerning the AFVG, the UK wanted their choice of airframe, fitted with their choice of engine; these being the English Electric P.45 and the Rolls-Royce RB 153 turbofan. However, following more negotiations during June 1966, the partners agreed to let the French, that is, Dassault, take the lead in the airframe and the British act as partner, with Rolls-Royce now teaming up with SNECMA for the engines. In August 1966 came a further turnaround, when once again Britain was given the lead as a sop for having cancelled the F-111K in favour of the AFVG; this time with engines provided by Bristol Siddeley/SNECMA. However in the October, Rolls-Royce absorbed Bristol Siddeley, its major engine competitor. Suddenly it became apparent to the French camp that this was becoming a very one-sided partnership, and in late 1966 the French Defence Ministry decided to pull out, putting its finances into an indigenous project, the swing-wing Dassault Mirage G.

Suddenly the RAF found itself without a viable strike aircraft to fulfil its near-future needs. Attentions were turned to the only project that was past the 'drawing board' stage – the Jaguar, which thankfully could, with relative ease, be developed into a potent offensive warplane. With that in mind the RAF altered its requirements, and on 16 January 1967 amended the original MoU, ordering ninety of a new 'S' (strike) variant, and 110 'B' trainers, effectively adding an extra fifty aircraft to the earlier order. The French also increased their requirements by ordering a further fifty aircraft, forty of these being a new 'M' (*maritime*) version to meet a carrier-based requirement from the French Navy, with the balance being two-seat trainers. With the balance of strike/attack aircraft in the UK's inventory again coming under Government scrutiny during 1970, the RAF again refined its requirement, this time to 165 single-seat strike versions and only thirty-five two-seat trainers, with an option to purchase a further three of the latter. This effectively ended the RAF's interest in the Jaguar as an advanced training aircraft, with the two-seaters now to be used as operational trainers for *ab-initio* pilots posted to the Jaguar.

During 1967, the French Government undertook a rationalization of its aircraft industry, and as a result Breguet were taken over, or 'merged', with Dassault, the company from then on being known as Dassault-Breguet (although the 'Breguet' half was dropped in 1992). Worth observing was the French Government's concern that Breguet Aviation, a small company with limited means, would not be able to measure up to a giant like the British Aircraft Corporation: the merger with Dassault was seen as restoring the balance. As already noted Marcel Dassault was none to pleased at loosing out on the ECAT contract. By the time of the take-over he already had numerous projects on the drawing board, and in reality was not too concerned about this 'joint little aircraft programme', but no doubt was happy about the revenue it would bring in. Dassault now found himself in control of a project, and a philosophy, he neither liked nor agreed with, in addition to which the Br.121 or Jaguar as it was now known, was perceived by BAC as a major player in the export field, where it would inevitably be in competition with Dassault's Mirage. As a partner in SEPECAT, Dassault knew every detail of any export Jaguar submission, a fact that was to have repercussions later. It is now generally recognized that had Dassault not been so intransigent about the overseas sales prospects for the Jaguar, it would have enjoyed far greater export success than it actually did.

In the UK also, changes were afoot in the aerospace community with the Government stepping in to nationalize the British Aircraft Company in 1971, making it part of the new British Aerospace (BAe).

Developing the Breed – Jaguar Design

During the various phases of the Jaguar's evolution there have been five separate versions of the aircraft These were:

Jaguar E An advanced trainer for the French Air Force, with twin Martin-Baker Mk4 seats, DEFA 30mm cannon, five external store points, a twin gyro platform with compass, no automatic navigation equipment, a TACAN and gyro gunsight and a runway arrestor hook stressed to 2g.

Jaguar A A single-seat strike version for the French, with Martin-Baker Mk4 seat, DEFA cannon, five stores points, a nav/attack system essentially that of the Mirage IV, twin gyro platform with Doppler giving inputs to the navigation and bombing computers, TACAN, VOR/ILS, ECM, computer for Martel ASM, internal IFR probe and runway arrestor hook stressed to 2g.

Jaguar M Single-seat carrier-based variant for the French Navy, with strengthened undercarriage and twin nosewheel and single mainwheels, Martin-Baker Mk9 seat, DEFA cannon, avionics the same as the Jaguar A, an undernose laser rangefinder, an internal IFR probe and aircraft carrier arrestor hook.

Jaguar S Single-seat version for the RAF, designated GR.1 in the UK, with Martin-Baker Mk9 seat, twin 30mm Aden cannon, five stores points, nav/attack system based on an internal platform and central nav digital computer, projected moving map display, head-up display, laser rangefinder, TACAN, internal IFR probe and runway arrestor hook stressed to 2g.

Jaguar B Two-seat trainer for the RAF, designated T.2, with single Aden cannon, Martin-Baker Mk9 seats, five stores points, nav/attack system the same as that of the Jaguar S, no laser rangefinder, and runway arrestor hook stressed to 2g.

From the outset, it was clear that the RAF's Jaguar S was set to be a far more complex attack aircraft than its French counterpart, and relied on some of the very cutting edge of the available digital avionics technology. As with all aircraft types, the Jaguar's shape was decided by the role it was to perform, and the basic Jaguar style is therefore

---

Naming the Beast

When jointly developing an aircraft, it is a difficult task to decide just what to call it, especially when the meaning must be the same in two different languages. Such was the problem that faced SEPECAT. About six names were forwarded, and *Etoile* (star) was suggested as a possibility by the French, but soon removed. The final three letters of the company's name, CAT, had an obvious influence, and the word Jaguar has the same meaning in both English and French. One problem emerged with this selection: Jaguar Cars already had quite a monopoly on the use of the chosen name. A call to the managing director of Jaguar Cars put all to rights, with the car manufacturer also making maximum PR from the deal, and the name 'Jaguar' became the official title for the Anglo-French project, being announced as such in time for the 1965 Paris Air Salon.

common to all types, individual users specifying the avionics and tactical systems to suit their own needs. The official line during the early days, described the Jaguar as:

An all metal–aluminium alloy with titanium alloy around the engine bay areas. Shoulder-winged aircraft with high lift devices, controlled by wing spoilers, with an all-moving tailplane and rudder. To enable the aircraft to operate from rough field sites the undercarriage is designed to accept a vertical velocity of 11.8ft/sec (3.6m/sec), with low pressure tyres fitted to the twin mainwheels and a single nosewheel. Ejection seats are of Martin-Baker Mk4 or Mk9 type, with a windscreen bullet-proof against up to 7.65mm rifle fire. Weaponry can include Martel ASM, Sidewinder AAM, two internal 30mm guns and all sizes of high explosive bombs or rockets, together with a dedicated reconnaissance pack, flares, unguided rockets and external fuel tanks. Flight controls are mechanically linked to 3,000lb/sq in (210kg/cm^2) Fairey Hydraulics power control jack rams that work in tandem within a double body, actuating the rudder, all-moving tailplane and spoilers. Artificial feel in three axis is obtained by means of springs. Armour is used in the front of the cockpit, and the windshield is also designed to be effective against bird strikes at up to 600kt (1,110km/h). Self-sealing fuel lines and internal fuel tanks are installed and fuel transfer is independent for each tank. Hydraulic and electrical systems are duplicated. Usable internal fuel comes from a 200 imp gal (909ltr) tank in the front fuselage, 258 imp gal (1,173ltr) in the centre fuselage, 252 imp gal (1,146ltr) in the rear fuselage and 210 imp gal (955ltr) in the wings.

The Jaguar would be able to operate a good basic tactical mission relying on internal fuel alone, and have a good weapon-carrying capability. In the realms of ground handling the philosophy was simple: engine changes in thirty minutes; access to engines without step ladders and plug-in equipment easily replaced; and a fifteen-minute turnaround, including re-fuel and re-arm. Engine access was excellent, via two upward-hinging panels that wrapped around the powerplants themselves, allowing not only for ease of maintenance, but also for groundcrew to be able to work at eye-level.

The Jaguar's perceived war role and training duties dictated a shoulder-winged design with a high wing loading, to reduce gust response at low level, where it was anticipated the Jaguar would spend most of its operational life. However, the aircraft also needed to have a good field performance, so a highly efficient 'thin wing' was developed for the aircraft which would not only lower take-off and approach speeds, but also have retractable slats on the outboard leading edge, full span double slotted trailing edge flaps, and a 40-degree quarter chord wing sweep with a 3-degree anhedral. The leading edge slats could also be partially extended during high 'g' turns to provide additional lift. Boundary layer control was at one time considered, but was dismissed because of its inherently complex nature and the loss of thrust it would cause through bleeding large quantities of air from the engines. As there was no room on the wing for conventional ailerons, roll power was provided by spoilers placed on the upper surface, balanced by differential movements of the tailplanes, and to counter any adverse yaw, both tailplane and spoilers were interconnected. Petal-type airbrakes were installed under the rear fuselage; these were originally of a plain design, but to reduce buffet they were later perforated. A taller fin was also introduced and a bulge incorporated in the spine to house the heat exchangers. The slab tailplanes themselves had a pronounced anhedral similar to those of the F-4 Phantom, in order to keep them below the wing wash at high angles of attack. Forward strakes were fitted to one of the prototype aircraft, but later removed; however, the rear underside strakes remained a permanent feature. Flying controls were designed to be powered with duplicate back-up systems, with a Smiths autostabilizer system operating the rudder and tailplanes, with a spoiler autostabilizer also being added to cope with turbulence at very low altitudes. The airframe was stressed to 8.6g limits, with a design maximum of 12g, which

---

The Measurement Problem

An interesting aside to the story is one of measurements. The French worked in the metric system while British engineers operated in feet and inches. The two teams achieved mutual understanding during the 'blackboard' phases, but although the first prototype was virtually hand-built using both systems, it was obvious that this could not continue into the production phase. With the UK's intention to 'go metric' in the early 1970s, it was widely anticipated that the Jaguar would follow suit. In fact, just the opposite happened. All the measurements used the English system, although they are also annotated in metric.

---

gives some impression of the strength of the aircraft.

The intakes were made wedge-shaped to take account of their greater efficiency at higher speeds, with two spring-loaded auxiliary inlet doors on each side. Splitter plates were initially added but later deleted, and even variable-geometry ramps were being considered at one time. With the airframe being designed with a 12g load factor at combat weight, each aircraft was calculated as having 3,000 flying hours for single-seaters and 6,000 flying hours for two-seaters.

Technical advances in the production of materials were also a key feature in the Jaguar's engineering, and it was the first production military aircraft on which BAC had used new bonding techniques which mated chemi-milled skin panels to an adhesive-bonded aluminium core. The bond between the honeycomb and the skin had to be constant, and this necessitated new inspection techniques. Developed by Ultrasonascope and BAC, a device was built using ultrasonic probes to pinpoint any bond failures. Apart from titanium used around the engines, the Jaguar was mostly aluminium clad sheets, drawn sections and forgings, the wing, fin and tailplane torque box skins being machined solid alloy. Stainless steel was used in the high-stress components such as the tailplane spigot housing and the fin and pylon attachment points. The total internal fuel capacity was set to 264gal (1,200ltr) and the fuel system was armoured in its important sections to prevent damage from ground fire.

The aircraft featured Messier Hispano Bugatti landing gear onto which are fitted twin Dunlop mainwheels, with low pressure tyres of 5.91kg/cm^2 (84lb/sq in) and anti-skid brakes, augmented by a 18ft-diameter Irvin brake parachute stowed in the extreme rear of the fuselage. The forward door on the mainwheel bay remains closed except when the leg is in motion, thereby reducing the risk of FOD (Foreign Object Damage) ingestion The landing gear's curious 'gangly' appearance affords the aircraft its superb rough field performance. The two-seat Jaguar's forward fuselage was carefully 'sculptured' so as to provide maximum forward vision for the back-seater, and minimum drag.

As Wg Cdr Clive Walker, the Officer Commanding the RAF's Jaguar Conversion Team, later commented, 'The designers have got their priorities absolutely right ... Everything that matters is right in front of you ... the object of the exercise is to put a bomb on the target ... something that Jaguar does better than anything else we currently have.'

Paving the Way – Prototype Jaguars

The shape of the Jaguar first emerged as a wooden mock-up representing the British two-seater. Built at Warton, the 'fake' Jaguar was designed basically to check the engineering, the layout and its compatibility, and was displayed at the 1967 Paris show. An agreement to cover the production of the first 400 aircraft was signed in London on 9 January 1968 by the then Secretary of State for Defence, Denis Healey, Secretary of State for Technology John Stonehouse and the French *Ministre des Armées* Pierre Messmer. By that date, the first of the 'real' prototypes was nearly complete, and to this another seven were to be added, four for the *Armée de l'Air* and three for the RAF. In all there were to be eight prototypes, and the programme was so integrated as to ensure there was as little duplication of effort as possible on both sides of the Channel. Construction was therefore to be shared as equitably as possible between the partners. The nose, fuselage, centre sections and undercarriage were to be made by Breguet, and the wings, tail unit, rear fuselage and engine air-intakes by BAC. These items were then exchanged across the Channel and mated together on two identical production lines set up at BAC's Military Aircraft Division at Warton and at Colomiers on the Toulouse-Blagnac airport site in France, where all the prototypes were to be built.

The first of the 'Cats', powered by the still-developing Adour Mk101, was a French two-seater, E-01 (coded 'B') F-ZWRB, which was rolled out on 17 April 1968, and for the start of static ground tests and engine running trials was sent to the Breguet factory at Velizy-Villacoubay near Paris. Painted up in grey and green disruptive camouflage with dull aluminium undersides, E-01 carried a rather splendid red, white and blue vertically striped rudder.

On completion of the ground testing phase it was dismantled and shipped by road to the *Centre d'Essais et Vol* at Istres near Marseilles. Its maiden flight was set for the early summer, but due to the state of near-revolution that existed in France

Jaguar E-01 demonstrates some of its features, such as the rough field landing gear, the shoulder-wing design and the full span double slotted trailing edge flaps. BAe

in middle of 1968 was delayed until the autumn. Preliminary taxi trials began in late August, and minor technical hitches prevented its appearance at that year's Farnborough Air Show. The first flight finally took place on 8 September 1968, with Breguet's chief test pilot, 42-year-old

Bernard Witt, at the controls. The flight began at 9.20am, the aircraft being taken up to 17,000ft for a 25-minute sortie, after which Witt reported he had no problems; however, further trials were not entirely satisfactory, as the Adour engines were not yet perfected, particularly with regard to

The first French Jaguar E two-seat prototype, E-01, being readied for flight by engineers at the Centre d'Essais et Vol at Istres. The first flight took place on 8 September 1968, with Breguet's chief test pilot, Bernard Witt, at the controls. BAe

fuel consumption and the afterburner. BAC Preston's chief test pilot, Jimmy Dell, accompanied the Jaguar in a Hunter chase aircraft.

On the aircraft's third flight it was taken supersonic, and thereafter was regularly flown by Witt and Dell, investigating the aerodynamics and handling qualities of the aircraft. The second prototype, E-02 F-ZWRC, was also a French two-seater, which first flew for sixty-five minutes on 11 February 1969, also from Istres, with Witt at the helm. The aircraft was subsequently presented at that year's Paris Air Show, wearing the side number '308'. It made its final flight on 28 February 1979, subsequently being air-freighted to the French Technical Training School at Rochfort on 7 June 1989.

The first of the single-seat aircraft, the French A-03 F-ZWRD, took to the air for the first time on 29 March 1969, once again with Bernard Witt at the controls.

The aircraft was airborne for just over seventy minutes, to glowing praise from its pilot, although it ended its life rather ignominiously after a heavy landing at Tarnos on 14 February 1972. A-04 F-ZWRE (coded 'E'), the second French single-seat prototype, flew on 27 May 1969 from Istres, with Jimmy Dell in the 'office', for a 45-minute trip; this aircraft was later retired and displayed in the *Musée de l'Air* at Paris-Le Bourget in 1979. This was followed in the November by the maritime variant, M-05, with Jaques Jessberger undertaking a 30-minute flight.

Around this time the Jaguars began putting in a few select public appearances, the first of these at the Paris Air Salon at Le Bourget, and later at the Central Flying School's 57th anniversary celebrations at Little Rissington, when a single-seater was flown by Jimmy Dell in the presence of the Queen, the Duke of Edinburgh and the Queen Mother.

The first British-assembled prototype, S-06 XW560, was rolled out at BAC Warton on 18 August 1969, and flew for the first time on 12 October, with Jimmy Dell at the controls, going supersonic at the first attempt. The aircraft was used for gunnery tests and stores trials before being burnt out during a ground fire at Boscombe Down on 11 August 1972. The second British prototype, S-07 XW563, did not get airborne until June 1970, and was later used for trials of the Matra Magic AAM before being flown to RAF Brüggen in January 1978 for use as an instructional airframe. S-07, built by the English Electric Division of BAC at Warton, was later to be fitted with the Elliott digital inertial navigation and weapon aiming system – the first such item of its kind to be produced in Europe. The aircraft featured the 'chisel nose' that was to become the main distinguishing feature of the RAF aircraft, albeit having the LRMTS windows faired over. Its nose and centre fuselage were later mated with 'bits' from other Jaguars and, painted up as XX822, it was put on static display on 25 October 1985. The eighth and final aircraft, B-08 XW566, the British two-seat Jaguar, was flown from Warton by BAC Preston's test pilot, Paul Millett, on 30 August 1971 on a 50-minute flight, and by this time eighty per cent of B-08's airframe was made up of 'production' parts. XW566 was put into store at Farnborough during 1985.

23 February 1971 saw Paul Millett take S-06 on a direct flight from Preston to Istres,

way, with S-06 and S-07 gaining 263 hours in the air as part of a 261-sortie package, S-07 making its 200th flight on 17 March. Changes were made to a few of the airframe parts from the development stage: the short nosewheel door with its unique twin landing light array was extended to full length; the intake splitter plates were deleted; perforations added to the airbrakes as a standard feature; and the original 'short tail' was modified on the two British prototypes to the current 'tall' standard, in order to give additional stability during manoeuvring. Starting with prototype B-08, the original

M-05   Maritime compatibility, catapult launches and arrested recoveries.
S-06   British weapons trials and IFR studies.
S-07   RAF navigation and attack system tests.
B-08   Training options and navigation and attack trials.

As has been discussed previously, the backdrop of the Jaguar prototype testing phase was overshadowed by the merger of Breguet and Dassault, and the associated problems this caused. Combined with that was the

The first of the single-seat aircraft, the French A-03 took to the air for the first time on 29 March 1969, with once again Bernard Witt at the controls. The second French single-seat prototype, A-04, flew on 27 May 1969 from Istres, with BAC pilot Jimmy Dell at the controls. BAe

its longest sojourn to date, and a journey of some 738nm (1,366km), with a duration of 1hr 25mins. Later that same month the RAF got their first real look at the Jaguar with S-07 at Warton, some twenty technicians taking the aircraft to pieces during a Servicing Appraisal Exercise (SAE), and came away with a very favourable report. Ground handling trials were also undertaken by S-07, proving the aircraft's compatibility with RAF flight servicing equipment. By the early spring of 1971, the British portion of the test programme was well under-

one-piece starboard hinging nosewheel door was split into a three-door unit.

The duties of the prototypes were as follows:

E-01   General systems tests, handling and control evaluation, and flutter trials.
E-02   Engine optimization trials and flight performance tests.
A-03   Navigation and attack systems for the French tactical aircraft.
A-04   Weapons and stores carriage, and weapon firing trials.

loss of the first Jaguar prototype, E-01, in an accident on 26 March 1970, when the aircraft suffered a catastrophic fire in its No.2 engine and crashed on approach to Istres. Later described as 'finger trouble' on the part of its French pilot, an engine bay fire warning light indicated a problem during a test flight and the pilot shut down the errant powerplant and selected the fire suppression system – losing in the process one of the two main hydraulic systems. The second engine was also shut down in order to reduce thrust as the aircraft came over the runway,

The first three Jaguar prototypes in close formation, a pair of two-seaters and a single Jaguar A. BAe

Single-seater A-03, used for navigation and attack system trials for the French tactical version. BAe

thereby losing the second hydraulic system as well. The pilot did not select manual emergency power, and with no automatic system available to operate the hydraulics the controls froze, and the pilot was left with little choice but to eject. This led to the installation of an automated electrical power system which cuts in if a double engine failure occurs. This mishap did not, however, detract from the onward march of

September 1971, flying the 600 miles (965km) from the Breguet airfield at Caza-ux, near Bordeaux, to Warton with Paul Millett at the controls and Brian McCann as his navigator. The aircraft was to join the Warton test programme alongside the RAF-specification Jaguars S-06, S-07 and B-08, and undertook engine development trials, staying in the UK until 1980 when it was returned to France.

aircraft, S1 XX108, made its maiden flight from Warton on 12 October that year in the hands of Tim Ferguson, BAC's Deputy Chief Test Pilot, being airborne for 1hr 11mins. S2 XX019, the second British production aircraft, and was the first aircraft to have the definitive LRMTS and full avionics package. The RAF's initial production two-seat Jaguar, T.2 XX136, first flew on 28 March 1972. The first batch of

One of the early production examples for the RAF, XW563, which was later retained by BAC as a trials aircraft. Note the early 'French style' nose, lacking the LRMTS, and the faired-over cannon ports. BAe

the Jaguar programme. With the cancellation of the Jaguar M, discussed further on pp.36–8, there were only to be two basic variants for full production, the tactical Jaguar A/S and the Jaguar B/E for training.

The French-assembled Jaguar E-02 travelled across the English Channel on 9

Initial Production Aircraft

The French Air Force were the first to receive the Jaguar, and the initial production A-model rolled off the assembly line at Mont-de-Marsan, near Bordeaux, on 4 May 1972. The RAF's first production

production aircraft were despatched to Boscombe Down for type proving before the aircraft was released for RAF service. Aircraft S4 XX111 was delivered to RAF Lossiemouth in Scotland on 30 May 1973 for ground crew training whilst S1 was retained by BAC for further trials work,

An impressive nose-on shot of Jaguar prototype S-07, loaded with four 1,000lb (454kg) bombs, four MATRA 155 rocket pods and a 264gal (1,200ltr) underfuselage tank. BAe

including being upgraded to become the first Jaguar International. Early British two-seaters initially had intake splitter plates fitted.

'Power Station' – The Rolls-Royce/Turbomeca Adour Engine

The powerplant for the new aircraft was also to be an Anglo-French effort as, with the airframe being an joint venture, it was natural that the engine should follow suit. Both governments had decided that only manufacturers willing to participate in a collaborative effort would be considered for any proposals, and to this end two joint companies were formed to compete for the contract. Bristol-Siddeley teamed up with the French company SNECMA, and Rolls-Royce joined forces with Turbomeca, with the latter pair being selected.

Turbomeca had been already involved from the French side, with their Turbo-

meca T-260 Tourmalet powerplant, which was the proposed but unsuccessful powerplant for the original Breguet Br.121 design as part of the ECAT submission, and the British had already been informed of Breguet's preference for their Rolls-Royce RB172 turbofan. It was therefore agreed that a joint company, which was registered in 1966 in the UK as Rolls-Royce/Turbomeca Limited, should develop an all-new powerplant to go into the latest airframe. Hereby came a problem, and one that aerospace companies almost always try to avoid: developing a new airframe and a new engine to power it at the same time. Within this context, the main problem became clear: as the powerplant was specific to the Jaguar, there were no flying test beds available to trial the engine, so all the air testing had to be done within the Jaguar's airframe evaluation programme.

supersonic operations, as well as meeting the demands of a low-level 'dash'. Production lines were established both at Derby in the UK and Tarnos in France and, working in parallel, development got underway.

The basic layout of the Adour was to be of twin-shaft design, with the main components being a two stage low pressure compressor, driven by a single stage low

9,600lb with reheat, the degree of which being variable under pilot control. All these features were squeezed into a small, short yet powerful engine.

Ease of maintenance was another issue high on the agenda. The initial specification called for the ability to make a simple engine change achievable within thirty minutes, and also to make use of plug-in-

Early production examples XW560 and XW563 in close formation. Of note is the high-gloss paintwork, which was later changed for a matt finish, and the original tall tail. BAe

With its basis in the RB172, and including parts from the Turmolet T-260, the new engine was named the RT172 Adour, after a French river – thereby continuing the Rolls-Royce tradition of naming engines after rivers – and was specifically sized to fit the Jaguar's airframe. It was to have good specific fuel consumption, with a high by-pass ratio, and at the same time be able to develop high thrust for take-off and

pressure turbine, and a five stage high pressure compressor driven by a single stage high pressure turbine, with the combustion system consisting of a single, fully annular chamber. By-pass ratio was 1 and the pressure ratio 9:6, with the engine not being fitted with inlet guide vanes so that it would be less prone to ingestion problems. Maximum dry thrust was in the order of 4,600lb, which could be boosted to

type support equipment. Therefore, each Adour was internally suspended within the airframe by three mountings, which included spherical bearings. The engine bay access panels were attached to the fuselage by means of special pins and could be hinged upward, positioned at 60 or 80 degrees and locked, or completely removed, for maintenance. The engine could be disconnected with the panels opened at 60 degrees, and could be removed with them positioned at 80 degrees. For the Adour engine, the design team were told to 'KISS' it – 'Keep It Simple, Son', yet make it rugged enough to achieve the target figure of 1,000 hours run time between overhauls.

Work on the engine was split between Rolls-Royce and Turbomeca, with Rolls-Royce being responsible for the combustion chamber, turbine, mixer and other components, and Turbomeca for producing the low and high pressure compressors, the intermediate casing, the gearbox, afterburner and jet nozzle assemblies. The

engines were then assembled on production lines at Derby and Tarnos. Twin-engine safety was one of the requirements given to the design teams, as it improved survivability over a single-engined aircraft. Maximum speed for the Jaguar with its twin Adour installation was to be of the order of Mach 1.1 at low level and Mach 1.7 at altitude, with a mission radius of, lo-lo-lo, some 410 miles (650km) with internal fuel or 530 miles (850km) with external fuel; lo-hi-lo, 780 miles (1,250km) with internal fuel or 1,030 miles (1,650km) with external fuel; and having a ferry range of some 2,800 miles (4,500km). The maximum dry thrust

for the Adour Mk102 was to be in excess of 4,400lb (2,000kg), with maximum reheat thrust in excess of 6,600lb (3,000kg).

The first Adour was successfully bench tested on 9 May 1967 at the Rolls-Royce Derby plant; however, it was noted that there were problems when reheat was selected. This problem also came to light during the air tests, when the reheat seemed to have little or no effect until 30 per cent reheat was selected. Thrust problems were found to be responsible for a heavy landing by the maritime Jaguar, which badly damaged the airframe. The initial specification had called for landings to be achieved on

Maintenance of the Jaguar's Adour engine has never been a problem thanks to the removable access panels, the easy working height and their semi-external location. The engine bay access panels were attached to the fuselage by means of special pins, and could be hinged upward, positioned at 60 or 80 degrees and locked for maintenance, or, as here, completely removed. Rolls-Royce

one engine using only dry thrust; however, development flying again showed this to be unsuitable with the aircraft at its all-up weight. The fuel efficiency of the engine was good, but in its Mk101 form the Adour, which had been tailored for the Jaguar's cruising flight, needed a powerful afterburner to meet the take-off and supersonic requirements. As designed, the Mk101's afterburner engaged at around 104 per cent rpm to give an immediate 30 per cent boost, being variable up to 50 per cent. However, on approach the aircraft's lift and drag characteristics were such that it needed more than the maximum available dry power and less than minimum afterburner for an immediate recovery following the failure of one of the engines. To allow for greater flexibility, and to solve the afterburner problems, a 'part-throttle reheat system' (PTR) was introduced on

making single-engine recoveries possible at higher weights. The Mk102 powered all the RAF Jaguars, and was introduced to the French aircraft from the thirty-six development engines and the forty Mk101s, and installed from the eleventh French Jaguar onwards.

A 'blip' occurred on 4 February 1971 when Rolls-Royce went bankrupt, but in an effort to save one of British industry's 'flagship' companies, their problems were soon addressed, when the UK Government stepped in and nationalized the firm. However, the French engine industry eagerly seized at the chance to push its SNECMA Atar engine, as an alternative for the Jaguar. Whilst having twice the thrust at half the cost of the Adour, the Atar would have been totally unsuitable for the aircraft's *raison d'etre* of low-level operations.

Jaguar Powerplants	
Jaguar Prototypes	Two Adour Mk101 turbofans
Jaguar GR.1	Two Adour Mk102 turbofans RT172-26
Jaguar GR.1A	Two Adour Mk104 turbofans RT172-56
Jaguar T.2	Two Adour Mk102 turbofans RT172-26
Jaguar T.2A	Two Adour Mk104 turbofans RT172-56
Jaguar GR.3/T.4	Two Adour Mk811 'hybrid' turbofans
Jaguar A	Two Adour Mk 102 turbofans
Jaguar E International	Two Adour Mk102 turbofans
Jaguar International Single-seat	Two Adour Mk804 or Mk811 turbofans

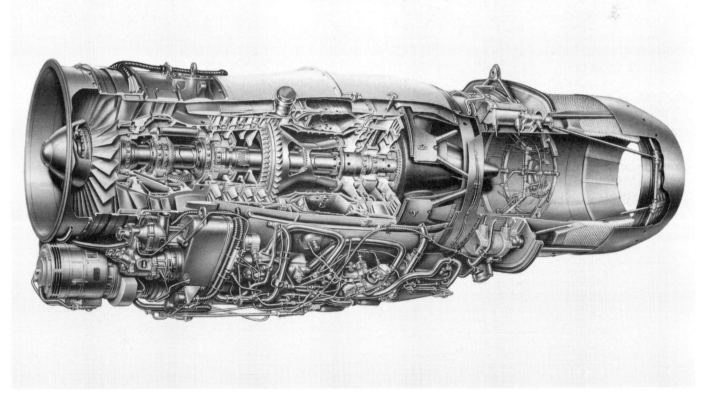

Cutaway section of the Adour. Rolls-Royce

the production Adour Mk102, allowing operations to be continued within the dry thrust range and permitting continuous power without extinguishing or having to re-light the engine to maximum, thereby

After what had been considered to be a 'shaky' beginning, the Adour has developed into one of the most respected engines in the world, and was the powerplant chosen for all versions of the hugely

successful BAe Hawk, including its McDonnell Douglas/BAe T-45 Goshawk variant, and it continues to be improved to meet new customers' requirements.

Omani Air Force ground crew 'check out' one of the Jaguar International's Adour Mk811 turbofans.
Rolls-Royce

The Means to Justify the End?

In 1971 French Government auditors examined the financial results of the development programme, and concluded that Jaguar had cost 1,200 million francs to produce, which, when compared to the more complex Mirage IV at 635 million francs and the Mirage F.1 at 670 million, seemed to be quite excessive. From the originally authorized finance for the design and prototype stage of 120 million, the figure had risen to over 864 million, thus spending had increased sevenfold, and the original costings were 'underestimated in a way that

did not seem entirely satisfactory'. The Jaguar project was not, as has been appreciated, without its problems, but at the end of the day was the collaborative project worthwhile? What began as a need for a common advanced training aircraft never materialized, with both the British and French two-seat Jaguars eventually being used only for conversion or continuation training; and what was presented as an urgent requirement in 1964 did not actually enter service until 1973. In addition to this, it was necessary for the partner countries to each go on and develop a new training aircraft as well; in the UK the Hawk,

and in France – in co-operation with Germany – the Alpha Jet. The Jaguar never achieved its potential in the export field, and lacked the drive to add much-needed avionics fits until the aircraft was called upon to go to war. As Dassault's Jaques Desmazures later explained:

> The Jaguar could have been an even greater aircraft, because it was a real 'bomb wagon', but having to increase its mass, it had far too much drag and was underpowered. As more speed was also required, plus a new wing design; these re-design features did not allow for sufficient augmentation, and the aircraft suffered as a consequence.

CHAPTER TWO

Les Felins Français

Armée de l'Air Jaguars

Deliveries of *Le Jaguar* to the French Air Force began on 4 May 1972, when the first of the production machines rolled out of the final assembly shop at Mont de Marsan, where the first pilots and groundcrew had also undertaken basic and advanced training in preparation for forming the first operational training unit at St Dizier in north-eastern France. Priority had been given to the manufacture of the Jaguar E two-seat version, and the total order for forty training aircraft was fulfilled by early 1976. Jaguar E1 first flew on 2 November 1971, whereas Jaguar A1 did not make its first flight until 20 April 1972.

Jaguar A

Unlike the Royal Air Force with its sophisticated avionics equipment fit, the French had opted for a far simpler mission suite, as they perceived the Jaguar A in the battlefield support/stand-off role, and therefore did not require the more complex systems of the GR.1. Likewise, the Jaguar E has only the most basic of flight systems, and is a 'basic conversion trainer', whereas the RAF's Jaguar T.2 was from the outset designed to have a full operational capability. This lack of parity, particularly between the French E and A models has been the source of considerable comment by the *Armée de l'Air* over the years, in that the training vehicle is not representative of the front-line version, but at this late stage in the Jaguar's career there seems little likelihood of change.

The Jaguar A, therefore, is fitted with the following: an SFIM 250-1 twin-gyro inertial platform; a Jaguar ELIDA air data computer system; a Thomson-CSF 121 fire-control sighting unit/weapons selector with an adaptor and a sighting camera; a Decca RDN 72 EMD Doppler radar; a Crouzet Type 90 navigation computer and target selector; a fin-mounted Thomson-CSF passive radar warning receiver; a Thomson-CSF 31 weapons aiming computer; a Thomson-CSF RL50Pj incidence probe with angle-of-attack indicator; a Thomson-CSF HUD; and a Dassault fire control computer for launch control of the Matra Martel anti-radar missile. Ejection seats were originally of the French-built Martin-Baker JRM4 type, capable of zero altitude use, but only at speeds below 104mph; these were later replaced by the more capable Martin-Baker FB9, with true 'zero-zero' capability. Also included was an Omera strike camera and a retractable IFR probe. Radios included VHF/UHF, VOR/ILS IFF and Tacan. Internally, the Jaguar A has twin DEFA 550 30mm cannon with 150 rounds of ammunition each, developed from the German MG213C design of World War II. It has an external stores load of some 10,000lb. As with the RAF Jaguars, the French aircraft were originally powered by the Adour Mk102 engines, which have subsequently been upgraded to Mk104 standard.

Beginning in February 1977 with airframe A81, the Jaguar As were fitted with a Thomson/CSF CILAS TAV-38 laser rangefinder in an undernose blister fairing with an optically flat circular aperture facing forward, an element 'borrowed' from the Jaguar M which in clear conditions has an air-to-ground range of some 6.3 miles (10km) and an accuracy to 16ft (4.8m). This equipment was also retro-fitted to a small number of earlier aircraft. The TAV-38s window should, however, not be confused with the window for the Omera 40 panoramic camera, which was moved to the rear of the blister fairing. Jaguars assigned to EC 1/11 and to 3/11 were retro-fitted with the nose camera in 1978, while those of EC 4/11, beginning with airframe A113, had them installed on the production line. Jaguar airframes A131 to A160 were also given the provision to carry the Thomson-CSF ATLIS I and later ATLIS II targeting pod, to be used either in conjunction with the Aerospatiale AS.30L

Specification – Jaguar A	
Type:	Single-seat tactical strike and ground attack fighter/bomber
Accommodation:	Pilot only, in Martin-Baker JRM4/FB9 ejector seat
Powerplant:	Two Rolls-Royce/Turbomeca Adour Mk102 afterburning turbofans
Performance:	Max speed 1,056mph (1,690km/h) Initial climb 30,000ft (9,100m) in 90sec Service ceiling 45,930ft (13,920m) Range 870 miles (1,392km) tactical
Weights:	Empty 15,432lb (7,000kg); normal 24,149lb (11,000kg); max 34,612lb (15,700kg)
Dimensions:	Length 55ft 2.5in (16.73m); span 28ft 6in (8.64m); height: 16ft 10.5in (5.11m)
Armament:	Two 30mm DEFA cannon with 150 rounds per gun, five external hardpoints for a total of 10,000lb (4,545kg) of stores. Capable of carrying ATLIS/AS.30L, bombs, rocket pods, Matra 550 Magic AAMs, Durandal and other non-nuclear munitions.

guided missile or for stand-off/self-designation of laser guided bombs. The aircraft can also carry up to three RP36 264gal (1,200ltr) external fuel tanks for roles that required intervention overseas, giving the Jaguar a range of 2,285 miles (3,650km) and an endurance of ten hours. It was envisaged that the Jaguar would have a specific reconnaissance role, possibly as a replacement for the Mirage IIIR, with a

tasked with carrying the French AN52 nuclear bomb; EC 1/7, 3/7 and 4/7 were therefore also assigned to nuclear strike. Their duty was to be that of clearing a path for the Mirage IVA strategic bombers, a role that was eventually withdrawn on 1 September 1991. For the nuclear role, the Jaguars would have been configured with a centreline AN52, two RP36 fuel tanks on their inner wing pylons, and two Phimat

retarded weapons; 400kg and 1,000kg laser guided bombs; Matra F1 pods containing thirty-six 68mm rockets or F2 containing six 68mm rockets; Matra F3 pods containing four 100mm rockets; Matra-Brandt Belouga BLG 66 grenade launchers; Brandt BAP-100 anti-runway bomblets; BAT-120 anti-armour bomblets; Matra Durandal runway denial rocket propelled bombs; and Matra 550 Magic AAMs.

Jaguar A4 carrying a pair of Aerospatiale AS.30L missiles and an underfuselage ATLIS targeting pod.
Aerospatiale

revised nose section fitted with a camera suite. The French military opted for the Mirage F1.CR to fulfill that role, with the Jaguar retaining a limited reconnaissance capability as a secondary mission, using a centreline-mounted RP36P camera pod.

In addition to its conventional strike/attack duties, it was announced that the *Armée de l'Air* Jaguars would also be

pods on the outer wing pylons. EC 2/11, who specialized in defence supression, carried in addition to their Martel missiles two Caiman (or CT51) jammer pods on their inner wing pylons, complemented by a pair of Barax deception/jammer pods on the outer wing pylons. Other offensive weaponry included 125kg GP bombs; Matra SAMP 250-, 450- or 750kg slick or

Self-protection aids included Phimat chaff or Bofors BOZ-103 chaff/flare pod; a 85kg Dassault Electronique Barracuda ECM pod; Thomson-CSF TVM-015 Barem or Remora wide-band ECM detector/jammer pod; a 56-cartridge Alkan 5020/5021 conformal chaff and flare launcher beneath each wing root; and occasionally an 18-cartridge Lacroix flare in the tailcone in place

Matra/Thomson Brandt BLG 66 Belouga Aeral Grenade Launcher

The *Bombe Lance Grenades de 66mm* (bomb for dispensing 66mm grenades) is the standard cluster bomb used by the French Air Force, and seven other export customers. The type was developed in the 1970s as a successor to the Giboulee CBU, the design objectives being to produce a weapon with lower drag, a larger ground 'footprint' and the ability to dispense its bomblets at high speed – anything up to 550kt (1,000km/h). The weapon is delivered as a certified round of ammunition, and the mid-section is filled with nineteen rows of rearward-facing ejector tubes containing 152 x 66mm bomblets, or grenades. This gives the Belouga its curious 'spotted' appearance. The bomblets are of three basic types: General Purpose Fragmentation (GPF) for attacks on vehicles; High Explosive Anti-Tank (HEAT) for armoured concentrations; and Area Interdiction (AI) for attacks on fixed

sites such as airfields and marshalling yards. Before release the pilot is able to choose from two operating patterns; either 131yd or 282yd (120 or 258m) in length x 47.5yd or 65.6yd (43 or 60m) in width. On release, a sensor in the weapon's nose deploys a drag 'chute to retard the bomb and allow the launch aircraft to escape, before ejecting the bomblets, which are spewed out at regular intervals each side of the dispenser. The individual bomblets are also retarded and reach the ground vertically: the GP bomblets detonate into a disc of horizontal fragments; the HEAT bomblets explode downwards hitting the top of the vehicles; and the AI fragment similarly to the GP. A typical *Armée de l'Air* Jaguar/Belouga stores load would be nine canisters, three each on two underwing stations and three on a centreline rail, plus a pair of Magic AAMs on the outer underwing pylons.

of the drag-chute, the suite being completed by the aircraft's own internal CF-TH RWR, with its receiver aerial mounted on the tailfin leading edge. For EW support, the Thomson-CSF Caiman or Basilisk pods could also be carried; the 550kg CT51J communication jamming pod has now been deemed obsolete and is only in limited use by EC 2/11. Weapons pylons consist of an Alkan 905 on the centreline stressed for 1,200kg, Alkan 900 on the inboard section of the wings stressed for 1,200kg and either an Alkan 610 or shorter Alkan 700 on the wing outboard section and stressed for 600kg. Typical war loads for the French Jaguar was considered to be eight 750kg; eleven 450kg or fifteen 250kg bombs for close support; two Matra 550 Magic AAMs for low- or medium-level air superiority; AS.37 Martel for low-altitude anti-radar penetration with two 264gal (1,200ltr) tanks, and three such tanks for overseas intervention along with in-flight refuelling, thus giving a range of 2,485 miles (4,000km) and an endurance of ten hours.

Thomson-CSF BAREM

The BAREM is the standard EW jammer pod carried by the French Jaguar, and is able to detect, analyse and identify signals emitted by tracking, fire control, pulse modulated, pulse Doppler and continuous-wave radars using its own threat library. It will automatically jam enemy radars and is able to be interfaced with decoy launchers. Its systems can also record the signals and the emitted response for later use.

An example of a single-seat Jaguar A from EC 3/11, fitted with a 56-cartridge Alkan 5020/5021 conformal chaff and flare launcher beneath each wing root. Author

(Above and below) **Jaguar As configured for EW support, carrying the large Thomson-CSF Caimen jammer pod on their inner wing pylons and the smaller BAREM on their outer wing pylons.** Thomson-CSF

Matra R550 Magic Air-to-Air Missile

Developed in 1968 as a competitor to the AIM-9 Sidewinder, the Matra R550 Magic has a genuine all-aspect ratio, a digital autopilot and an active proximity fuze. Instantly recognizable by its cruciform control surfaces, it carries a 27.6lb (12.5kg) warhead and is powered by a SNPE Romeo single-stage solid propellant rocket motor. The missile entered service as the Magic I in the late 1960s, but has now been replaced in French service by the Magic II, an enhanced version with a new digital autopilot, active radar proximity fuze and improved SNPE rocket motor. The Matra Magic is the standard self-defence missile for the *Armée de l'Air* Jaguars. It has a length of 9ft 1in (2.8m), a diameter of 6.18in (15.7cm) and weighs 198lb (90kg).

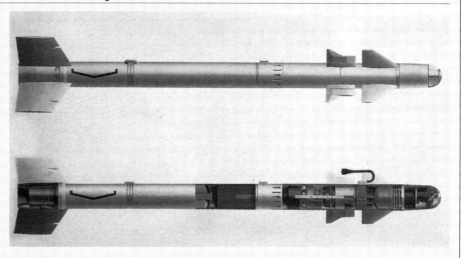

The Matra R550 Magic missile. MATRA/BAe

Matra Durandal

This effective runway-cratering weapon was developed by Matra in conjunction with SAMP and Thomson-Brandt, and as it is carried on NATO standard 14in (35.5cm) suspension lugs it requires no special control equipment in the carrier aircraft. Durandal can be released from any altitude down to 195ft (60m) and at any speed between 351–551kt (650–1,020km/h). On launch the weapon is retarded by a double parachute which drags it back and pitches it to a nose-down attitude. When optimum angle of penetration is reached without the chance of a ricochet (between –20 and –30 degrees)

Durandal fitted to an F-15E. via Paul Jackson.

the parachute is released and a SNPE Hector internal rocket motor is ignited. This accelerates the Durandal to its impact point on the runway at a velocity of some 853ft/sec (260m/sec). The weapon's kinetic energy is sufficient for its forged steel warhead to pierce 400mm (16in) of concrete, and a one-second delay fuze built into the system detonates as it impacts under the runway, the resulting explosion creating a crater 16ft (5m) wide and 6ft (2m) deep, with 'heave' extending the sphere of damage to 23ft (7m), with further fractures enlarging the total damage area to over 300sq yd (250sq m). Designed for multiple use to maximize the destructive effort, six Durandals are considered the best way of rendering a standard runway inoperative for at least one day. The Jaguar is able to carry up to eleven of the type, each of which has a weight of some 482lb (219kg), of which 220lb (100kg) is the warhead section.

Armed with an ATLIS II laser pod and Martel missiles, a Jaguar A from EC 3/7 'Languedoc', one of the three surviving French Jaguar units. SIRPA Air

---

Thomson-Brandt BAT-120

The 'brother' to the BAP-100 the BAT-120 (*Bombe d'Appui Tactique 120mm*) carries a parachute retarder and rocket motor. The weapon detonates just above the ground by means of a pizeo electric fuze, and the front and rear charges produce two near horizontal discs of fragments moving at 3,940ft/sec (1,200m/sec) to a radius of 100ft (30m). The BAP-120 comes in two variants: the BAT-120ABL for use against light armour and the BAT-120AMV for use against unarmoured targets. Nine rows of three weapons can be fitted into a Thomson-Brandt 30-6-M2 launcher.

Jaguar E

The two-seat Jaguar E trainer is basically the same as the 'A' in its general appearance. However, to accommodate a tandem, raised second place, the fuselage was stretched to 57ft 8in (17.57m), including the pitot/probe, and features a lengthened bubble canopy with two opening sections, the second seat replacing one of the internal fuel cells and being raised some 15in (38cm) higher than the front seat. The 'E' has a wheel track of 7ft 10in (2.39m) and a wheelbase of 18ft 7in

(5.66m). Early Jaguar Es did not have any IFR capability, unlike their RAF counterparts which boasted the same fit as the single-seat aircraft, but from airframe E27 onwards a fixed probe was factory-fitted in place of the nose pitot – an item later and uniquely added to two of the Omani Air Force Jaguar International trainers. Unlike its RAF counterpart, the Jaguar E has twin DEFA cannons, with 130 rounds of ammunition. Completely differing philosophies were employed in the avionics applied to both the British and French trainers. The

26

Specification – Jaguar E	
Type:	Two-seat advanced and operational conversion trainer
Accommodation:	Pilot (front seat) and instructor (rear seat) in tandem, on Martin-Baker JRM4/FB9 ejector seats
Powerplant:	Two Rolls-Royce/Turbomeca Adour Mk102 afterburning turbofans
Performance:	Max speed 1,056mph (1,690km/h)
Weights:	Empty 15,432lb (7,000kg); maximum 34,612lb (15,700kg)
Dimensions:	Span 28ft 6in (8.64m); length 57ft 6.25in (17.43m); height 16ft 0.5in (4.86m)
Armament:	Two 30mm DEFA cannons with 150 rounds of ammunition per gun

French 'E' was to have the simplest possible fit, based on a master gyro and TACAN. Therefore, the avionics were to include a VHF/UHF radio, VOR/ILS, IFF, TACAN, a SFIM 250-1 twin-gyro inertial platform, an ELIDA air data computer, and a Thomson CSF-121 fire control/sighting unit/weapons selector. Engines were the Adour Mk102, later uprated to the Mk104.

Service and Unit History

The *7ème Escadre de Chasse*, which was then located at Nancy-Ochey, had been selected to be first operational unit to receive

To accommodate a second seat, the fuselage was stretched to 57ft 8in (17.57m) including the pitot/probe, and features a lengthened bubble canopy with two opening sections, the second seat replacing one of the internal fuel cells and being raised some 15in (38cm) higher than the front seat.
f4 Aviation Photobank

A low-angle shot of the French Jaguar E, this particular example being one of the later models with a fixed IFR probe fitted to the nose. f4 Aviation Photobank

the Jaguar, and preparations were made for its service entry with air and ground crews from the *7ème* starting their practical training on the prototype Jaguars, and initial production Jaguar Es, then operated by the CEAM (*Centre d'Experiences Aériennes Militaires*) at Mont de Marsan. The *7ème* squadrons 1/7 'Provence' and then 3/7 'Languedoc' were the first to receive the new aircraft, the units being grateful to trade in their ageing Mystère IVAs. Both units then moved to their new operating base, St Dizier. On 19 June 1973 the Jaguar officially entered service, amidst much pomp and ceremony, with the French Armed Forces Minister Robert Galley and General Claude, Chief of the French Air Staff, amongst the dignitaries invited. An impressive array of ten Jaguars were lined up for inspection, with Commandant Max Simon, the OC of EC 1/7, showing off the aircraft's flying capabilities. General Grigaut gave an address which expressed his admiration for the collaborative project and commented that the Jaguar was already proving to be a fine strike aircraft,

capable of carrying an impressive payload over greater distances than contemporary French aircraft. The *7ème* was soon operational with three two-flight squadrons, the initial two squadrons being joined by 2/7 'Argonne', which had been re-numbered from EC 1/8 based at Casaux, and then added peacetime training to its wartime role of tactical support. 1/7 and 3/7 were now given a nuclear role, and the wing was finally brought up to full strength with the addition of a fourth squadron, EC 4/7, in 1980. Jaguars of *7ème Escadre* had amassed 50,000 hours by January 1977, 100,000 by January 1983 and 200,000 by December 1989.

The second wing to form on the Jaguar was the *11ème Escadre*, based at Toul-Rosiers, which began to convert to the aircraft in 1974, retiring its American-built F-100 Super Sabres. EC 3/11 'Corse' was the first squadron from the wing to convert, being operational by 1976, followed by EC 1/11 'Roussillon', and EC 2/11 'Voseges' by the end of the same year. EC 4/11 'Jura' was added to the wing's

complement at a later stage, but had its home base at Bordeaux, where it replaced the *92ème Escadre* and its Sud-Ouest Vautors in 1978. As the most recent of the Jaguar units, EC 4/11 received the later, updated versions of the aircraft.

The third, and final, wing to be equipped with the Jaguar was *3ème Escadre* 'Ardenne', which received the type during 1977 and was based at Nancy. Its first unit to convert was EC 1/3 'Navarre', followed by EC 2/3 'Champagne', replacing Mirage III fighters.

The Jaguar wings are incorporated in the *Force Aériennie Tactique* (FATac), the tactical air arm of the *Armée de l'Air*, the majority of units coming under the *1er Commandement Aérien Tactique* (CATac), with EC 4/7 and 4/11 being assigned to *2ème* CATac until its absorption by *1ème* CATac in 1987.

Pilot conversion in the *Armée de l'Air* commences with EC 2/7, the Jaguar OCU, and begins with two weeks of ground school and sixteen simulator sessions. This is followed by a flight conversion phase consisting of forty trips over two months for young pilots, fifteen missions over one month for existing pilots, or ten sorties for experienced pilots with at least 1,500 hours in their log books. Their first flight is from the rear seat of a Jaguar E, with a brief to 'watch and not touch'. They then have three familiarization flights, each of

men to maintain it than the older, and less complicated aircraft types that it was to replace.

As well as their conventional and nuclear strike roles, several of the Jaguar units were given specific tasks, with the aircraft of *11ᵉᵐᵉ* having perhaps the most diverse, in being tasked with overseas support of

back to demonstrate the French arm of the UN peacekeeping force's ability to call for a swift response if needed. Perhaps the most memorable of the early Jaguar exploits came when a single Jaguar A from CEAM at Mont de Marsan, flown by Captain M. Gauthier, conducted the first live drop of the French AN52 free-fall nuclear

A pair of French Jaguar Es of Escadrille 2/7 'Argonne' in formation, captured at the point of lowering their undercarriage. f4 Aviation Photobank

an hour's duration and these trips include navigation, blind flying, air-to-ground firing, with the younger pilots being allowed to go solo after ten flights. Training then moves to its final phases which include tactical work and weaponeering before the pilot finally passes to an operational unit.

Ground crew training had problems early on, due to lack of numbers, however, it was soon discovered that despite being a new aircraft, together with its anticipated teething problems, it required no more

French interests, direct army support and anti-radar/ECM duties. EC 3/11 undertook the first operational overseas Jaguar deployment in 1977 when aircraft operated out of Senegal against rebel forces in Mauritania in Operation *Lamentin*. Another milestone for the Jaguar occurred on 19 January 1984, when four fully-armed aircraft from EC11, with tanker support (using five 'prods') flew a non-stop reconnaissance mission, Operation *Chevense*, from Solenzara in Corsica to Beirut and

weapon in an operation codenamed *Maquis* over the Mururoa Atoll in French Polynesia on 24 July 1974. Interventions by French forces have been commonplace in its former colony of Chad in North Africa, where *Armée de l'Air* Jaguars have undertaken combat missions in the 1970s and 80s, In Operations *Manta* and *Epervier*, the *Armée de l'Air* lost at least three of their aircraft through accidents or ground fire. (Operations in Chad are dealt with in greater detail on pp.40–3.) The largest

Armée de l'Air operation since World War II was their participation in Operation *Desert Storm*, their role designated Operation *Daguet*, which again is dealt with separately, on pp.139–50. This was soon followed by Operation *Aconit*, as part of the UN's joint Operation *Provide Comfort* over Iraq, policing the no-fly zones, and latterly over the skies of Bosnia-Hercegovina in Operation *Crecerelle*.

At its peak the *Armée de l'Air* operated nine fifteen-aircraft squadrons of Jaguars, totalling 135 airframes, out of the original order for 200. The remaining seventy were stored at the Chatendun Centre in individual 'cocoons' to aid their maintenance until 'rotated' into squadron service, thereby giving the *Armée de l'Air* a built-in reserve stock and attrition replacements. At the beginning of the 1980s a modernization programme was envisaged for the remaining French Jaguars, with upgrades to the engines and a new avionics suite based around the Sagem INS. The Air Force General Staff sought to persuade the Ministry of Defence to authorize the spending of over a billion francs to modernize at the very least the single-seat aircraft, but as French policy was already framed in the context of only 'defence', it was against augmenting the 'offensive' capabilities of the aircraft and the modernization was not undertaken; the Air Force was instructed to used its funds elsewhere. As an immediate result of the ending of the Cold War, the force was reduced by three squadrons, and following the Gulf War and the now seemingly permanent outbreak of peace in Europe, the *Armée de l'Air* decided to further rationalize its Jaguar units: as there was little prospect of any upgrades, having all the aircraft in one location would make them easier to manage, in terms of operations, logistics, spares and training. As a result, sixty Jaguar A and E airframes were allocated to the three units of the *7eme Escadre* at St Dizier; the balance being either put into storage or dispatched to ground training units. Under the *Assault Conventionnel* banner, EC 1/7 'Provence', the first Jaguar unit to form, then assumed responsibility for operations concerning the AS37 Martel missile, whilst EC 3/7 'Languedoc' undertook the AS.30L and ATLIS II illumination mission, with EC 2/7 'Argonne' continuing to train new pilots assigned to the Jaguar, and it is with this unit that the bulk of the remaining two-seaters can be found.

Armée de l'Air Jaguar Units' Histories, Duties and Aircraft Markings

The French Jaguar units are divided as follows. A wing (*escadre*), is divided into three or four squadrons (*escadrons*) each of which have two flights (*escadrilles*). *Escadron* aircraft are 'pooled' and carry both *escadrille* insignia on their tailfins, *1e Escadrille* on the left side, and *2e Escadrille* on the right side.

Aircraft carry individual codes, for example 'A148 11-YD', where A = Jaguar A; 148 = build number; 11 = *escadre* number; and YD = individual aircraft identity.

The individual squadrons are usually named after regions in France, e.g. 'Provence', whilst bases are numbered, and since 1984 also named in honour of famous aviators. With a few exceptions Jaguar A aircraft above airframe No. A-81 are assigned to *11eme Escadre*, those below to *7eme Escadre*. It is customary that the aircraft's code letter/number combinations are applied to the engine intake sides, with the aircraft's individual airframe number being applied to the mid-section of the rudder. Generally, national insignia is applied either side of the rear fuselage, and above the port and below the starboard wings.

11eme Escadre de Chasse 'Res Non Verba'

Based at *Aérienne 136* 'Colonel Georges Phelut', at Toul-Rosiers, EC 11 was originally equipped with F-100 Super Sabres, the last of the type retiring in 1973. EC 11 did not have a nuclear role, but it did operate all other types of munitions in the French inventory. EC 1/11 and EC 3/11 were ATLIS-equipped with EC 1/11 assigned to European operations, while EC 3/11 was assigned to the *Force d'Action Exterieure* in the overseas intervention role. EC 2/11 were the defence suppression specialists armed with Martel anti-radar missiles, CT51 and Barracuda jammer pods. EC 4/11 was attached to BA106 at Bordeaux/Meringac and had the additional role of tactical reconnaissance using the RP36P camera pod. *11eme* have been involved in most of France's overseas actions, deploying to Africa as well as the Gulf.

Escadron de Chasse 1/11 'Roussillon'
1eme Escadrille – GCIII Markings: African mask on port side of tail

2eme Escadrille – GCIII Markings: mask of comedy starboard side of tail
Aircraft coded 11-EA to 11-EZ

EC 1/11 converted to Jaguars beginning on 10 October 1975, with its prime task of supporting the Army. The unit has seen combat in the Gulf War and in Chad.

Escadron de Chasse 2/11 'Vosages'
1eme Escadrille – SPA91 Markings: vulture clutching a skull on starboard side of tail
2eme Escadrille – SPA97 Markings: pennant charged with ermine on port side of tail
Aircraft coded 11-MA to 11MZ

Received its first Jaguars on 3 November 1976, and fully equipped by June 1977, led by Commandant Sanchez. The unit was the first equipped with the laser rangefinder nose, with other EC 11 squadrons trading their earlier aircraft for newer models similarly equipped. The unit was tasked with providing ECM support and defence suppression, taking over the Martel commitment from EC 3/3 in June 1987.

Escadron de Chasse 3/11 'Corse'
1eme Escadrille – SPA88 Markings: snake on port side of tail
2eme Escadrille – SPA69 Markings: cat's face (?) on starboard side of tail
Aircraft coded 11-RA to 11-RZ

Began equipping with Jaguars in February 1975 under Commandant Sauvebois with seven 'A' and eight 'E' models, in order to practise intensive IFR training, later being equipped with thirteen 'A' and two 'E'. The unit deployed to Senegal and operated against rebel forces in Mauritania in 1977, and also participated in the support of the UN in Beirut in 1984.

EC 4/11 'Jura'
1eme Escadrille – SPA158 Markings: secretary bird on port side of tail
2eme Escadrille – SPA161 Markings: sphinx on starboard side of tail
Aircraft coded 11YA to 11YZ

Detachment Air 15/531 formed at Bordeaux in 1978 to start working up on the Jaguar. On 12 December 1978 it became EC 4/11, taking over the number from the last Super Sabre squadron under Commandant Argelier. Because of its 'detached' position at BA106 Bordeaux/Merignac away from its other wing members, and as a result of Cold War force reductions, it was disbanded on 30 June 1992.

Note
The Toul-based component of EC 11 are involved with regular exercises with the 1st Armoured Division of the French Army, whilst before its disbandment EC 4/11 was assigned to support the 11th Parachute Division.

Escadron de Chasse 3/3 'Ardennes'
1ᵉᵐᵉ Escadrille – Markings: a wild boar and blue bar on the port side of the tail
2ᵉᵐᵉ Escadrille – Markings: a wild boar and red bar on the starboard side of the tail
Aircraft coded 3-XA to 3XZ

service, converting to the Mirage IIE in commonality with the other units of the wing, its tasking passing to EC 2/11.

7ᵉᵐᵉ Escadre de Chasse
Now the sole operators of the Jaguar in the French Air Force, four squadrons from EC

A Jaguar E from EC 2/7 'Argonne' taxies back to its ramp, the twin canopies 'cracked' open to allow a cooling breeze into the jet. f4 Aviation Photobank

3ᵉᵐᵉ Escadre de Chasse
Operating from Nancy-Ochey 113, this wing was assigned to defence suppression duties with the Martel missile, and was unusual in having a mixed force consisting of two squadrons of Mirage IIIEs and a single squadron of Jaguars.

'Ardennes' reformed with the Mirage V in January 1974 and re-equipped with the Jaguar in March 1977. EC 3/3's Jaguars reportedly launched a Martel strike against a Libyan radar site in Chad in 1987, but the squadron's Jaguars were withdrawn on 1 June 1987, after ten years'

7 have flown the Jaguar, including EC 4/7, which was detached to Istres, away from EC 7's home base of Aérienne 113 'Commandant Antoine de Saint-Exupery' St Dizier/Robinson. EC 1/7, 3/7 and 4/7 were assigned to nuclear strike until this task was withdrawn in September 1991. Their

role was that of clearing a path for the Mirage IVA strike aircraft. EC 2/7 remains the French Jaguar OCU, whilst EC 4/7 was disbanded in 1989.

Escadron de Chasse 1/7 'Provence'
1ème Escadrille – Markings: bayard's helmet on port side of tailfin
2ème Escadrille – Markings: Cross of Jerusalem on starboard side of the nose
Aircraft coded 7HA to 7HZ

Pilots earmarked for EC 1/7 were the first to operate the Jaguar and underwent training at Mont de Marsan's CEAM (*see* below). The first aircraft to arrive was E7 7-HA on 15 March 1973. Following re-equipment with the Jaguar the unit moved to St Dizier, being declared operational on 1 September 1974. EC 1/7 is now the sole operator of the AS.37 Martel missile.

Escadron de Chasse 2/7 'Argonne'
1ème Escadrille – Markings: Greek archer on port side of tail
2ème Escadrille – Markings: cock's head on starboard side of the tail

Aircraft coded 7PA to 7PZ

Third of the *7ème* to form, on 11 October 1974. It initially used aircraft borrowed from other units until receiving its own. Pilots fresh out of basic training come to EC 2/7, flying some sixty hours before being posted to a squadron.

Escadron de Chasse 3/7 'Languedoc'
1ème Escadrille – Markings: blue and gold shark on starboard side of tail, facing either direction
2ème Escadrille – Markings: Lorraine thistle on port side of tail
Aircraft codes 71A-71Z

Became operational on 1 July 1975, and is tasked specifically with ground attack, rather than tactical support. Now the sole operator of the AS.30L missile.

Escadron de Chasse 4/7 'Limousin'
1ème Escadrille – Markings: eagle on the port side of the tail
2ème Escadrille – Markings: desert fox on the starboard side of the tail
Aircraft coded 7NA to 7NZ

The final Jaguar squadron to form, on 1 April 1980. Originally based at St Dizier, moving later to Istres/Le Tube. Together with EC 4/11, formed part of the French Rapid Reaction Force and was assigned to the low-level nuclear strike role. The unit's last Jaguar sortie was flown on 17 July 1989 and the unit disbanded on the last day of that month, one aircraft being painted up in an anniversary colour scheme shortly before disbandment.

Other Jaguar Units

Centre d'Instruction Tactique 339

CITAC 339 Markings: a bat on a terrestrial globe
Aircraft codes 339-WA to 339-WZ

Based at 'Lt Col Papin' Luxil/St.Saveaur, *Centre Prediction et d'Instruction* flew five Jaguar Es to teach low-level all weather penetration techniques.

An EC 3/11 'Corse' Jaguar wearing the Gulf War-style camouflage, complete with Barax jammer pod and Alkan conformal chaff/flare dispensers. Author

Painted in what appears to be a three-tone Gulf camouflage scheme (actually the paintwork had been touched up with a different shade), this Jaguar E of EC 2/11 was used for familiarization training for aircraft bound for the Gulf. There were reports that Jaguar Es took part in Operation Daguet, **but due to their non-combat status this seems very unlikely.** via Gary Madgwick

Centre d'Experiences Aériennes Militaires – CEAM

CEAM markings: figure throwing a thunderbolt, kneeling on gears below clouds and stars

CEAM 330 is located at Base Aérienne 118 'Capt K W Roland' Mont de Marsan, and tests air force equipment. CEAM trials involved Jaguar prototypes E02 and A04, as well as early production aircraft. E2 was the first production Jaguar to arrive at CEAM, on 4 May 1974. A CEAM Jaguar also made the first live AN52 nuclear weapons drop and all CEAM Jaguars were transferred to other units as the need for them receded.

CEAM 330's aircraft were 'owned' by *Escadron de Chasse* 24/118, with 118-A codes, but on 15 October 1987 they were

designated an operator in their own right, becoming EC5/330.

Escadron de Chasse 5/330 'Cote d'Argent'
Markings: tiger on the port side of the tail
Aircraft codes 330-AA to 330-AZ
Centre d'Essais en Vol – CEV
Markings: none

In contrast to the work undertaken by CEAM, CEV tests the airworthiness of items of equipment destined for the *Direction Technique des Constructions Aeronautiques*, operating from Bretigny-sur-Orge. CEV conducted the ATLIS and AS.30L missile trials, and has on strength Jaguars E-01, A3 and A4. E-01´has been modified with the taller production tailfin and the removal of the intake splitter plates.

Armée de l'Air Jaguar Camouflage

On entry to service, the Jaguars were camouflaged to suit the European terrain that they were expected to operate over, and as such received a tactical paint scheme of, initially, gloss dark green/dark grey disruptive pattern on their upper surfaces with aluminium on their lower surfaces and wing pylons, similar in style to that applied to the RAF aircraft, but having a lighter hue. The gloss finish was later replaced by a more conventional matt. As more 'out-of-area' commitments began to be undertaken by the aircraft, most notably in Africa and the Middle East, then more suitable colours were applied, and these

(Above) **A two-seater Jaguar E in desert garb, reported to have taken part in Operation** Daguet. **However, due to its lack of RWR and other defensive systems, this seems unlikely.** via Gary Madgwick

The interior of the wheel bay, and also the underside of the Alkan conformal chaff and flare launcher beneath the wing root and one of the twin DEFA cannon ports. John Blackman

The Jaguar A's cockpit. John Blackman.

schemes are dealt with in later chapters. Grey/green aircraft still proudly wear the stylized 'Jaguar' logo on their noses, but this has been lost on the 'out-of-area' aircraft.

Like those of the RAF, the *Armée de l'Air*'s Jaguars have competed in many internal and international exercises, also participating at the US-hosted 'Red Flag' at Nellis AFB in Nevada in 1980 and 1982, with EC 11 being the first French Jaguar unit to attend. In addition to the 'Flags', the French Jaguars have also been embarrassed winners of the *Armée de l'Air Comete* and *Tactique* trophies. During 1980 at the *Congres de la Chasse* at Cazeaux, the Jaguars soundly beat off various types of Dassault Mirage to sweep the board, taking the two top prizes. EC 2/7 took the *Coupe Comete* and EC 3/3 the *Coupe Tactique*, and, as if to add further insult to the bruised egos of the Mirage units, the *Coupe*

Tailfin of a desert-camouflaged aircraft from the Armée de l'Air's **first Jaguar unit, EC 1/7 'Provence', denoted by the bayard's helmet on the port side.** John Blackman.

Comete is an air-to-air gunnery contest, something which the Jaguar is hardly the best equipped aircraft to win!

Jaguar M: SEPECAT's 'Sea Cat'

The Jaguar M (for '*màrin*' – maritime), was a one-off single-seat prototype aircraft built to fulfil a requirement from the air arm of the French Navy, the *Aèronavale*, for an aircraft to replace its Etendard IVs: one that would possess excellent attack capabilities and twin engines for operational safety. Early in 1967, based on the promise of what a production aircraft could achieve, fifty of the proposed Jaguars were earmarked to be produced for seaborne duties. Of these, forty would be single-seat strike/reconnaissance aircraft

and ten would be land-based two-seat trainers. A 'one-off' prototype, coded Jaguar M-05 F-ZWRJ and carrying the letter 'J' on its intakes, was produced by Breguet in France; it undertook its maiden flight on 14 November 1969 from the airfield at Melun Villaroche, with *Breguet Avions* test pilot Jaques Jesberger at the controls, the aircraft being airborne for just over thirty minutes.

The main visible difference from the Jaguar A was in the undercarriage, the M version having a smaller, twin nosewheel and larger single mainwheel arrangement to facilitate catapult launches and arrested recoveries; the land based version had a single nosewheel and twin mainwheels to cater for rough field operations. The Jaguar M's undercarriage legs were also different, with the mainwheel structure sitting fairly 'straight out' from the wheel-wells, unlike

the A and S models, whose legs have a more angled and squat stance. These units were suitably strengthened to accommodate a higher sink rate on landing, from 11.8ft/sec (3.6m/sec) to 19ft/sec (5.8m/sec), and the nosewheel gained an extendible oleo to give the aircraft the correct angle of attack for catapult launches from the smaller French aircraft carriers (similar to the nosewheel arrangement used later by the British Phantom FG.1). It is interesting to note that whilst nosewheel doors were built for the aircraft, they were seldom fitted, especially during its trials phase, and had a far more 'cut-out' shape than the other prototypes. The arrestor hook, which had a far thicker section than the overshoot hook on other aircraft, was stressed to take 5.5g during 'trapped' landings aboard ship, and had a much stronger root fairing between the engine exhaust nozzles. Catapult strop attachment points were added to the airframe and located on the underside, forward of the mainwheel doors.

Other general structural strengthening was undertaken to give the M's airframe the ability to withstand catapult forces and, as it was a prototype, the aircraft also sported the intake splitter plates that were to be deleted on the later production models. Avionics were similar to those fitted to the Jaguar A, but with the addition of a laser rangefinder and camera port in a bulged fairing beneath the tip of the nose, which thereby gained a smaller profile as a result. Radio and navigational aids were tailored to maritime operations. For communications, a single blade aerial was fitted behind the canopy. Martin-Baker provided their Mk9 'zero-zero' ejector seat for the aircraft, and provision was made for twin DEFA cannons, though the external cannon ports were actually faired over, and evidence suggests the actual guns were never fitted. A retractable in-flight refuelling probe was fitted beneath the windshield and provision was made for the M to carry a 'buddy-buddy' aerial refuelling pack on its centreline. The twin Adour engines had not at that point been 'navalized', but plans were well advanced for them to have components that would be salt water corrosion-resistant. The M also began its prototype stage with the original, shorter, fin, but was retrofitted with the taller 'production' fin before undertaking sea trials, and the designers took the opportunity to fit the aircraft with restyled, kinked, stabilizers at the same time. The airbrakes had the original style of four rows of perforations, rather than two rows found on the other prototypes.

Having spent much of its early life practising deck landings both at Istres and Nimes/Garons naval base, on 20 April 1970 the aircraft was flown across the Channel to the Royal Aircraft Establishment at Bedford for initial carrier deck-

complete success', and following another series of trials at Bedford, the way was paved for the next phase in the test procedures: operating from a ship at sea. On 8 July the Jaguar M was flown out from Lann-Bihoue to the aircraft carrier *Clemenceau* as it sailed of Lorient, and between the 8th and 13th conducted a

Vaisseau Daniel Pierre. For take-off, the pilot would position the aircraft on the steam catapult track, and once fixed in position the nosewheel leg would be extended under the watchful eye of the launch officer, who would confirm the correct angle. To facilitate this procedure a series of coloured lights were added to the

The Jaguar M framed by the overshoot net aboard Clemenceau. **Worth noting from this shot are the open main- and nosewheel doors, very seldom seen 'hanging' when the aircraft is on the ground (or, as in this case, deck).** BAe

landing trials using the RAE's land-based dummy deck, which was a fully-equipped catapult track built on raised steel girders to simulate the 'cat-shots' from a real aircraft carrier. The Anglo-French team reported that the tests were a 'total and

total of twelve full-reheat catapult-assisted launches and arrested landings, as well as deck handling assessments and compatibility tests with the ship's deck lifts.

The first catapult launch at sea took place on 10 July, flown by Lieutenant de

nosewheel leg, contained in a white oblong box, and to observe the launch and weapons-carrying characteristics, a rearward-facing test camera was installed in an orange fairing on the underside directly beneath the cockpit; similarly, a forward-

A fine study of the Jaguar M as it arrives at the RAE in Bedford for a 'conventional' landing. The 'beefed-up' landing gear is readily apparent. BAe

looking camera was installed on the rear underfuselage just ahead of the engine access bays. The aircraft was flown in turn by Capitaine de Corvette Yves Goupil, Lieutenant Daniel Pierre and Jaques Jessberger, and were operated with a wide variety of weapons and fuel tank fits, and were once again declared a complete success. M-05 returned to Bedford for more preparations for a second series of twenty launches and landings from *Clemenceau* between 20–27 October 1971. The reheat problems associated with the early Adour engines were to prove the near undoing of the maritime prototype when on one occasion the arrestor hook failed to trap a 'wire' and the throttle response was not sufficient to prevent the aircraft sinking dangerously close to the sea, a problem exacerbated by the Mk101 Adour's continuing thrust problems.

Despite the Jaguar's many impressive qualities – which stood it head and shoulders above its contemporaries – the Navy were unhappy with the aircraft's costs; which meant that it could only afford fifty fighters, rather than the hundred they needed. The French Government therefore cancelled the Jaguar M in January 1973, citing their main reasons for ditching the project, apart for the cost factor, as the need to reinforce the catapult and deck of the aircraft carriers and, most notably, their 'dissatisfaction with the single engine recovery characteristics of the aircraft', which gave insufficient recovery power in the case of one engine shutting down during deck landings. Therefore, after looking at other options, such as the McDonnell Douglas Skyhawk and the Vought Corsair, they opted for the single-engined Dassault Super Etendard as its replacement; this despite Dassault being directed by the French Government not to promote its aircraft against the Jaguar only two months earlier! M. Dassault was probably rubbing his hands together! The additional fifty-

aircraft naval Jaguar allocation was transferred to the French Air Force.

Again, political pressures and heavy lobbying by Dassault themselves for a 'totally French'-designed and -built aircraft to spearhead the nation's seaborne power, rather than having a collaborative effort fell on sympathetic ears. Despite holding a fifty per cent stake in the Jaguar, Dassault wanted the hundred per cent that the Super Etendard gave them, an attitude that was to have repercussions in later export dealings. (On the subject of exports, it was hoped that the maritime Jaguar would interest the navies of Brazil and Argentina, who were also looking to upgrade their equipment; these hopes were dealt a severe blow by the project's cancellation.) The aircraft was relegated to test flying after its cancellation and made its last flight on 12 December 1975; it was consigned to technical training at Rochfort, having been delivered there by road on 28 November.

One of the many compatibility tests undertaken aboard Clemenceau was of the aircraft's handling aboard
ship and its ability to be easily moved around and operated on the deck lifts. BAe.

Engineers position the aircraft onto the RAE's catapult test track for a trial launch, giving a good insight
into the Jaguar M's nose-on aspect. Note the nose-mounted laser rangefinder and lack of nosewheel door.
BAe

Launching into the dusk, the blue afterburner plumes from the Adour engines searing the deck, the white- and yellow-tailed Jaguar M at the point of launch. BAe

(Below) **'Trapping' onto the deck.** BAe

Camouflage and Markings

The prototype Jaguar M was painted up in gloss French Navy dark blue-grey uppersurfaces and gloss white lower surfaces, the upper surface colour wrapping around the underside of the wing leading edges. White also featured on the underwing pylons and underfuselage strakes, with *Aèronavale* roundels located above and below the wings and on the rear fuselage sides, with the stylized 'Jaguar' logo applied to the nose, and 'SEPECAT Jaguar' and 'M-05' stencilled onto the tailfin. Either side of the nose were a number of white, red and blue markings, perhaps denoting the number of sorties undertaken by the aircraft. Warning and rescue markings were in full colour, with 'captive' trials weaponry being blue and fuel tanks silver. During its time aboard

Clemenceau the Jaguar M also gained an all-white rudder with four horizontal golden yellow stripes applied across it, with the latter colour also being added to the braking parachute housing below. The intakes also sported the insignia of the *Clemenceau*, and was 'zapped' with badges by the resident Etendard squadrons, *Flotille* 14F being one, plus the emblem of the RAE. During a visit to the RAE at Bedford in its trials phase, the Jaguar M wore broad (approx. 12in/30cm wide) red, white and blue stripes painted from behind the cockpit to just behind the second of the auxiliary inlet doors, across the top of the wings and fuselage and across the rear fuselage from just behind the roundel to the mid-section of the ventral fins. On the tail was a large, crudely painted French roundel, and the nose carried the legend '1789 14 July' in red.

Force d'Action Exterieure – French Jaguar Operations 'Out of Area'

Chad 1978

Soon after Chad, a poor, landlocked country in north central Africa, gained its independence from France in 1960, tensions arose between the Christian-led population of the south, and the Moslem-orientated population in the north. Fighting soon broke out, and the then President François Tombalaye, unable to put down the rebellion against his government by the Libyan-backed FROLINAT (FROnt de LIberation NAtionale du Tchad), called on France for help. Air support was provided by four ageing Douglas AD-4 and AD-4N Skyraiders from EC 1-21, who were despatched to Djibouti for 'flag flying' operations. Later, this detachment was enlarged into the *Escadrille Lagere d'Appui Aérien 1-22* in March 1969, the aircraft later being given to the Chadian Government. The first of France's 'Chad Interventions' ended in September 1972.

In 1973 Libya, relying on an un-ratified post-World War II treaty, annexed a 62-mile(100km)-wide strip in northern Chad which could provide bases for Libyan forces and the Chadian rebels. With this tension still apparent, French aircraft remained on detachment at Djibouti until 1975. Two years later, in April 1978, the *Armée de l'Air* was back again. Under Operation *Tacaud*, eight of the EC 3/11 Operation *Lamentin* Jaguars (*see below*), still based at

(Above) **On the ramp at N'Djamena, an already weary-looking Jaguar from EC 2/11 'Vosages', shares space with a similarly camouflaged Mirage F.1CR, whilst in the background stands a Breguet Atlantic. To the left of the picture is one of Chad's ageing Skyraiders, outclassed by Libya's supersonic jets.** SIRPA Air

A Jaguar standing ready for an armed patrol mission, carrying six 500lb (227kg) slick bombs, and Phimat and Barax jammer pods. SIRPA Air

Dakar in Senegal, were detached to N'Djamena to back up the ailing Chadian government of President General Malloum, whose forces were under attack from guerrillas backed by Libya. A further twelve Jaguars from EC 2/11 'Vosages' arrived at Djibouti in late April 1978. However, the French forces failed to stem the tide and in the process lost a Jaguar to an SA-7 'Grail' SAM on 31 May, a second during a reconnaissance flight on 8 August, a third in a collision on 23 August and a fourth on 14 October. Malloum subsequently fled the country, to be replaced by a coalition government led by former northern rebels Goukion Oueddi and Hissan Habre. The French subsequently withdrew in 1980.

The 'peace' did not last for long, and the frail coalition fell apart, with Oueddi eventually asking for Libyan support to help quell a Habre-led rebellion. Most Chadians were not in favour of this, and the Libyans were angrily forced to withdraw in 1981, giving Habre the opportunity to drive Oueddi and his GUNT (*Government d'Union Nationale du Tchad*) forces back into the north. On 17 June 1983 Oueddi and his Libyan-backed GUNT went on the counter-offensive from the Aouzou strip. Advancing rapidly, they captured the strategically-important oasis of Faya-Largeau, and continued to push south, capturing the town of Abeche. Habre's forces countered and re-took Abeche and Faya-Largeau, but Libya, unwilling to let the GUNT forces suffer defeat, sent their ALN (*Armée de Liberation Nationale*) air force into the fray. The veteran Chadian Skyraiders left by the French years earlier were no match for Libya's modern, supersonic, Mirages, MiGs and Sukhois. Therefore, Habre requested help from France and President Mitterand, who had two alternatives in hand, decided that a major intervention package was required to support the Government and ordered Operation *Mamba*.

Chad 1983 – Jaguars in Operation Mamba

On 12 August 1983, as part of a larger tri-service force, four *Armée de l'Air* Jaguars from EC 4/11 'Jura' were made ready for Operation *Mamba* and stationed at Libreville in Gabon, with four other Jaguars, three KC-135F tankers and two Breguet Atlantic aircraft being based at Bangui Airport, Djibouti. By 21 August, six other Jaguars from EC 3/11 'Corse', four Mirage F.1Cs and a single KC-135F were also operational from N'Djamena, followed

later by a Breguet Atlantic. The Jaguars went into action on 2 September 1983, 'buzzing' rebel forces who were attacking Oum Chalouba, their remit being to only deter the attackers. After much posturing on both sides the French forces established a 'Red Line' drawn across northern Chad, roughly along the fifteenth parallel from Tourdoum to Oum Chalouba. On 25 January 1984, before the *Mamba* forces could intervene, the ALN over-ran the FANT (*Forces Armées Nationale Tchadieenes*, the Chadian Army) garrison at town of Ziguey, taking a number of prisoners including a Belgian doctor and nurse. The reaction was swift. That morning two 11e Jaguars, escorted by two Mirage F.1s and refuelled by a KC-135F were despatched to find the aggressors, and successfully located a twenty-vehicle ALN convoy near Torodoum. The aircraft kept the convoy under surveillance, and whilst awaiting orders, the rebels fired off SA-7 missiles at the aircraft with no effect; the French responded by calling in an armed Gazelle helicopter which destroyed a Honda four-wheel-drive vehicle with a HOT missile. A hour later, authorization was finally given to a similar formation of two Jaguars and two Mirages (which were now on station, replacing the original force) to stop the convoy. During the action one of the two Jaguars of was struck in its main hydraulic system by 23mm gunfire (although other reports indicate this may have been an SA-7 missile). Despite ejecting, the pilot, Capitaine Michel Croci, was killed as his aircraft, which was in a tight banking turn just prior to being hit, was too close to the ground when he initiated the 'get out' sequence. The remaining Jaguar and the two Mirages strafed and stopped the convoy, despite one of the F.1s also being damaged by gunfire. Capitaine Croci was posthumously awarded France's *Legion d'Honneur* medal in February 1984.

Following this incident further troops, helicopters, Mirages and Jaguars were sent to Chad to counter any other moves, and went onto full alert for possible operations against Libya. During this time a further Jaguar was lost on 16 April during a probing flight sixty-two miles from the 'Red Line', when Commandant Bernard Voelckel flew his aircraft into a sand dune near Faya Largeau. Reason finally prevailed between the two sides and a French withdrawal got underway in September, the last Mirage aircraft leaving on 1 October and the last Jaguars following two days

later under Operation *Silure*, even though evidence existed that the Libyan forces would continue to occupy the Aouzou strip and the northern third of Chad.

Chad 1986 – Operation Epervier

Within a matter of weeks of the departure of the last of the French forces from N'Djamena in November 1984, the Libyans began, with East German assistance, to construct a military airfield at Quadi Doum in northern Chad, from which tactical aircraft could reach well into the country. Completed in 1985, the site was also provided with Soviet-built radar systems such as 'Flat Face', 'Spoon Rest', 'Long Track' and 'Straight Flush', together with SA-6 'Gainful' SAMs, and 23mm and 14.7mm AAA batteries. During the early part of 1986, Goukouni Ouddei, the leader of the overthrown GUNT, Chad's Government of National Unity, and the commander of the rebel forces occupying the north of the country, crossed the cease-fire line originally set up during Operation *Mamba* three years earlier. Ouddei's forces, supported by Libya's Colonel Gadaffi, attacked on three fronts, threatening the nation's capital, N'Djamena.

Once again at the request of the President of Chad, Hissen Habre, elements of the French Army, Navy and Air Force stationed at Bangui M'Opoko Airport in Djibouti were put on full alert to support their African ally. By the middle of February twelve Jaguar As from EC 2/11, EC 3/11 and EC 4/11, four Mirage F.1Cs, three KC-135F tankers and six C-160 Transall transports were ready to be called upon if needed. The air element was also joined by two *Aéronavale* Atlantic ASW aircraft for use as airborne command posts for the fighters and bombers in the area. As the immediate threat to the capital receded, the French forces turned their attentions to the rebel airfield at Quadi Doum, an oasis some 155 miles (250km) from the sixteenth parallel.

The French launched the first mission of Operation *Epervier* ('Sparrowhawk') at 8am on 16 February when eight Jaguars of EC 3/11 'Corse' flew from their Djibouti base, covered by Mirage F.1Cs, refuelled by KC-135F and guided by the Atlantics in a five-hour round trip, and attacked the rebel airfield. Six of the Jaguars, each carrying two 264gal (1,200ltr) fuel tanks, a Phimat chaff dispenser, a Barracuda ECM pod and Lacroix tailcone flare launcher, dropped eighteen Thomson-Brandt BAP-100

Thomson Brandt BAP-100

The BAP-100 (*Bombe Accélerée de Penetration 100mm*, or 100mm anti-runway bomb) was designed in the mid-1970s and provides the French Air Force with a lightweight runway-denial munition as a counterpart to the heavyweight Durandal. The weapon is released as the carrier aircraft approaches the runway on a diagonal course, the launch altitude being between 165–260ft (50–80m), at a speed of 340–551kt (630–1,020km/h). The weapon's sequencer is activated 0.5sec after release and allows the tail braking parachute to deploy, pulling it clear of the aircraft. The weapon is now armed, the parachute falls away and a rocket motor in the tail ignites for 0.3sec, accelerating the weapon obliquely downward at 65 degrees, penetrating the runway surface at a velocity of between 755–853ft/sec (230–260m/sec). The weapon can penetrate up to 1m(3ft)-thick concrete and is capable of destroying an area of 60sq yd (50sq m). Delay fuzes can also be fitted, timed for up to six hours. As each round is light, the BAP-100 is designed for multiple carriage, with nine weapons in a Thomson-Brandt 14-3-M2 or 30-2-M2 carrier, of which three are usually mounted on the Jaguar's centreline.

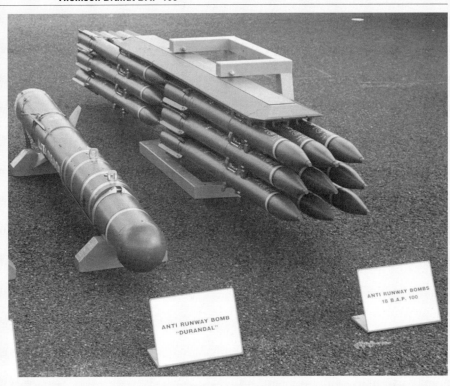

BAP. via Paul Jackson

runway cratering munitions with great accuracy, the other two Jaguars being armed with 882lb (400kg) retarded bombs instead of the BAPs. After refuelling at 17,000ft (5,180m), the Jaguars dropped to low-level and made their attack, completely surprising the Quadi Doum defenders. Crossing the runway at 170 degrees relative to its axis, they dropped their weapons in a single pass, putting the airfield out of action for several days. Despite intense, but fortunately inaccurate, anti-aircraft fire, all aircraft returned safely back to base. In response, a Libyan Tu-22 'Blinder' bombed the capital's airfield, but with little effect. On 7 January, responding to an air raid by Libyan MiG-21s and -23s, another major air strike was mounted, this time against Libyan-operated radar installations at the Ouadi Doum, airfield by ten Jaguars of EC 4/11 (some sources say EC 3/3), armed with Martel anti-radar missiles, along with Mirage 5Fs and reconnaissance Mirage F.1CRs. Another Jaguar crashed, soon after take-off from Banjui airport, on 27 March, the pilot ejecting after he reported a technical failure. The crippled fighter hit an Islamic religious school on the outskirts of the city killing twenty-one people, many of

them children, and injuring over thirty more, sparking off violent anti-French demonstrations.

During 1987 the Chadian Army pushed back the rebels, supported again by the French Jaguars and Mirages, and despite other incursions, which resulted in a HAWK battery downing a Libyan Tu-22, the war virtually ended with the Army overrunning rebel positions and capturing no fewer than twenty-three Libyan aircraft. Although tension has eased, Jaguars and C-160s remain at Djibouti on semi-permanent detachment in case of further incursions. Jaguars from 3eme have made a number of detachments to Chad and 3/3 'Ardennes', specializing in the use of the Martel anti-radar missile, have flown a number of effective missions that would again prove the effectiveness of the French resolve should the rebels use their radar systems to lock onto the aircraft.

Mauritania, Togo and the Ivory Coast

Continuing the support of its former African colonies and protectorates, the *Armée de l'Air*'s Jaguars have also operated in other areas of the continent. EC 3/11

flew three Jaguars on a 'proving trip' to Djibouti in 1975, followed by a further sortie to Senegal and the Ivory Coast in 1976 as part of Exercises *N'Diambour* and *Abidjan*. Jaguars also participated in exercises in Gabon – *Estuaire*; the Ivory Coast – *Bandama*; and Togo – *Mangrove* and *Murene*.

Senegal

EC 3/11 also undertook the first operational overseas Jaguar deployment in October 1977 when aircraft operated out of Dakar, Senegal against rebel forces in Mauritania in Operation *Lamentin*, acting against the Algerian-backed Polisario guerrillas who were attacking Mauritanian territory in the former Spanish Sahara. Two Jaguars were shot down in December 1977, and another on 3 May 1978 during the fourth French air strike against guerrilla positions. The Polisario Front constantly accused France of blatantly attacking its forces with its Jaguars and Mirages, reportedly using napalm and phosphorus bombs along with other weapons against them in the western Sahara. In these attacks, the Polisario guerrillas, who had been consistently harassing Mauritanian forces, claimed two Jaguars were shot down, with the loss of at least one pilot. In Paris, the French denied any such losses by its air forces, and said that French support for Mauritania had been 'very limited', and any such claims had been 'largely invented'. However, the *Armée de l'Air* admitted that four Jaguars of EC 3/11, refuelled by a KC-135F tanker and accompanied by a C-160 Transall, had deployed to Libreville for a joint exercise, Operation *Abidjan*, with Gabon. Similarly, in January 1977, four more Jaguars from *11ème* had been

Jaguar As and ten Mirage F.1CRs, supported by KC-135 tankers, took up station at Kisangani Air Base near Goma to provide reconnaissance and air support (if needed) to the troops giving aid to the population.

'Out of Area' Camouflage Schemes

For their initial deployments overseas in the 1970s the *Armée de l'Air* Jaguars wore the traditional grey, green and aluminium colour scheme. Subsequent deployments

having light/pale blue undersides, and at least one aircraft carried an experimental colour of pale turquoise FS 35622, which was not retained. The colour confusion may lie in the shade applied to the Mirage III and Super Mystère, which carried a pale blue FS 35414 hue on their undersides for their operations when stationed at Dijbouti.

African Scheme, circa 1970s
Dark grey, dark green, and aluminium.

Jaguar A142 11-RO of Escadrille SPA69 from EC 3/11 'Corse' in the chocolate brown and cream colour scheme adopted for operations in Africa. The aircraft carries the centreline-mounted Thomson-Brandt BAP-100 runway cratering munitions, used with such great effect against the rebel airfield at Quadi Doum in northern Chad during Operation Epervier. Dassault via Paul Jackson

deployed to the Ivory Coast following a similar reinforcement flight in April to Senegal under Operation *N'Diambour*.

Rwanda 1994 – Operation Turquoise

On 24 June 1994, as part of the United Nations humanitarian effort in the beleaguered African country of Rwanda, ten

saw the lessons from the African terrain taken into account and the aircraft were given a more appropriate colour scheme of brown and cream disruptive uppersurfaces and aluminium undersides. Deployments since the Gulf War have seen a standard beige FS 33617 and light stone FS 33531 disruptive scheme with aluminium undersides. Some references quote the Jaguars as

Chad Scheme, circa 1980s.
Upper surface: cream FS 33798 and chocolate brown FS 30125
Lower surface aluminium FS 17178

African Scheme, circa 1990s
Upper surface: beige FS 33617 and light stone FS 33531
Lower surface: aluminium FS 17178

CHAPTER THREE

Royal Air Force Jaguars

A menacing four-ship of Jaguar GR.1s at low-level. Not so much a 'ground attack' aircraft as a 'total weapons system', and its various characteristics must be considered as part of a whole giving it the ability to deliver a fast, accurate and powerful punch, even in adverse weather. GEC/Marconi

Background

Once brought into service, *panthera onca*, the Jaguar, was destined to be the most important strike aircraft in the RAF's inventory throughout the mid-1970s and early 1980s, with 165 single-seat and thirty-five two-seat aircraft being purchased. Three more two-seaters were later acquired for operations in test and evaluation units

directly linked to future advancements for the Jaguar. The largest user of the type was to be RAF Germany (RAFG), which formed part of the Second Allied Tactical Air Force under the Supreme Allied Commander Europe (SACEUR) and was to be concerned with interdiction, battlefield support and reconnaissance. It operated four squadrons of Jaguars in the strike role and one for reconnaissance. In mainland

Britain, No.1 Group, RAF Strike Command, operated four squadrons – three strike and one reconnaissance – which formed part of the Allied Commander Europe's 'ACE' Mobile Force in conjunction with the 3rd Division of the British Army. In addition to the front-line units, the UK was also home to the Jaguar OCU, which in time of war could provide additional crews from their instructor staff, and replacement aircraft. During its early days of service in Germany, the Jaguar was partnered by the Harrier, Buccaneer and Phantom, eventually replacing one squadron of Harriers, and supplanting the Phantoms in the strike/attack/reconnaissance role, freeing them to take up air defence duties in both Germany and the UK.

The Jaguar is not so much a 'ground attack aircraft' as a 'total weapons system', with its various characteristics needing to be considered as part of a whole, endowing it with the ability to deliver a fast, powerful punch at low level, in adverse weather, and even in the face of hostile SAMs and fighter defence. There is also a limited STOL capability within the Jaguar's repertoire: in 'clean' configuration it can be landed inside 450yd (410m), the aircraft's slow approach speed, energy-absorbing undercarriage and braking systems being ideal for this type of operation, and take-off with a respectable load can be accomplished in around 600yd (550m).

Jaguar GR.1

As has been mentioned in earlier chapters, the RAF's Jaguar S, or to give it its official title, the GR.1 (Ground Attack/Reconnaissance Mark 1), was far more sophisticated, technically advanced and expensive than its French counterpart, the

Jaguar A. Where the French had opted for a simple avionics fit, the Royal Air Force fitted their Jaguars with one of the most comprehensive and accurate computerized digital navigation and attack systems that was available anywhere in the world at the time. With an inertial platform that neither transmitted nor received signals which could be disturbed by enemy jamming, the avionics were designed to provide the Jaguar with the maximum possibility of making a successful first-pass attack without reference to TACAN or any other ground-based aids, which may not be available in times of war. An automatic moving map display was also seen as essential: as the pilot would be operating mainly at low level – where he would need to be able to establish his position with the minimum of effort – he needed to avoid having to shuffle through a 'leg-full' of maps. Central to this requirement was the Marconi NAVWASS (NAVigation and Weapons Aiming Sub-System) and the Marconi-Elliott MCS 920M computer into which the pilot enters waypoint and target co-ordinates before the mission gets underway.

The NAVWASS gave the Jaguar the ability to hit a target with pinpoint accuracy without needing to use a (detectable) radar system. The fit consisted of: the Marconi-Elliott Avionics Systems E3R three-gyro inertial platform; a projected map

display; a navigation control unit weapon aiming mode selector; a hand controller and air data computer; the Sperry Gyroscope Divisions gyromagnetic compass; and a Smiths Industries diffractive-optics head-up display (HUD). The HUD uses a low-light-level TV camera, which compared with the standard refractive-optics type offers a wider field of view, improved optical characteristics and a brighter (green) display, exhibiting vital attack and flight information, focused at infinity. Also fitted was a horizontal situation indicator; ARI 23232 radar altimeter; ARI 23205/4 TACAN; Ferranti ARI 23231/3 laser rangefinder and marked target seeker; a fin-mounted Ferranti ARI-18223 radar homing and warning receiver (RHWR); with the tailfin also playing host to the VOR/ILS aerials. Radios included an ARI 23181 HF, ARI23315/4 VHF, ARI 23159 standby VHF, ARI 23134 SSR identification friend or foe (IFF), and a Vinten 1200-04 cockpit voice recorder. Both single- and two-seat British aircraft were originally fitted with the Martin-Baker Mk9 zero-zero ejector seat and the Adour Mk102 engine giving 5,115lb (2,325kg) of dry thrust and 7,305lb (3320kg) with afterburner. The reconnaissance Jaguars of Nos 2(AC) and 41(F) squadrons in Germany and the UK respectively, were equipped with a centreline-mounted BAe reconnaissance pod, details of which can be found in Chapter 4.

The Jaguar GR.1's Tactical Edge – the NAVWASS

As the then Chief of the Air Staff, Air Chief Marshal Sir Neil Cameron, enthused in 1977, 'With the Jaguar the RAF is now in the "bomb-in-a-bucket" era.'

The means by which the Jaguar delivers its various types of weapon onto target sets it apart from many of its contemporaries, and many other aircraft since. The navigation and attack avionics are designed for single-pilot operation, and for any mission the pilot relies on the information given to him by the extremely sophisticated NAVWASS. Much of the mission information is plotted by the pilot on the ground, when his maps are drawn up and he inputs the waypoints and target information into a ground computer station, from where they are transferred into the cockpit via a small portable unit called a 'brick'. The Marconi-Elliott NAVWASS system contains the E3R inertial platform,

Specification – Jaguar GR.1A	
Type:	Single-seat tactical strike and ground attack fighter/bomber with secondary reconnaissance capability
Accommodation:	Pilot only, on Martin-Baker Mk9B zero/zero ejector seat
Powerplant:	Two Rolls Royce/Turboméca Adour Mk104 afterburning turbofans rated at 5,320lb (2,418kg) dry and 8,040lb (3,655kg) with afterburner
Performance:	Max speed 1,056mph (1,690km/h) Climb rate 30,000ft (9,100m) in 90sec Ceiling 45,930ft (13,920m) Range 334 miles (534km) lo-lo-lo, 875 miles (1,400km) hi-lo-hi and 2,190 miles (3,504km) ferry
Weights:	Empty 15,432lb (7,000kg); normal 24,149lb (11,000kg); max 34,612lb (15,700kg)
Dimensions:	Length 55ft 2.5in (16.73m); span 28ft 6in (8.64m); height: 16ft 10.5in (5.11m)
Armament:	Twin 30mm Aden cannon with 150 rounds per gun, plus five external hardpoints for a total of 10,000lb (4,545kg) of stores, including CRV-7 air-to-surface rockets, over/under wing Sidewinder AAMs, CBUs, and standard and laser-guided bombs, non-nuclear

(Above) The Royal Air Force fitted their Jaguars with one of the most comprehensive and accurate computerized digital navigation and attack systems available at the time, the Marconi NAVWASS, which led one senior RAF officer to comment that the RAF had entered the 'bomb-in-a-bucket' era. GEC/Marconi

Jaguar GR.1 cockpit, showing the central moving map display, the traditional needle-and-dial instruments and the g-load meter above the coaming. BAe

with a fully manoeuvrable four-gimbal gyroscopic platform using three single-degree accelerometers. Information is passed to the pilot giving heading, velocity and acceleration via the platform electronic unit and the interface unit via the 920M computer. The 920M's central computer had an 8,912-word store machine which receives inputs from fourteen different sources through the interface unit.

The NAVWASS was replaced by the Ferranti FIN 1064 INAS in 1979. The INAS can give 20 types of information on the NCU and PMP which shows the aircraft's present position, track and direction to selected waypoints, and these are presented to the pilot on his HUD which, in addition to the 'regular' flight information, also shows angle of attack, vertical speed, time to go and weapons aiming information.

Jaguar T.2

Externally similar to the GR.1, the T.2 is an operational conversion trainer which first flew in 1971. The aircraft features an elongated nose section to accommodate an extra seat for pilot training. The two crew are accommodated in a pair of Martin-Baker Mk9 ejector seats within separate and divided cockpits, housed beneath a large bubble canopy which features two rear-hinged opening sections, the aft section of which has been raised by 15in (38cm) to

Specification – Jaguar T.2A/B	
Type:	Two-seat operational conversion trainer with secondary strike and ground attack capabilities
Accommodation:	Pilot (front seat) and instructor (rear seat) in tandem Martin-Baker Mk9B zero/zero ejector seats
Powerplant:	Two Rolls Royce/Turbomeca Adour Mk104 afterburning turbofans rated at 5,320lb (2,418kg) dry and 8,040lb (3,655kg) with afterburner
Performance:	Max speed 1,056mph (1,690km/h) Climb rate 30,000ft (9,100m) in 90sec Ceiling 45,930ft (13,920m) Range 334 miles (534km) lo-lo-lo, 875 miles (1,400km) hi-lo-hi and 2,190 miles (3,504km) ferry
Weights:	Empty 15,432lb (7,000kg); max 34,612lb (15,700kg)
Dimensions:	Span 28ft 6in (8.64m); length 57ft 6.25in (17.43m)
Armament:	One 30mm Aden cannon with 150 rounds of ammunition, plus five external hardpoints for 10,000lb (4,545kg) of stores

One of the RAF's early unmarked Jaguar GR.1s, in its early style three-tone camouflage. via Gary Madgwick

The raised height of the T.2's rear cockpit can be appreciated in this shot, as can the superb view. Also of note is the re-styled nose section and the 'flat' undersides. f4 Aviation Photobank

allow good vision from the instructor's (aft) position. Avionics are the same as for the single-seat version, though there is no internal RWR, giving it a limited operational role in wartime, and allowing for a smooth transition from training to front-line aircraft. The T.2's fit originally featured the Elliott MCS 920M system, but this has been upgraded in line with the GR.1's to the Ferranti FIN 1064 INAS, giving a re-designation of T.2A. The T.2s all have a retractable IFR probe, but only a single 30mm Aden cannon, and again were originally fitted with the Rolls-Royce Adour Mk102 engine. Most T.2s are located at RAF Lossiemouth with No.16(R) Squadron, the Jaguar OCU, with the three Coltishall units each having at least one 'T-Bird' on strength. In addition to the original order for thirty-five T.2s a further three were acquired for use by specialist RAF units, one at the Institute of Aviation Medicine and two at the Empire Test Pilots School at Boscombe Down.

Jaguars in the UK

The first of the production Jaguars to reach the RAF was S-4 XX111, originally flown in by Sqn Ldr John Preece, arriving at RAF Lossiemouth in Scotland on 30 May 1973 to begin the process of groundcrew training. The Jaguar Operational Conversion Unit (JOCU) under the leadership of Wg Cdr Clive Walker had been established at the base in March 1973, with initial pilot training being the responsibility of BAC Warton. The first single-seat deliveries to the unit were XX114 (S-7) and XX115 (S-8) which arrived on 13 September 1973, flown in by Sqn Ldr Preece and BAC test pilot Jerry Lee, and JOCU was redesignated No.226 OCU from late 1974, taking over its identity from the former Lightning OCU.

The first operational Jaguar unit was No.54 Squadron, which was re-formed at Lossiemouth on 29 March 1974 under the leadership of Wg Cdr Terry Carlton, albeit

for the interim with some aircraft borrowed from the JOCU, and others that did not have the LRMTS nose or RWR fin. The squadron's service entry was marked by an official ceremony which included dignitaries from both partner companies and a line-up of visiting French Jaguars, plus a sneak preview of one new RAF Jaguar, XX726 (the twenty-third production model) which was in the colours of No.6 Squadron, the second Jaguar unit which re-formed under the command of Wg Cdr John Quarterman at Lossiemouth on 30 September – the aircraft publicly displaying the Jaguar's laser nose for the first time.

In August 1974 No.54 Squadron left its Scottish home and moved south to RAF Coltishall in Norfolk, and was subsequently declared combat-ready on 1 January 1975, in line with the original targets set in 1972. No.6 Squadron also left Lossiemouth in November – leaving the OCU as the

A pair of early RAF Jaguars assigned to the JOCU at Lossiemouth. Of note are the faired-over cannon ports and the lack of the LRMTS on the nose. BAe

An early Jaguar line-up of 226 OCU aircraft at RAF Lossiemouth in Scotland. The Jaguar Operational Conversion Unit (JOCU) was established at the base in March 1973, and was subsequently redesignated No.226 OCU from late 1974, taking over its identity from the former Lightning OCU. via Gary Madgwick

only permanent Jaguar resident – and was later joined by No.41(F) Squadron, which re-formed at Coltishall on 1 April 1977 and whose primary function was to be tactical reconnaissance. Jaguars from No.54 Squadron took part in their first NATO exercise, *Bold Guard*, in September 1974, and paid their first visit to *Red Flag* in 1978. These three units, part of No.1 Group, Strike Command, formed the 'Coltishall Wing', assigned to the NATO-driven Regional Reinforcement and the Allied Commander Europe's Mobile Force, capable of rapid deployment overseas in times of crisis.

The RAF's Jaguars have been maintained at three different sites in the UK

Jaguar, XZ399, departing on 24 February 1992. The task of maintaining the Jaguar fleet currently rests with the Engineering Wing at RAF St Athan.

With the ending of the Cold War in the early 1990s, the Government issued a White Paper entitled *Options for Change*, in which it set out the face of the Royal Air Force's future standing, now that the threat from the former Soviet Union had diminished. For the UK's Jaguar force however, this was to have little effect on their numbers, and the three Coltishall-based units were to see an increase in their out-of-area commitments. The most significant squadron change came to No.226 OCU at Lossiemouth, which gained the number-

support. Early aircraft included the Atlas, Audax, Hector and Lysander. A role change saw the 'Saints' tasked with reconnaissance in World War II, flying the Tomahawk, Mustang and Spitfire, moving to RAF Germany postwar to fly the Tempest, Vampire, Venom, Canberra, Buccaneer and Tornado.

No.16(R) Squadron's markings consist of two yellow crossed keys on a black disc, a yellow 'Saint' motif on a black disc, and a red and blue tartan design across the RWR. No.226 OCU markings were a shaft of arrows and a beacon torch crossed and intertwined with a belt, usually painted on the tailfin, and for a brief period the unit carried a leaping Jaguar on the nose. With

XZ109/EN in the colours of No.6 Squadron. Author

over the years. No.60 MU (Maintenance Unit) at Leconfield took on its first Jaguar, XX111, from No.226 OCU on 2 December 1974, with the last to receive the unit's attention being XX729 of No.6 Squadron, in 1976. Servicing then switched to the Engineering Wing at Abingdon, with its No.1 AMU (Aircraft Maintenance Unit) accepting XX732 of No.54 Squadron on 3 June 1976, reaching the milestone of one hundred 'major' Jaguar services with XX847 on 19 January 1990. With the rationalization of RAF bases during the early 1990s, Abingdon was closed, its final

plate of No.16 (Reserve) Squadron, following the disbandment of four of RAF Germany's Tornado GR.1 squadrons, and their standards being passed on to non-combat units in the early 1990s.

UK Units

No.16(R) Squadron (formerly No.226 OCU)

Originally established at St Omer in France during 1915, the squadron has traditionally been associated with Army

the advent of the two-tone permanent grey colours replacing the tactical grey/green scheme, the tail-applied 'tartan' has, at the time of writing, been withdrawn, but the high-visibility No.16(R) markings remain.

No.6 Squadron

The longest-serving RAF squadron, No.6 is unique in having never been disbanded since it originally came into service at South Farnborough on 31 January 1914. Operating overseas for most of its life, the squadron was equipped with the 40mm cannon-armed Hurricane IID during World War II and fought in the famous desert campaigns, earning its nickname, the 'Flying Can Openers'. Postwar, the squadron operated the Vampire, Venom, Canberra and Phantom FGR.2, which it retained until re-equipped with the Jaguar at Lossiemouth, before moving to its current Norfolk home.

Markings are red zig-zag 'gunners' stripes across a light blue background applied to the RWR, and a red outlined winged 'can

No.41(F) Squadron

Formed at Gosport in July 1916, No.41 has been a fighter squadron for most of its life. It reformed in 1929, flying Snipes, Siskins, Bulldogs, Demons and Furies before receiving Spitfires during World War II. Postwar it operated Tempests, Spitfires and Hornets, and later Meteors, Hunters and Javelins. After a spell as a Bloodhound missile unit it re-formed in 1972 on the Phantom at RAF Coningsby, moving to the Jaguar on 27 April 1976.

No.54(F) Squadron

Another 'always a fighter' squadron, No.54 flew Pups and Camels in France during World War I, re-forming in 1930 with Siskins, Bulldogs, Gauntlets and Gladiators, receiving Spitfires before World War II. After the Battle of Britain the unit moved to Australia, eventually returning to the UK to fly Tempests, Vampires, Meteors, Hunters and Phantoms. The unit converted to the Jaguar in 1974 at Lossiemouth before moving to Coltishall.

A Jaguar T.2 in the markings of No.54 Squadron. Author

opener' motif applied to the intake sides. Early No.6 Squadron Jaguars had the blue and red zig-zags applied either side of the squadron motif on the engine intakes, which was later changed to a red bar either side, before settling on their current design. Allocated code letters: EA–EZ

Markings consist of a red cross of St Omer (being taken from the town's coat of arms) surmounted with a crown and Roman numerals representing the squadron number superimposed. This marking is carried on the tailfin and intake sides, flanked by red bars outlined in white. Allocated code letters: FA–FZ

Markings consist of a heraldic blue-coloured lion rampant superimposed on a yellow shield on the aircraft's nose, with blue and yellow chequers applied to the engine intake walls and repeated across the RWR fairing on the tail. Allocated code letters: GA–GZ

No.54 Squadron's 75th Anniversary Special

No.54 Squadron was the second of the Coltishall Wing to celebrate its 75th Anniversary, on 15 May 1991, following No.6 who had their celebrations in 1989. To mark the event a GR.1, XZ112, received a special commemorative scheme. The basic concept was quite simple, consisting of a large squadron badge applied to an all-blue tailfin, with the unit's blue and yellow chequers carried across the RWR fairing, and a yellow shield containing the unit's emblem on the nose. The *pièce de resistance*

was, however, the application of the chequerboard markings to two underwing fuel tanks, which added some real spark to the aircraft. The chequerboard is a fairly recent addition as far as RAF heraldry goes, having been first applied to the squadron's Vampires in the early jet days following World War II. The scheme lasted for just over a year, but the RWR chequerboard has remained a permanent feature on all No.54 Squadron jets.

No.54 Squadron's dramatic 'anniversary' jet. BAe

No.41(F) Squadron's 75th Anniversary Special

In the same year as No.54 Squadron's 75th birthday, No.41(F) Squadron also celebrated their 'three-quarters' anniversary and to mark the occasion a single GR.1, XZ398, also received a special commemorative paint scheme. The aircraft featured an all-red spine and tailfin, with the squadron's Cross of Lorraine crest applied to the centre of the fin, outlined with a blue laurel and 'capped' with a gold crown. The RWR, which was also red, carried the legend '75 Years 1916–1991' in gold lettering, and either side of the unit a white stripe was applied. The usual fin flash was outlined in white, with the remainder of the airframe retaining its tactical camouflage of dark green and dark sea grey.

No.41(F) Squadron's red-tailed cat. via Gary Madgwick

XZ104/EE in an early incarnation of a desert sand colour scheme. Author

A No.6 Squadron Jaguar T.2B (T.4) on finals, resplendent in the two-tone Jaguar '96 colour scheme.
f4 Aviation Photobank

UK Camouflage

The Jaguar began life with the traditional RAF scheme of disruptive dark sea grey and dark green uppersurfaces with light aircraft grey undersides. When originally delivered the Jaguars wore a gloss finish to their paint schemes, though XX760 received an overall matt finish in 1976. XX728 was used to experiment with a suitable underside camouflage colour, which eventually led to the upper surface scheme being extended in a wraparound pattern, which also made the aircraft less visible when making turns at low level. 'Out-of-area' camouflage has included a washable coat of white for Arctic operations; an all-over 'desert sand' ARTF (Alkaline Removable Temporary Finish) scheme for operations in the Gulf region since 1990; light grey ARTF for operations over Bosnia since 1993; and all-over permanent UOR Jaguar '96 colours of two-tone low infra-red dark camouflage grey and medium grey for aircraft coming out of a modification phase and being used for continuing operations around the Adriatic. The latest Jaguar '96 scheme has the dark camouflage grey on all upper surfaces, around the canopy and windshield and following the rear fuselage contours around the tailfin, with the tailfin itself being painted medium grey. Some of the 1,200ltr wing tanks have also received an 'upper' and 'lower' half-grey camouflage colour. The fin, tailplanes and underfuselage strakes have also had a black radar-absorbing SWAM finish applied to their leading edges.

It is interesting to note that well before the Gulf War, at least one Jaguar, XZ104/EE from No.6 Squadron, had been painted up in an experimental light desert sand colour, for its participation in a 1989 Middle East exercise, though it retained its squadron markings.

Two Arctic-clad GR.1As taxi back onto the Coltishall ramp. f4 Aviation Photobank

Jaguars in Germany

The insignia of RAF Germany has a simple motto – 'Keepers of the Peace' – and this aim has remained unchanged since its inception post-World War II. Its tactical air element's principal role was that of strike/attack, air defence and reconnaissance, and the introduction of the Jaguar gave its commanders a powerful and flexible new asset. Five operational Jaguar squadrons were destined for Germany-based operations, flying from Brüggen and Laarbruch, both close to the Dutch border. The first of the Jaguar units, No.14 Squadron, re-formed at Brüggen on 7 April 1975 with the arrival of XX836, and was operational by the end of that year. It was followed by Nos 17, 31 and 20 Squadrons, all units being up to strength and declared combat-ready by 1978. Laarbruch's sole Jaguar unit was No.2 Army Co-Operation (AC) Squadron, which like its UK-based counterpart, No.41(F), was tasked with tactical reconnaissance. All of the Germany-based units were included in the 2nd Allied Tactical Air Force (2ATAF). With the exception of No.20 Squadron, the new Jaguar units had previously operated

A Jaguar pilot in full NBC rig climbs aboard his aircraft inside its HAS. He carries his portable oxygen system with him until he connects to the aircraft's own system. Note also the dual language – English and German – yellow warning panels.
via Gary Madgwick

(Below) XX756, one of the many redundant ex-RAF Germany airframes at No.2 SoTT Cosford, where the engineering apprentices use them to learn their trade. Author

the Phantom in the strike/attack role, No.20 being a former Harrier close air support unit.

Like all of the front-line aircraft based in Germany, the Jaguars enjoyed the accommodation of TAB-V Hardened Aircraft Shelters (HAS), which could each accommodate two aircraft. 'Hardened' means protected against the effects of nuclear, chemical or biological contamination. In wartime the crews would live and work in their Personal Briefing Facility (PBF), located next to the HASs, using NBC (Nuclear, Biological and Chemical) masks and portable oxygen systems to get to and enter their aircraft if necessary. On the nuclear theme, RAF Germany's Jaguars were able to carry the British WE177 free-fall tactical nuclear weapon, a responsibility later turned over to the Tornado.

Throughout the next decade the Jaguar performed its duties in Europe quietly and professionally, achieving all that was asked of it. However, the introduction of the multi-role Panavia Tornado during the mid- to late 1980s saw the Germany-based Jaguars being replaced by the newer aircraft, and the unwanted airframes were either put into storage at RAF Shawbury, or passed to one of the Schools of Technical Training at Cosford and Halton.

The first Tornado unit to form was No.20 (Tornado Designate) Squadron at Laarbruch during early 1984, with No.20 (Jaguar) Squadron at Brüggen thereby disbanded on 29 June 1984 and thus becoming a Tornado squadron on the same day. No.31 Squadron were the first to receive Tornados at Brüggen, in June 1984, followed by No.17 and then No.14 before the end of 1985. That left No.2(AC) Squadron the sole operators of sixteen Jaguar GR.1As in Germany, which they continued to do at a base now dominated by the Tornado. However, the days of the 'Recce-Jag' were to be short-lived, its retention being only a stop-gap until the more capable Tornado GR.1A, which was still under development, could be introduced to service. No.2(AC)'s Jaguars finally bowed out of RAFG on 31 December 1987.

RAF Germany Squadrons

No.2(AC) Squadron

Since its inception in 1912, the squadron has operated almost entirely in the reconnaissance role, seeing extensive service in France in both World Wars, operating in World War II the Lysander, Tomahawk,

Mustang and Spitfire. Postwar operations were conducted entirely in Germany until 1992 when the unit returned to the UK with its Tornado GR.1As. Former aircraft have included the Meteor, Swift, Hunter, Phantom, and Jaguar. The Jaguar took over the reconnaissance role from the Phantom under Wg Cdr 'Sandy' Wilson on 1 October 1976.

Markings consist of a white disc on the engine intake flanked by white triangles on a black rectangle, the disc containing the 'Hereward's Wake Knot'. Individual aircraft codes are contained within a black-edged white triangle on the tail, which when lined up in the correct manner spelled out 'SHINEY TWO JAG IIER' (the II being Roman numerals). The squadron later swapped its tail letters for numbers. This tail marking was also repeated on the nosewheel door. During 1988 the squadron celebrated 75 years of service, and painted the tailfin of XZ104 all black and applied a large squadron crest to it.

No.14 Squadron

Formed at Shoreham in February 1915, the unit saw action in the Middle East flying DH9s, Bristol Fighters, Fairey 111Fs and

No.14 Squadron Jaguar undergoing maintenance. Graham Causer

Gordons, operating the Martin Marauder during World War II. Re-established post-war, they have operated the Mosquito, Vampire, Venom, Hunter, Canberra and Phantom based in Germany, and flew the Jaguar from April 1975 before converting to the Tornado in November 1985.

Markings consist of a winged crusader's shield, surmounted by a yellow helmet and shoulder piece from a suit of armour, flanked by blue diamonds, carried on the intakes. Allocated code letters: AA–AZ.

converted to the Tornado GR.1 and disbanded its Jaguars on 1 March 1985.

Markings consist of the squadron badge of a mailed red glove on the intake sides flanked by white rectangles containing black zig-zags. Allocated code letters: BA–BZ.

No.20 Squadron

Established at Netheravon in September 1915 with the Bristol Fighter. The squadron later moved to India, flying bor-

Markings consist of the squadron emblem, a swooping eagle carrying a sword, flanked by blue, red, white and green bars applied to the engine intakes. Allocated code letters: CA–CZ.

No.31 Squadron

The 'Gold Stars' were the first RAF unit to serve on the North-West Frontier in India, in 1916 with the BE2. These were superseded by Bristol Fighters, Wapitis and Vincents. They then became a transport unit

No.17 Squadron Jaguar. Author

No.17 Squadron

Formed at Gosport in February 1915 and saw action in the Middle East. Took part in the Battle of Britain and flew later marks of Spitfire in Burma. It was assigned reconnaissance tasks postwar with the Canberra, and found a new role as a strike fighter with the Phantom FGR.2 before converting to the Jaguar as RAF Germany's second Jaguar unit in June 1975 with the arrival of XX840. It also received the 100th production aircraft, XX818, on 15 August that year. No.17 Squadron

der patrols. In World War II it flew in Burma, and postwar was re-established in Germany flying Sabres, and then Hunters. A brief move to Singapore was followed by a return to Germany to operate the Harrier before moving to Jaguar on 1 March 1977, with the arrival of XZ374. The unit disbanded on the Jaguar on 24 June 1984, re-forming on the Tornado, before again disbanding as part of 'Options For Change', re-appearing as No.20(Reserve) Squadron, the Harrier OCU at Wittering.

flying Valettas, DC-2s and Dakotas, before returning to the UK to become the Metropolitan Communications Squadron operating Ansons, Devons and Chipmunks until 1955 when they moved to Germany with the Canberra PR.7. They changed to Phantoms in 1972, changing again in January 1976 to the Jaguar with the arrival of XX970. No.31 Squadron relinquished its Jaguars to become a Tornado unit on 1 November 1984.

Markings consist of a five-point golden yellow star surrounded by a green laurel

Pictured just prior to the Jaguar GR.1 taking over the No.20 Squadron badge from the Harrier GR.3.
GEC/Marconi

wreath, flanked by green and yellow chequers, and applied to the engine intakes. Allocated code letters: DA–DZ.

Camouflage in Germany

As with the UK-based aircraft, during their time in Germany the Jaguars either carried the dark sea grey, dark green and light aircraft grey colour, or the two-tone disruptive grey/green scheme. Rescue, caution and warning markings applied to all Germany-based Jaguars were annotated in both English and German.

Jaguar GR.1A

Beginning in 1983, the RAF's remaining Jaguar GR.1s had their original Elliott MCS 920M computer replaced by a Ferranti FIN 1064 INAS (Inertial Navigation

and Attack System) NAVWASS II unit, which was some 50kg lighter and occupied one-third of its predecessor's space. First flown on 31 July 1981, it has increased the effectiveness of the overall systems of the NAVWASS, and created the designation of Jaguar GR.1A. The FIN 1064 INAS was introduced to aircraft from No.54 Squadron in 1983. The conversion work was undertaken on eighty-nine aircraft by the Jaguar Maintenance Unit (JMU) at RAF Abingdon. The FIN 1064 is a far more reliable and accurate piece of kit than the NAVWASS, offering a 99 per cent servicability rate, and a maximum one mile drift per flying hour without needing to be updated. Another new feature introduced during the 1980s was the Ferranti TABS (Total Avionics Briefing System) which is a ground computer linked to a digitizing map table. By placing the computer's cursor over a point on his map, the pilot can plot

his route, and the computer in turn displays the completed route, annotating any threats and giving error and time-on-target cues. A hard copy is presented to the pilot with grid references, targets and turns, and these are also down loaded into a Ferranti PODS (POrtable Data Store) a 32K erasable memory module or 'brick' that can be inserted into the aircraft's computer via an interface and allows up to thirty-one targets or turning points to be stored. The aircraft were also given a 'battle fit' consisting of a Westinghouse ALQ-101 jammer pod and a Phimat chaff dispenser on their outer wing pylons, together with two Tracor AN/ALE-40 flare dispensers scabbed onto the underside engine access panels. Provision to carry the AIM-9G Sidewinder missile was also added. RAF Germany GR.1As also had a rather crude five-shot chaff/flare dispenser which could be carried in place of the braking parachute.

An impressive line-up of Jaguar GR.1As and T.2As from Nos 6, 41 and 54 Squadrons on the ramp at RAF
Coltishall. Author

A 'scrubbed' ex-Gulf War Jaguar GR.1A. Author

UK and Europe – 'In the Field' Trials

XX109 is 'hidden' and armed under a bridge on the M55 motorway in Lancashire. BAe

The much-vaunted 'rough field' capability of the Jaguar was amply demonstrated on many occasions, as was the aircraft's ability to operate from 'non-standard' runways. In 1973 Tim Ferguson, a BAC test pilot, landed XX109/09, one of the early production machines, on an unopened stretch of the new M55 motorway near Blackpool in Lancashire, with a landing run of only 450yd (410m) using the brake parachute. The aircraft was then turned around and fitted with four captive flight cluster bombs and a 264gal (1,200ltr) fuel tank on the centreline. The return take-off run began beneath a road bridge, in full afterburner, and the aircraft was airborne in around 600yd (550m), causing no damage to the road surface.

Drawing upon the conclusions of Ferguson's trial, four Jaguars from No.31 Squadron practised emergency landings and take-offs from a new German Autobahn between Bremen and Bremerhaven in September 1977. A second series of tests was carried out by the UK Aeroplane and Armament Evaluation Establishment (A&AEE) at Boscombe Down, also in the autumn of 1977. Using both single- and two-seat Jaguars, the aircraft were operated from a specially prepared surface with all manner of obstacles, such as shallow ditches and rabbit holes, scattered along its way. The pilots quickly adjusted to the effects on the aircraft caused by the undulation, and were able to taxi, land and take off, thus proving the Jaguar's flexibility, which could only be matched by the V/STOL capabilities of the unconventional and unique Harrier.

(Below) **With afterburners blazing, Tim Ferguson rotates the Jaguar, after a take-off run of only 600yd (550m). Maybe not a Harrier, but when you consider that a similarly armed V/STOL aircraft would need the same take-off run, it's a pretty impressive performance.** BAe

Jaguar GR.1s taxi out from what seems to be a wooded site, but is in fact the perimeter track to RAF Coltishall's runway. RAF

The Mk102 standard Adour engines were replaced by the improved Mk104 (RT172-26), a powerplant roughly similar to the export Mk804, giving the Jaguar extra available power, in a programme that began in 1978 with the re-engining of all RAF Germany's Jaguars; the Mk104 engines were eventually retrofitted to all the aircraft. However, had the RAF been a little more patient, they could have used the even better Adour Mk811 (RT172-58), which was fitted to the Jaguar International aircraft supplied to Oman and Nigeria (*see* Chapter 5). The Mk811 featured an increase in its operating temperature, and revision dynamics in its low pressure compressor.

Jaguar T.2A

In line with the upgrading of the single-seat GR.1 to GR.1A standard, so the T.2 underwent the same process to keep the two-seaters representative of the front-line aircraft. Therefore, they had their original

Elliott MCS 920M computer replaced by the Ferranti FIN 1064 NAVWASS II, and the original Mk102 standard Adour engines were replaced by the improved Mk104.

Training to Fight

Following the introduction of the Jaguar into RAF service in 1974, the provision of the necessary organization to train future pilots was given careful consideration. The selection of a suitable base was dictated by the need to practise low-level training and to have easy access to a weapons range. RAF Lossiemouth on the Moray Firth in Scotland proved to be the ideal choice, lying as it does in the middle of the finest low-flying areas in the UK, with two air-to-ground weapons ranges on its doorstep, at Tain and Rosehearty. Tain is only four minutes' flying time from Lossiemouth and here the use of the aircraft's LRMTS is permitted. Much of the flying over

Scotland is cleared down to 250ft (75m), with minimal airspace restrictions. One area in the west of Scotland, officially referred to as 14 Tango Tactical Training Area – known also as 'moon country' – is cleared, with special permission, for flights down to 100ft (30m).

It was at Lossiemouth that the Jaguar Conversion Team (JCT) was formed-up, a small team consisting of experienced ground attack staff who were tasked with writing the rule book for the Jaguar, and planning its training regime. As such the JCT opened its doors as No.226 OCU in February 1974. Initially the OCU had two flights (No.1 and No.2) as there was a large introductory requirement for the RAF to man eight Jaguar squadrons in Germany and the UK. Since the introduction of the Tornado, the heady days of intensive work-up are gone, but the OCU, now numbered No.16(Reserve) Squadron still has the task of turning out 'top-up' aircrew for the three units at Coltishall, as well as

RAF Jaguar GR.1 Mission Systems: Hit Hard, Hit Fast

After suiting-up into the necessary combat gear, briefing, producing his maps, and arming the TABS 'Brick' with the relevant INAS information, the pilot walks to his aircraft. He enters the weapon loading onto indicators inside the nosewheel compartment, and climbs aboard. To allow for accurate alignment of the INAS each HAS, hanger or hardstand has its exact geographical location painted on the floor, giving latitude, longitude, magnetic variation and a true heading stripe. Pre-flight, the pilot 'winds up' the computer systems and the magnetic compass, plugs the PODS 'brick' into the Ferranti FIN 1064 INAS, and starts up the engines. A Microturbo air generator fires up the powerplants, (an ideal piece of equipment for off-base operations) and when the 'NAV' light illuminates on the instrument panel the pilot knows the INAS has correctly aligned, and he selects his first turn point. Take-off is in full afterburner, which is cancelled at 300kt (555km/h) to save fuel, and the wheels and flaps come up immediately. The HUD and HSI then give the pilot all the necessary flight information in his line of sight and his projected map display shows his turning points, IPs (initial points) and targets; but the pilot always carries the traditional 'legfull' of maps – just in case! The HSI gives him a

fed into the weapons aiming mode selector (WAMS) and all relevant ordnance details are presented in the HUD.

In a planned attack, when the 'IP to target' point is reached, the pilot manoeuvres the Jaguar onto its run-in heading with the HUD now displaying its attack symbology: a drift-compensated 'bomb fall line' and a target bar showing a continuously computed impact point (CCIP) for the chosen weapon. The aircraft is then flown so that the target is visually acquired and kept on the bomb fall line, with the target bar being moved up and down by the pilot's control inputs so that the target coincides to give range information. Weapon delivery is achieved as the correct range is reached, with the pilot depressing the 'pickle' button to commit the automatic system to release.

The Jaguar's accuracy is enhanced by the LRMTS. With the laser giving accurate range information, the pilot can use the target bar to direct the laser as he flies, as information is being fed directly into the weapons system. With the marked target seeker, a ground or airborne laser can designate a target, and its reflected energy is acquired by the seeker system and is locked up to provide automatic ranging.

A Jaguar pilot checks out his systems before a mission. Author

digital readout of the distance to turns in relation to the aircraft's position, which is why it is so crucial that the INAS has the correct information.

The Jaguar is excellent at low level and easily cuts through turbulence, giving a comfortable and rock-steady ride. As the aircraft comes to within seventy seconds of each turning point the HUD automatically generates a time-to-go circle with an 'X' marker indicating the computed position of the turning point. The circle then winds down, and on reaching the turn the next waypoint is selected. During the 'attack phase' of the mission the HUD again automatically changes from navigation mode to close navigation mode; and as the target is approached it converts into attack mode. The pilot is shown each turn denoted by an 'X' marker in the HUD, and he can then select two attack options: either a planned attack (PA) or a target of opportunity (TGT OPP). His choice is

For a target of opportunity, much of the same applies, except that the target's position is not known to the computer: the WAMS displays attack symbols in the HUD, but without the 'X' marker, so the pilot must provide the system with range and track information.

As soon as the weapons are released the HUD reverts to navigation mode again, and multiple targets can be plotted into the system.

Jaguar attack sorties are almost always flown as pairs or as part of a package, so formation flying is a big part of training, as is mutual defence and low-level flying. Until recently, Jaguars would always have made their attacks at 250ft (75m) or below, and 'amongst the weeds' is still a vital part of RAF Jaguar operations, but the face of the battlefield has now raised the operational threshold to medium level.

The 'T-Bird' cockpit provides excellent vision for both student and instructor. f4 Aviation Photobank

running postgraduate Weapons Instructor and Instrument Rating Examiner courses. With the recent upsurge in Jaguar activity, the introduction of the GR.1B and delays with the introduction of the Eurofighter 2000, slots with No.16(R) Squadron's conversion course are still very much in demand, and it will allow the RAF to keep its Jaguars viable and effective until the introduction of the Eurofighter.

The OCU is equipped with ten aircraft, five single-seat GR.1As and five two-seat T.2As, (which can alter due to throughput of students), plus two flight simulators. The latter have full visual and motion systems and are most suitable for preparing the students for every aspect of flying on the unit. The OCU staff itself consists of eleven pilots and over sixty NCOs and airmen.

The students arrive for the OCU Long Course, the unit's primary course, having completed their Hawk-based tactical weapons course at RAF Valley with some 300–350 hours in their log books. They begin with ten days of intense ground school, followed by at least six simulator 'rides' before being progressed to the flying stage. There are eight separate phases to the course including the actual 'conversion' to type, and several hours of flying are also allocated to mastering the techniques of using a HUD. These phases include instrument flying, formation flying, night low-level navigation, weapons, simulated attack profiles, tactical manoeuvring and operational flying.

Conversion is said to be (relatively) painless, once the aircraft's angle of attack has been mastered and the HUD work is familiar, with most students going solo after three dual sorties, though these *ab-initio* pilots do have to work at a 'geometric rate'. Following some instrument flying, the student is introduced to the Jaguar's INS and trained to make the best use of it during low-level navigation sorties. This leads onto the weapons phase where the full facilities of the navigation and weapons aiming sub-system are investigated. This phase then sub-divides into level bombing, shallow dive bombing, toss bombing and strafing with 30mm cannon. Bombing does not involve live weapons: 6.5lb (3kg) smoke-generating 'bean tin bombs' are used, delivered from CBLS (carrier bomb light stores) pods under the wings or centreline, the attributes of which simulate retarded 1,000lb (454kg) bombs or CBUs. The larger 62lb (28kg) practice bombs are used in toss (released under 3g) or loft (released under 1g) attacks. Throughout the course, the students are taught how to use the LRMTS.

Following about four weeks of intensive weaponry come the simulated attack profiles (SAPs). This is arguably the most important phase of the course, as it puts together all that has gone before, and it is during this time that the students' real capabilities are established. The instructors pick a bridge or power station to be used as a target, and the student must plan and launch an attack, including a first run attack (FRA) onto one of the ranges.

are taken 'down to the dirt' where they practise low-level evasion, plus a run through the ECM range at Spadeadam to give them the feel of what could be encountered in a high-threat environment. This is usually done in pairs or a four-ship, with an instructor flying another aircraft to simulate a fighter 'bounce' – arriving unannounced!

The course culminates in an operational phase, in which the full potential of

time-limited environment. Sqn Ldr Andy Cubin, a former flying instructor with the OCU, takes up the story:

[The] Jaguar has very few vices, but it must be handled with respect. Not being blessed with Specific Excess Power (SEP) when carrying tanks or any stores, its 'G' and 'Alpha' are limited and a departure at high angles of attack can lead to a spin. It's a hard and demanding course, however, the Jaguar is the last single-seat non-

The OCU is equipped with ten aircraft, five single-seat GR.1A/Bs and five two-seat T.2A/Bs. Author

Accurate navigation, low-level formation flying and weaponry skills are all required – the basics of flying are taken for granted. Next comes tactical manoeuvring, where the students are taught advanced handling. After some medium-level work they

the Jaguar is demonstrated and exercised. This ties together the whole of the syllabus, and these last sorties are extremely busy. To make the trips as realistic as possible, detailed intelligence scenarios are simulated, briefed, planned and flown in a

V/STOL aircraft in the RAF's inventory, and it's a prized posting for the ambitious pilot. One of the final sorties the students fly comes in the evasion phase, it's a four-ship, with a fifth aircraft tasked as the 'bounce'. A target will be presented to them, two-and-a-half hours prior to

Flt Lt Andy Cubin acting as the 'bounce' during a low-level sortie. Andy Cubin

the mission, with current intelligence on the area. As we will be working over Scotland, a major feature is chosen, say Balmoral Castle, which will simulate an airfield, or main installation, and it will be the student's job to plan how best to attack such a position. They will look at simulated troop positions, installations, missile systems etc., and they will draw up a detailed map for the trip. Each individual will have his own task during the planning, so nothing should be left out. As they will be flying at seven miles a minute, navigating at speed is essential, and once the target is acquired the idea is to put the weapons aiming symbology through the target and simulate weapons delivery. Each aircraft has its own HUD video, which is later carefully scrutinized.

During this final phase of the trip the bounce is in their area and can 'hit' at any point. His job is to provide a realistic aid to the scenario, not to merely 'hack-off' the students, and he will also check to see that they are performing mutual support of each other. If they see the 'bounce' early enough, the objective is to 'step around' and not get

involved in a furball, however if the bounce 'gets in' the remit is to evade effectively by getting a 180 on him inside his missile envelope and run away. In the event that the bounce gets into your 'shorts' i.e. close in, the deal is to hit him with a 'knickers' option, that is to release a bomb into his face, so he gets caught in its debris hemisphere as he tracks through. Fundamentally speaking, pilots are trained to overcome the Jaguar's limitations, and to survive in a hostile environment, a process that recognizes the aircraft's more positive qualities such as solid low-level performance, an accurate kit and excellent weapons delivery.

On completion of the course, the students are well prepared for the advanced training that will be given by the squadrons they are posted to, and will reflect that unit's particular speciality. By that time some four months have passed (depending on the Scottish weather) and the student has an additional eighty-five flying hours to his credit. During its time of operation the Jaguar OCU has trained in excess of 800 pilots from five different

No.16(R) Squadron Jaguar Training Courses as at November 1997

Ab Initio (Long) Course
Three courses per year – ten students in total

Phase	Dual Hours	Solo Hours
Conversion	5.20	3.30
Instrument Flying	9.10	
Formation	2.30	3.45
Low Level	2.40	5.05
Weapons	7.10	12.15
SAPS	2.35	7.45
Air Combat	1.40	
Evasion	8.30	
Total	**39.35**	**32.20**

Short (Refresher) Course
Three courses per year – six students in total

Phase	Dual Hours	Solo Hours
Conversion	2.00	1.00
Instrument Flying	3.30	
Formation	1.20	1.20
Low Level	1.30	1.25
Weapons	2.20	5.50
SAPS	1.30	2.45
Air Combat	1.00	
Evasion	1.15	
Total	**14.25**	**12.20**

Qualified Weapons Instructor Course
One course per year – four students in total

Phase	Dual Hours	Solo Hours
Local Area Familiarity	1.00	
Retard & Strafe	1.30	7.30
Freefall/Dive Toss	4.05	1.10
Toss Loft	3.35	1.15
Night	3.00	
Air to Air Gunnery	3.20	1.40
Tactical Manoeuvring	5.40	3.00
Missile Practice Camp	1.50	0.40
Applied Weapons	11.55	
Total	**35.55**	**15.15**

Competent to Instruct
Two courses per year – variable number of students

Phase	Dual Hours
Conversion	4.00
Instrument Flying	3.00
Formation	2.40
Low Level	2.40
Weapons	3.50
SAPS	2.40
Air Combat	1.00
Evasion	4.20
Qualification/ Evaluation	2.20
Total	**26.30**

Instrument Rating Examiners Course
One course per year – four students in total

Phase	Dual Hours
Instrument Flying	6.00

T.2A XX141/Z displays the 'old' OCU markings and the 'Lumsden Tartan' on its tailfin. Author

One of the 'Saints' flashes across the Scottish countryside. RAF

nations. Obviously, the majority of pilots go to the RAF, but the unit also trains aviators from the air forces of Nigeria, Ecuador, India and Oman.

The No.16(R) Squadron Jaguars still carry the tartan band on their RWR-equipped GR.1As and across the tails of the non-RWR T.2As, retained from the original markings of No.226 OCU. The tartan is something that was instigated Wing Commander John Lumsden, the commanding officer of the OCU from April 1980 to December 1982. He obtained permission from the Lumsden clan chief to use the 'Lumsden Tartan' to adorn the OCU Jaguars.

in 1990, following Saddam Hussein's invasion of Kuwait, the Jaguar force was to prove its worth to the RAF. Following their success in *Desert Storm*, the Jaguars were detached to Incerlik AFB in Turkey to provide a policing presence over northern Iraq, and were later given the same task, operating from Italy in the skies above Bosnia-Hercegovina. For GR.1A operations in the Gulf and over Bosnia, urgent 'war' modifications were made including improvements to the ARI-18223 RHWR, which was upgraded to 'Sky Guardian 15' standard, and the addition of a colour video recording facility to the HUD. Other items such as

West to exercise with the Egyptian Air Force.

During the mid-1990s, under the Jaguar GR.1B programme, GEC's thermal imaging and targeting system was added to some aircraft, with a wide angle HUD and a colour multi-function display. Also included in this project was a new Ferranti moving map display with symbol generator, a global positioning system (GPS) which will be linked to a modified 1065 inertial navigation system and a 1553B databus, with the overwing Sidewinder missile rails now becoming a permanent feature. Many of the lessons learned from operations both in the desert and over the Balkans have been

Following their success in Desert Storm, **the Jaguars were detached to Incerlik AFB in Turkey to provide a policing presence over northern Iraq, and were later given the same mission above Bosnia-Hercegovina.**
BAe

Jaguars 1990–95

After many years of uneventful European service, the Jaguar was seen to be rather in the twilight zone of its career. However,

overwing Sidewinder launch rails and engine enhancements were also rushed through. Out-of-area exercises were also a part of the Jaguar operations, with one notable deployment being made to Cairo

adopted as policy, with, amongst others, the Jaguar now embracing medium-level operations, changing tactics and revising their SOPs to suit, and practising air-to-air refuelling on a far more regular basis.

Showing off the latest Jaguar '96 two-tone LIR scheme is this T.2A from No.6 Squadron. f4 Aviation Photobank

Weaponry

In order to perform its strike mission, the Jaguar is cleared to carry a wide variety of weaponry, apart from its twin internal 30mm Aden cannon, which are very useful for strafing, keeping the enemy's heads down and, in the case of an unwary aircraft, in air-to-air combat. 1000lb (454kg) GP bombs, either free-fall or retard, can be carried on the inner wing pylons and on the centreline, either singly or on tandem beams. The aircraft are also cleared for the use of Hunting BL755 cluster bombs, or American CBUs, in addition to their latest piece of hardware, the Canadian-built Bristol Aerospace CRV-7 2.75in (7cm) high-velocity rocket, of which nineteen were fitted into an American-designed LAU-500B/A pod; the more traditional SNEB rockets can also be carried. Laser-guided bombs are also now a major part of the inventory, and AIM-9 Sidewinders are routinely fitted to the overwing pylons. The addition of the Sidewinder has added

Aden Cannon

Like the DEFA series, the Aden owes much to the German Mauser MG 213c revolver cannon of World War II, and is a useful weapon even today. The name is taken from the Armament Development Establishment and 'ENfield' where it was built.

Low-angle shot reveals one of the Jaguar's twin Aden cannons. f4 Aviation Photobank.

Jaguar XZ364 fires off an AIM-9 Sidewinder AAM from its overwing pylon, against a towed target over the Aberporth range in North Wales. BAe

Hunting BL755 Cluster Bomb Unit (CBU)

This dual-role weapon provides the British forces with a high kill probability against a considerable range of both hard and soft targets. Designed for release from low level, one of four time delays is selected for the weapon before take-off to ensure the delivering aircraft is well clear of the blast zone. Therefore, the aircraft flies with the primary striker armed, and on release this fires the primary cartridge which generates gas pressure to blow off the two-part body sides and then fire the main cartridge, which ejects the bomblets carried in the weapon's twenty-one bays. The bomblet ejection from each of the bays is varied in velocity so as to ensure the attainment of the desired pattern on the ground. Each bomblet has a 68mm diameter; its length enlarges as the spring-mounted tail and nose probes deploy. Each individual bomblet arms itself as it falls and detonates on impact with a shaped charge warhead able to penetrate at least 250mm-thick armour, as well as scattering a cloud of some 2,000 lethal fragments.

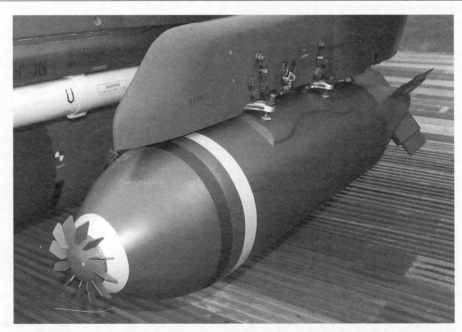

Hunting BL755. Author

another option to the Jaguar's already impressive capacity; however, it is recognized that the Jaguar is not the ideal machine in which to engage in air-to-air combat. As a result, the philosophy is, if bounced by fighters, evade – or as the Jaguars boys themselves will readily admit, 'run away bravely' – and as quickly as possible, thereby living to fight another day!

The Jaguar LRMTS

The GEC Marconi Laser Ranger and Marked Target Seeker (LRMTS) is designed to give accurate information to fast, low-flying ground support aircraft. The marked target seeker locks onto a laser spot placed on the target by a ground-based FAC, whilst the laser ranger operates by directing pulses of infra-red energy (1.06 microns) from a neodymium-doped YAG laser at the target. Range is then measured by calculating the time interval between transmitted and received pulses. The equipment is gyro-stabilized to produce instant and accurate ranges, even during heavy manoeuvring in flight, and has an effective range up to 9km.

LRMTS. GEC

Matra/BAe MARTEL Missile

The MARTEL – Missile Anti-Radar TELevision – grew from an independent British and French study in the early 1960s, and was then jointly developed as one of the first European collaborative weapons programs. The British version, the AJ.168, used command guidance by virtue of a small TV camera in the nose of the missile, which fed a picture to a small screen in front of the operator, who then fixed the target into the missile before launch. The missile then flew under an autopilot, being steered by the operator in the launch aircraft using a data-link pod. The French version, the AS.37, is designed for anti-radar use with a broad-spectrum passive seeker.

This can be used in the air to search for pre-set frequencies to look for a suitable transmitting target. Once acquired, the seeker is locked and the missile fired. Alternatively, the seeker can be pre-locked before launch, if a specific target is to be engaged. The AS.37 carries a 330lb (150kg) proximity-fused warhead and weighs 1,200lb (530kg). Powered by a Hotchkiss-Brandt/SNPE Basilie composite solid propellant booster rocket and a single Hotchkiss-Brandt/SNPE Cassandra composite solid propellant sustainer rocket motor, the MARTEL is 13ft 6in (4.1m) long and has a speed of Mach 2 plus.

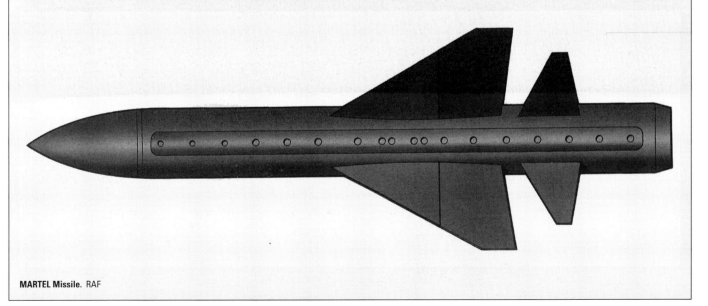

MARTEL Missile. RAF

'Cool For Cats' – RAF Jaguars in the Arctic

As with the RAF's Harrier force, one of the prime tasks for the Jaguar is defending NATO's northern flank, operating some 120 miles inside the Arctic circle in the inhospitable, snowy wastes of northern into service, and it is the Coltishall-based No.41(F) Squadron who are the declared Arctic specialists within the Jaguar wing; although in order to maintain the overall rapid deployment capability of the whole Jaguar force, both Nos. 6 and 54 Squadrons also make regular trips to Norway.

terrain in the world. The weather patterns are constantly changing, from clear skies with bright sunshine to impenetrable snow storms, in a matter of minutes, and the available daylight can be restricted to a mere three hours per day. The air temperature is so cold that it will freeze your breath against your face and makes touching any sort of

A No.41(F) Squadron aircraft, complete with reconnaissance pod displaying an Arctic 'blotched' effect, with the white overwash being picked out by the permanent camouflage underneath, obliterating all but the aircraft's rescue markings. RAF Coltishall

Norway. Regular annual deployments are made to the Royal Norwegian Air Force Base of Bardufoss, where the cold weather skills of the pilots and groundcrews alike are tested to the limit. The Jaguar has been visiting Bardufoss since its entry

The Jaguar force awards the title of 'Arctic Warrior' to any pilot and support personnel who has gained experience in the unique style of operations required for northern Norway, where can be found amongst the most spectacular and hazardous

bare metal surface extremely hazardous, lest you become frozen to it! Therefore, flying and operating combat aircraft in this sort of environment require special methods and tactics. From the pilot's perspective, the approach to Bardufoss's easterly runway is made down an imposingly steep hill, and whilst the aircrew are happy to launch and recover from these snow-packed operating areas, the taxiways and ramps regularly turn to sheet ice, which makes for some very 'sporty' returns. The major hazards to flying operations are the practically invisible high-tension wires which criss-cross

and -Bs being deployed to Bardufoss to participate in Exercise *Battle Griffin*. The combined skills of both Nos. 41(F) and 54(F) Squadrons were used on a routine yet vital test of NATO's ability to swiftly reinforce this strategically important region. This exercise also involved a significant number of Army and naval units manoeuvring in

high-explosive weapons as part of their close air support training, and also flew night attack sorties against airfields using their electro-optical equipment. Many of these airfield targets were well defended by such advanced systems as the Euromissile Roland SAM. Typically, each trip would involve eight Jaguars and four Harriers, sup-

Another variation on the same theme, this time a very effective one, sees the speeding Jaguar, captured in a frame from a recce pod camera, almost disappearing into the background. This particular camouflage effect is a more angular affair; again the white overwash is predominant, masking all of the unit's markings. RAF Coltishall

the Norwegian fjords and which are always a pilot's worst nightmare, especially when well hidden from above by the changing terrain.

One typical detachment was undertaken on 5 March 1996, with nine Jaguar GR.1As

the areas between Bardufoss and Bodo. Also taking part were Harrier GR.7s from No.1(F) Squadron and F-16 Fighting Falcons from the RNorAF. The Harriers and Jaguars operated as 'packages' with the F-16s flying top cover, and together delivered

ported by F-16s with AWACS and EW jamming cover. Some of the sorties incorporated live firing of CRV-7 rockets and the release of 1,000lb (454kg) bombs on the local training ranges. As has become the norm with the Harrier and Jaguar, an

For the 1995 series of Arctic exercises, the Jaguars from both No.6 and No.41 Squadrons again received the standard Arctic scheme, covering their green wraparound colour with white. This time, rather than the more usual 'hard edge' to the white overwash, a more feathered 'soft edge' was applied, giving the aircraft a more 'snow-swept' look, as can be seen here with XX767/GE of No.54 Squadron. Author

A reconnaissance-configured 'all-grey' aircraft from No.54 Squadron is readied on Bardufoss's icy ramp.
RAF

Arctic camouflage scheme was applied to some of the *Battle Griffin* aircraft. This applied to the GR1A aircraft which retained the traditional dark grey and dark green paint scheme, whereas the new permanent dark grey scheme on the GR.1B

(pilots visual reports) and close scrutiny of the infra-red sensor imagery provided by the systems of No.41(F) Squadron's aircraft. The exercise was declared a success, and a high sortie rate of twenty trips per day was achieved by the Jaguars.

accommodate the underside as well. Worth a note is that the 'whitewash' in some cases also covers the black anti-glare panel ahead of the windshield. However, during early 1982, XZ358 was painted in a one-off experimental light blue and light

In full reheat, a No.41 Squadron recce-jet gets airborne from Bardufoss. Note the 'hard edge' camouflage.
RAF

aircraft was deemed quite adequate for the snowy conditions.

During the *Battle Griffin* exercises the Jaguars also flew tactical reconnaissance sorties in addition to their attack missions, operating in support of the 'Green' forces which in this exercise were attacking the 'Blue' forces. The intelligence gathered by the reconnaissance systems provided a valuable tactical picture for the commanders, this being achieved by both 'Vis-Reps'

Arctic Camouflage Schemes

Over the years a wide variety of camouflage patterns have been applied to the Jaguars that have taken part in Arctic exercises. The standard Arctic scheme consists of an 'overwash' of white ARTF which is applied to the grey camouflage colour, leaving the green still visible. This colour also adorns the drop tanks, weapons pylons, and in some cases 'wraps around' to

grey temporary scheme for Exercise *Alloy Express*. As the arctic forays would be peacetime exercises, the normal full-colour squadron markings were retained on all of the aircraft, and in some cases where the ARTF threatened to obliterate the units markings, the finish was applied around the emblems. On certain occasions it has been the norm to paint up one Jaguar in a more adventurous scheme, to test its suitability against the Arctic conditions.

Trailing its 18ft(5.5m)-diameter brake parachute – very useful on icy runways – an 'Arctic Warrior' from No.41 Squadron eases in. RAF

Exercising the 'Cat'

The precision of the Jaguar's attack systems has often been proven during exercises, often to the embarrassment of supposedly more powerful aircraft. In 1975 and 1976 No.14 Squadron took the prizes in RAF Germany's annual navigation and bombing competition for the Salmond Trophy, flying against Harriers, Buccaneers and Phantoms, and during 1977 the Jaguars achieved the first four placings, the results giving the RAF and the Jaguar force just cause for optimism. Jaguars regularly participate in the UK's *Mallet Blow* exercises, where the aircraft perform precision bombing from low level against various targets on the Otterburn Ranges in Northumberland.

In the 1980 Tactical Air Meet at Ramstein AFB in Germany, No.31 Squadron won two of the coveted awards: the Canberra Trophy for retarded low-altitude

bombing and the Broadhurst Trophy for conventional bombing, with Flt Lt Kevyn Broadhurst achieving the maximum points total of 400. The same year, the Jaguars took their expertise abroad to compete, when six aircraft from No.20 Squadron and six from No.6 Squadron flew to the Royal Canadian Air Force base at Cold Lake to take part in Exercise *Maple Flag*. The Jaguars were pitted against RCAF CF-5s, CF-104s, CF-101s and C-103s, as well as USAF F-15s and F-5E Aggressors. In the first two weeks of the exercise the pilots of No.20 Squadron operated in some atrocious weather to notch up some sixty-one sorties, while in the second phase Jaguars from No.6 Squadron achieved some seventy-five sorties in improving conditions. The results were again impressive, particularly where the Jaguars had consistently claimed victories in poor conditions where others had failed.

Exercise Red Flag

Tucked in beside the gambling capital of the world, Las Vegas, is Nellis Air Force Base, home of the USAF's Fighter Weapons Centre, and the operating base of the 'Red Flag' exercises. Beginning life as a purely USAF competition, the *Red Flag* 'battles' that are fought across the Nevada plains are now the yardstick by which many NATO countries measure their training. For the RAF Jaguars, deployment to 'the Flag' can involve up to ten aircraft and twenty pilots, supported by VC-10 tankers and C-130 Hercules transports and a host of groundcrew. The flight out to Nellis begins with a transatlantic crossing to the Canadian base at Goose Bay, with reconnaissance and control being provided by an RAF Nimrod, followed by an overnight stop and then transit through Canada into the USA and on to Nellis. The crews usually have a few days' break before taking up the cudgels in the pre-exercise work-up. After two weeks of exercise over the ranges, the personnel change over with another of the Jaguar units deploying to Nellis for the second period.

For the players at *Red Flag* the rules are strict and must be stringently observed. Before they even begin, pilots must have a minimum of 500 hours, and all participants are required to 'work down' to 100ft (30m), allowing the pilots to become familiar with

system, enabling them to use their evasion tactics. Terrain masking is one of the Jaguar's many tricks, and the use of chaff and flare, are allowed but only in certain areas. The USAF has also developed the 'Smokey SAM', a replica missile made of polystyrene and cardboard with a firework in its tail, that is launched skyward to replicate the firing of a man-portable SAM missile and is described as 'a true heart-stopper for any pilot – real or not!'. Threats from

missile body with an active seeker, and an ACMI (air combat manoeuvring instrumentation) pod, which datalinks the aircraft to the *Red Flag* computer's measurement and debriefing system (RFMDS) for analysis in either 'real time' or during a post-mission debriefing. As the Jaguars lack the ability to carry an ACMI pod, they are tracked using their IFF transponder codes.

The RAF first sent its 'Big Cats' to *Red Flag* in 1976, and during the period of 17

The sign in the foreground sums up the 'live' nature of Red Flag, as groundcrew prepare aircraft from No.31 Squadron. via Gary Madgwick

the terrain and the ATC procedures. Day One is no more than getting to know the area, while Day Two sees the base height dropped from the initial 500ft to 300ft 150–90m); on Day Three it drops to just 100ft. Hazards are plentiful, threat simulations abound and the pilots can experience being locked-up by a missile's guidance

interceptors are also realistic, including F-5Es or F-16 aggressors, who use Soviet-style tactics as they attempt to 'bounce' the attacking forces. Most weaponry carried is inert, but the Jaguars do have the opportunity to drop at least one live 1,000lb (454kg) bomb. All the fighters carry Sidewinder acquisition rounds, an inert

January–28 February deployed eight Jaguar GR.1s from RAF Germany – five from No.31 Squadron and three from No.17 Squadron at Brüggen, the aircraft being ferried to the USA by tanker-qualified pilots from No.41(F) Squadron. During the period at Nellis pilots from No.2(AC), No.41(F), No.17, No.31 and No.6

The Nevada mountains make a picturesque backdrop to the Nellis flightline. via Gary Madgwick

Sandwiched between two F-4E Phantoms from Seymour Johnson AFB. via Gary Madgwick

Groundcrew work to prepare two aircraft from No.17 Squadron for their next Red Flag **hop.** via Gary
Madgwick

**A Jaguar from No.31 Squadron, the 'Gold Stars', heads out for another 'Flag' sortie, complete with practice
bombs in the underfuselage CBLS pod.** via Gary Madgwick

Squadrons flew as part of the 'Blue' force, operating with F-4E Phantoms as part of the primary air-to-ground exercise, as well as taking part in large composite attack forces.

During 1980 No.54 Squadron also took part in a *Red Flag* exercise, operating within the purpose-built range area, which includes fifty different types of target, including airfields, industrial sites, convoys, railways and replica armoured vehicles, all of which are 'defended' by tracked anti-aircraft guns, and up to thirty-five other threat simulations, which look similar to, and behave electronically like, Soviet equipment. Early warning radars and airborne AWACS protected the approach corridor to the range and informed the 'Red' Force defenders, which included the F-5E Soviet-painted interceptors, of the impending arrival of the Blue Force attackers. Initially, No.54 Squadron entered the arena with some trepidation, being tasked to attack a 'convoy' some 100 miles (160km) from their base. Flying at high transonic speeds and hugging the terrain, they arrived 'on the dot' without being tracked or intercepted. This achievement was a surprise to the defenders, but the Jaguar pilots modestly claimed their success was due to the local situation and a brief patch of 'typically European' weather; but in reality the aircraft's size, its radar signature and its ability to fly at low level and merge with ground clutter was the real reason. Further embarrassment followed a year later when No.54 Squadron's Jaguars returned to *Red Flag* and in the process 'gunned down' a pair of American F-15 Eagles!

There is little doubt as to the value of exercises such as *Red Flag*, *Maple Flag* and the RAF's own competitions, and the pilots' exposure to the simulated threat environment should stand him in good stead if he were ever called upon to perform in such a hostile atmosphere. It gives the planners and commanders the opportunity to put their training to the test in the most realistic way possible without actually going to war. The lessons learned from the conflicts that have occurred during the early to mid-1990s are now being applied in the planning of such exercises.

Air Warriors

In addition to the USAF's *Red Flag* exercises, comes close air support training with the United States Army, under the banner of their *Air Warrior* exercises, of which twelve are held annually at the Fort Irwin National Training Centre. The 594th Joint Training Squadron, based at Nellis, is the driving force in the *Air Warrior* programme, with its sophisticated computer system that links the the USAF's ACMI system – that of *Red Flag* fame – to the Army's Instrument Combat Training Centre at Fort Irvine. Designated the NTC/Air Warrior Measurement and Debriefing System, it allows both air and ground commanders to monitor in real time the effects of close air support, and allows for the exercise 'players' to review their own performance. The major development for the Army's training has been the MILES (Multiple Integrated Laser Engagement System) 2000 system, a laser 'shooting' and 'detection' system which allows the users to see what 'kills' have been made, and when they have 'knocked out' a target; the system it also tells the 'victim' what scored the hit. The MILES system is, however, not linked to the aircraft's cockpit, so pilots must rely on ground agencies to inform them of a 'hit', and whether they are 'out of the game'.

Air Warrior operational aircraft are of a lesser number than at *Red Flag* exercises, though the aircraft make multiple passes across the area to simulate a squadron-sized attack. Jaguars participated in recent exercises, coded by year and month e.g. '*Air Warrior* #96-10'. Close air support missions are flown by up to ten Jaguars from the Coltishall wing, supported by elements of the USAF such as F-16s or OA/A-10 'Warthogs'. Jaguars generally support 'Red' Force, the F-16s typically 'Blue' Force. The Jaguars operate over the ground troops, and during their missions their 'kills' are assessed by the *Air Warrior* computers in the command post at Nellis, who then 'talk' to the computers at Fort Irwin, giving a real-time look at the unfolding picture on the 'battlefield'.

Displaying the Jaguar – 'Cubin's Black Cat'

'Tower ... Jaguar Lima 272 ready for display.'

'Roger 272, clear take-off, surface wind is 230 degrees at 12kt.'

'Roger, take-off Lima 272 ... A superb day for a display', comments Sqn Ldr Andy Cubin as he lines up his sleek, black Jaguar GR.1 on the runway at RAF Lossiemouth. He settles himself back in his ejector seat and runs through the final take-off checks.

'Strobes on ... flaps set ... final check ... OK ... three, two, one, here we go ... REHEAT!'

Two plumes of bright orange flame burst from the Jaguar's engines, the brakes are released and the aircraft hurtles down the tarmac. As the speed hits 150kt (280km/h) Cubin hauls the 'Black Cat' into the air. The Jaguar accelerates smartly to 250kt (460km/h) and, flying level at a mere 100ft (30m), the gear is selected 'up', 60 degrees of bank is applied and a 60-degree turn initiated, pulling the aircraft away from the display line. The afterburners are wheeled around to point at the crowd, and the shock waves and noise produce a mind-numbing, ear-splitting announcement – 'Jaguar airborne'.

Cubin glances over his shoulder to pick up the display line, and having done so pulls the aircraft round to produce three 'spot rolls' along the display line, keeping the aircraft level at 500ft (150m).

'Going right ... three rolls ... one, two, three, REHEAT ... pull ...'

The aircraft heaves away from the crowd and into a 40-degree pitch up with wing over; Cubin again checks over his shoulder to pick up the display line, and pushes the aircraft back down. '500ft ... 380kt ... speed's good ... level ... SLOW ROLL ... lots of cross-wind ... up ...'

The slow roll is co-ordinated so the aircraft is inverted at crowd centre, ending in a 'Derry Wing-Over'. Reheat comes back on, and the Jaguar is manoeuvred round for a high-speed run. The aircraft accelerates quickly to 550–620kt (1,020–1,150km/h) (dependent on the air temperature and the airfield's elevation). Flying at 100ft at these sorts of speeds is quite taxing on the pilot as the aircraft is highly responsive to pitch at that stage. 'Now the hard work,' says Cubin.

Just abeam crowd centre in the high-speed run, the engines are brought back from max-reheat to 'idle', while 'Cubes' 'stands the aircraft on its ear' – the air-brakes flip out and with a 7g pull, the classic 'break back' manoeuvre is performed.

'High speed run ... looking for crowd centre ... 100ft ... at 100 ... crowd centre ... ONE OUT, TWO OUT, PULL AIR-BRAKES ... 7G!'

The discomfort is instant as Cubin's body suddenly becomes seven times heavier than normal as the Jaguar soars upwards. Climbing high the speed bleeds off to 115kt (210km/h) in the vertical, and 'Cubes' rolls back into position for a more sedate slow fly-past in a 'dirty' condition with flaps and gear down, and nosewheel lights on.

Wheeling around the Scottish Highlands, 'Cubes' shows off his 'Black Cat'. Rick Brewell

One of the highlights of the UK's air-show scene is the continued participation by many of the RAF's fast-jets, bringing the front line into full view of the public, and giving credence to the men and machines of Britain's air force. Each year senior flyers are invited to apply for the position of Display Pilot, and once selected they carry out the job of planning and executing a flying routine to be performed at major and minor air events both in the UK and abroad. Each of the RAF types has its own dedicated crew, and for the 1993–96 Jaguar display, this task was entrusted to Andy 'Cubes' Cubin, an instructor from No.16(R) Squadron, the Jaguar OCU at RAF Lossiemouth.

The display Jaguar selected for the three seasons, XX116, is usually displayed with 3,530lb (1,600kg) of internal fuel – half its normal load – and also has its internal cannons stripped out to save weight. The inner wing pylons are also removed though the outer ones stay in place to aid stability during tight turns. To make the aircraft more conspicuous for the display events, a striking all-black colour scheme was chosen, with a large bright yellow 'Saint' caricature on the tailfin, taken from the Squadron's *nom de guerre*, 'The Saints'. The unit's heraldic cross-keys emblem, also painted in yellow, was to be found on the engine intakes, which also had a yellow band painted around them, together with yellow

serial number and a yellow-outlined RWR fairing atop the tail. Also of note were the blue-and-red roundels, which for this occasion were also outlined in yellow. Andy Cubin was in fact the second display pilot to use the all-black Jaguar, as the scheme was pioneered during 1992 by that year's Jaguar Display Pilot, Flt Lt Gary Miller. During the 'triple seasons', 'Cubes and the Black Cat' worked nearly every weekend from May to October – a huge commitment for any airman and his family, as this 'voluntary' work is in addition to normal flying duties, and the phrase 'maxed out' seems pretty inadequate to describe the year end. So weekdays were spent in the rear seat of Jaguar T.2A, and weekends at

Pilot Profile – Squadron Leader Andy Cubin

Andy Cubin is a 34-year-old Shetland Islander who has been around aeroplanes and airfields all of his life, primarily as his father was a meteorological officer with the Ministry of Defence. He joined the RAF straight from school at 18 and took the standard route to fast-jet flying through Cranwell with the Jet Provost, the Hawk at RAF Valley and then a posting to the Jaguar OCU at Lossiemouth in 1984. His first operational tour was flying reconnaissance with No.41(F) Squadron at RAF Coltishall, before being offered an exchange posting with the Sultan of Oman's Air Force, where he spent two years flying the Jaguar in the desert with No.20 Squadron, based at Thumrait. He returned to the UK with the Central Flying School, then based at RAF Scampton, where he gained his QFI (Qualified Flying Instructor) rating, moving quickly to RAF Valley before another posting took him back to the Jaguar at Lossiemouth. He was again offered the opportunity to return to Oman as a Jaguar QFI teaching *ab-initio* students, again at Thumrait, this period including the time just prior to and just after the Gulf War. He returned to a posting at RAF Coltishall, only to find himself despatched back to the Gulf as part of Operation *Warden* where he flew some eighty-eight armed patrols from Incerlik in Turkey. Returning to the Jaguar OCU in 1993, he held the post of STANEVAL (Flying) and was the CFS agent for the Jaguar. On completion of his three year stint as display pilot, Andy was selected to join the prestigious Red Arrows aerobatic team during late 1996.

Andy Cubin. RAF Lossiemouth

the sharp end in a GR.1A! To remain current Andy Cubin needed to fly the routine every seven days, in view of a senior officer, with planning for events usually being undertaken 'after hours' on the squadron, and any display practices flown before the working day began.

'Full flap ... gear down ... crowd centre ... REHEAT ... Check ... Derry ... MAX RATE TURN ... coming down ...'

Abeam crowd centre the reheat is engaged and the aircraft accelerates away, winging-over and positioning for an inverted pass, which rolls out level again at crowd centre. Cubin snaps the Jaguar into a maximum-rate turn at 300ft (90m), pulling around again and rolling out at datum. Wings now level again and speeding along at 340kt (630km/h), a 60-degree pitch-up is applied, rolling away through 90 degrees and con-

verting that position into a turn for 'finals'. Easing the 'Cat' onto the runway, 'Cubes' keeps the nose high as an aid to braking, and as a final gesture to the crowd, dropping the nosewheel as he passes crowd centre.

'As a display platform the Jaguar is very good, although problems do occur. Because of its small wings, it has difficulty getting around corners – but then again its not an F-16,' concludes Cubin.

Sitting sedately on the Lossiemouth ramp, the black-and-yellow 'Black Cat' basks in the afternoon sunshine, awaiting its next display. Author

Replica Jaguars

In addition to the wooden mock-up mentioned in an earlier section, the RAF Exhibition, Production and Training Unit (EP&TU) at St Athan have two plastic 'Jaguars' used for exhibition work. XX725 is stored at St. Athan, whilst XX110 resides with No.1 School of Technical Training at RAF Cosford. The aircraft were built from plastic mouldings by Specialised Mouldings of Huntingdon, and are marked exactly as the aircraft they mirror in squadron service.

A 'Gulf Falsie' painted up for the 1991 RAF Cosford Open Day. Author

Experimental and Test Jaguars

Active Control Technology Demonstrator XX765

One of the most important projects undertaken by the Royal Aircraft Establishment (RAE), later to become the Defence Research Agency (DRA), was a programme that looked at the future of control systems for the next generation of combat aircraft. To accommodate one of the test programmes, a single Jaguar GR.1, XX765, was taken from the RAF's original order of 165 to become a flying testbed for the active control technology (ACT) systems programme. XX765 was a full production aircraft complete with tail-mounted RWR fairing. However, the aircraft had both of its cannon ports faired over and the glazing associated with the LRMTS blanked off. During its time with the RAE, XX765 was considerably altered from the original standard, and installed with one-off systems which were to be of immense help with the European Fighter Aircraft (EFA) programme.

The aircraft featured a so-called fly-by-wire (FBW) system, which was an advanced, all-digital quadruplex management unit, requiring no form of emergency back-up equipment. A fully-working 'FBW' system was flown aboard XX765 for the first time anywhere in the world on 20 October 1981 by BAe's senior test pilot, Chris Yeo, from Warton airfield. The project had originally been instigated by the Ministry of Defence back in 1977, and after favourable results were achieved by the BAe team, it was given full Government support. The project's major subcontractors were the Combat Aircraft Controls Division of Marconi Avionics, who provided the avionics and high-speed digital computers, and Dowty Boulton-Paul who provided the servo actuator controls for the spoilers, rudder and tailplane.

The FBW control system replaced the mechanical units and control rods which operate the Jaguar's conventional flying surfaces on the wings and tail. In their place were fitted four independent electrical channels which relay digital instructions to the control surfaces via electronic impulses generated by four high-speed self-monitoring computers. These computers were also linked to twin subsidiary actuator drive and monitoring computers and other 'fail-safe' compensating equipment, so that the whole system could automatically survive all probable system failures, and therefore no emergency back-up was deemed necessary.

Instructions to the various control surfaces are provided through the electronic systems not only by direct inputs from the pilot, but also produced automatically by the on-board computers if they detect, via external sensors, any uncommanded motions by the aircraft. The response to all these commands is instantaneous, and the computers are programmed to ensure that they only issue commands which are within the aircraft and airframe limits. One of the main advantages of the FBW system is that it saves on weight, doing away with the conventional 'hardware' normally associated with the mechanical operation of the aircraft's control surfaces.

Another advantage is that it allows an inherently unstable aircraft to fly, a vital component of future aircraft designs, as the Americans have already demonstrated with the F-117A Nighthawk. During 1984 XX765 was configured for a flight programme that explored the unstable aspects of aircraft design, by installing concrete

Fitted with large, rounded leading-edge root extensions and tail ballast to render the aircraft unstable, to test the FBW control systems, XX765 gets airborne from Boscombe Down. BAe

ballast in the rear fuselage and fitting large rounded leading-edge root extensions along the upper portions of the engine inlet trunks. The aircraft was also bombarded with simulated lightning strikes to test the ACT systems in differing atmospheric conditions, and all the trials undertaken by the aircraft proved a huge success.

The ACT Jaguar was retired from test flying in 1984, and after a period in storage at BAe Warton was loaned to Loughborough University of Technology's Engineering Department on 16 January 1991, being subsequently donated to the Aerospace Museum at RAF Cosford in September 1996, where it is now on display in their 'Experimental Aircraft Hangar'.

During its time with the RAE, XX765 wore the unit's traditional 'raspberry ripple' colour scheme of high gloss bright blue

which it still carries at Cosford. Gone are most of the markings, save the British Aerospace logo on the nose. The tail now carries the 'ACT' legend in white, and there is a brass plaque fitted to the port side of the nose denoting its presentation to the university by BAe. The cannon ports have also been un-faired, and the LRMTS glass re-fitted.

Empire Test Pilots School/DRA Boscombe Down

The ETPS is based at the Defence Research Agency, Boscombe Down, and is under the control of the Air Operations Directorate. The ETPS was the first dedicated test pilots school in the world when it was founded in 1943. It moved from the Boscombe Down site during the ensuing

During the course of 1996 students included pilots from South Africa, India and Finland. Currently on strength with the ETPS remain Jaguar T.2s XX145 and XX830, which are fully-instrumented 'flying classrooms', each fitted with a HUD video recorder and used for a variety of test flying tasks, aircraft performance, NVG operations and weapons delivery exercises. The aircraft are also used for continuation training and weapons release by the co-located Fixed-Wing Test Squadron.

Both aircraft carry the standard high-gloss 'raspberry ripple' scheme described earlier. XX145 has the 'Empire Test Pilots School' legend applied in red on the engine intake trunking under the wings, which is repeated in red on the two external wing-mounted fuel tanks, and particular markings are also found on XX830.

Resplendent in its 'raspberry ripple' colour scheme, XX830 taxies out at the start of another training sortie.
Author

undersides and lower fuselage, a bright red cheat line along the fuselage with bright red also applied above and below the tailplanes, the outer sections of the wings with all-white upper surfaces and a bright red tailfin with a black tip, plus a matt black anti-glare panel. Markings included full-colour roundels on the sides of the nose and above and below the wings, the RAE insignia and BAe logos on the forward nose and the 'FBW' legend in white italic lettering on the tailfin.

The aircraft was repainted at Loughborough University in a very unglamorous overall matt dark green colour scheme,

years, locating to Farnborough, then Cranfield, before returning to Boscombe in 1968. The ETPS trains around twenty fixed- and rotary-winged student test pilots per year, nearly half that number coming from overseas. After qualification these pilots return to their respective countries to undertake the exacting test flight roles their nations' industry or armed services demand. To expand their fleet, the ETPS ordered two Jaguar T.2s, XX915 and XX916, which were delivered in 1976 and 1977 respectively, but both were subsequently lost in flying accidents. These were replaced by XX145 and XX830.

Institute of Aviation Medicine

The IAM is involved in research into the psychological and physiological effects upon aircrew of service flying. It operated Jaguar T.2 ZB615 for a period at RAE Farnborough, before switching to BAe Hawks: the Jaguar carried the standard 'raspberry ripple' colour scheme.

Fast Jet Test Squadron (FJTS) DTEO – Boscombe Down

One of the most important trials units within the RAF is the Defence Research

Agency's FJTS, which is responsible for air-testing and evaluating any new aircraft or item of hardware or software that is destined for RAF front-line service. Before anything can be passed onto an operational evaluation unit, the FJTS must be happy with it and be assured that it meets the MoD's exacting standards. The FJTS operates a number of Jaguars, and at the time of writing these included GR.1As XX108/A, XX979 and XZ372, GR.1B XZ738 and T.2 ZB615.

Harrier, Tornado and Jaguar, and consideration was at one point given to the formation of a Jaguar Flight within the unit, as the number of new updates to the aircraft warranted closer inspection.

One of the major tasks of the Jaguars at the SAOEU during the early 1990s was to trial and test the proposed TIALD modifications and the cockpit additions for the Jaguar GR.1B. On strength with the SAOEU have been Jaguar GR.1Bs XX748, XX962, XX723 (in Jaguar 96/7 camouflage),

TIALD pod was fitted to the centreline pylon of the aircraft.

All of the SAOEU machines carry their standard in-service colour scheme, which, in the case of the Jaguars is normally dark grey and dark green, or more recently two-tone grey. The grey/green camouflage is also applied to XX833, the Night Cat Jaguar. The latest SAOEU markings consist of a stylized blue tailflash onto which is applied a white sword with three wings along its length. On the nose of the aircraft can be

XZ358/L on the SAOEU ramp, still in the markings of No.41 Squadron. Author

Strike Attack Operational Evaluation Unit (SAOEU)

One of the largest RAF units based at the Boscombe Down site, the SAOEU is part of the RAF's Waddington-based Air Warfare Centre, and is charged with testing and evaluating equipment and weaponry before it is released to active service. The unit irons out the 'bugs' and writes the operating procedures; being located with the Fast Jet Test Squadron helps it in its task of investigating the possibilities and assessing the potential of particular items of kit. The unit operates a mix of the current front-line combat aircraft, such as

XZ725, and XZ381, some of which they have also shared with the DRA Air Fleet and the FWTS for single-seat TIALD integration trials. The Jaguars, like the other aircraft assigned to the unit, are merely 'on loan' from their respective front-line squadrons; nevertheless, they receive the full SAOEU markings. During the initial trials for TIALD operations in 1992–3, the SAOEU had on loan from the DRA at Farnborough XX833, the so-called 'Night Cat' Jaguar T.2, which was used for single-pilot operations to prove the effectiveness of the TIALD pod system and the associated NVG and cockpit upgrades later to be fitted to the GR.1Bs. The BAe-supplied

found a blue triangular marking, edged in yellow, carrying a black Tornado, over which is superimposed red Harrier – but no Jaguar! Early in 1996 the SAOEU received Jaguar XZ358/L, which still carried the full markings of its 'owner', No.41 Squadron, and by late December the aircraft was fully marked as an OEU bird. During a series of weapons trials at China Lake in the USA during September 1997 under the codename 'Highrider', Jaguar XX723 carried the two-grey Jaguar '96 camouflage, with only a yellow 'SAOEU' legend applied to the RWR, and XX725 carried the same logo on a standard grey/green camouflaged jet; neither aircraft carried any unit markings.

CHAPTER FOUR

Photo Jaguars

The 'Recce Cats'

Royal Air Force Jaguar Reconnaissance

Viewing the lessons that had been learned in conflicts during the 1960s and early 1970s, particularly in the Middle East, it became clear to defence planners that tactical reconnaissance was a priority that could not be ignored, particularly in the era of the Cold War, when in the event of a conflict in Europe, discovering what your enemy was doing would be of paramount importance. The RAF already had high-flying reconnaissance aircraft in the photographic reconnaissance versions of the Canberra; but high-speed, low-level forays were not part of their operational procedures. The Jaguar, however, with its excellent 'tree-top' performance seemed an ideal choice for the tactical reconnaissance role. The introduction of the Jaguar to the reconnaissance role necessitated the design and construction of an externally carried pod, as there was no room in the aircraft's tightly packed interior for any more sensors. The workload in the recce Jaguar is by necessity high, so only the 'sharpest' pilots are selected to fly this demanding mission.

The BAe Reconnaissance Pod System·

The Jaguar's reconnaissance pod was specially designed and built by British Aerospace at their Weybridge site. Flight trials were carried out with the pod in the spring of 1975, with a view to service entry in mid-1976. To permit the Jaguar to operate low-level reconnaissance missions at speeds approaching Mach 1, the pod incorporated a BAe Dynamics Series 401 Infra-Red Linescan System (IRLS) which is carried in the rear section, allowing the Jaguar to make high-speed, ground-hugging reconnaissance runs in virtually all weathers. The

IRLS is 'fed' with all the relevant flight information that is stored in the aircraft's NAVWASS, or the later FIN 1064 Inertial Navigation System, including height, latitude, longitude and attitude. The IRLS gives 60 degrees of coverage to each side of the centreline – and roll stabilization allows the aircraft to use up to 35 degrees of bank without loosing image continuity – and increases the daylight and low-visibility effectiveness of the Jaguar. As a rough guide, the IRLS can cover a strip of ground as wide in metres as the aircraft's altitude in feet and has a 120-degree track field of view which can be off-set 30 degrees to port or starboard to allow a coverage capability of 180 degrees in 120-degree segments.

The pod's five optical cameras back up the IRLS, giving horizon-to-horizon coverage. They are carried in two rotating drums, viewing the ground through ground-glass windows whilst in the operating position but otherwise remaining covered for protection against damage by debris. A single Vinten F95 Mk7 camera with a 6in (15cm) F28 lens is mounted in the nose of the pod to give oblique coverage, and immediately behind this are two low-oblique Vinten F95 Mk10s, each with 1.5in (3.8cm) F2.8 lenses which give low 130-degree cross-track coverage during medium/low-level missions. The rear rotating drum accommodates two more cross-track Vinten F95s with 3in (7.6cm) F2 lenses to give high oblique coverage. The two rear F95s can also be replaced by a single Vinten F126 semi-survey camera for medium-level photography. The F95 cameras are capable of shooting between two and twelve frames per second. Because the recce pod is linked to the INAS, each negative frame and each strip of linescan film are marked with a latitude, longitude and details of which camera the image came from, in addition to which the pilots are also able to 'mark' the films via a cockpit prompt, designating any area requiring special attention, which can

later receive detailed inspection; the film can also be used to help strike targets with pinpoint accuracy.

Attaching the 1,100lb (500kg) pod to the Jaguar is a quick and simple procedure, with the aid of a special ground-handling trolley. The air pipe engages automatically, while easy access is provided for the electrical connections, enabling the film to be changed while the pod remains on the aircraft.

A Jaguar reconnaissance mission is very similar in nature to normal attack sorties in the use of the aircraft's avionics, the major difference being that a recce sortie is generally flown as a singleton, rather than a pair, taking photographs rather than dropping bombs. Turning points and IPs are input via the Ferranti PODS (POrtable Data Store), and subsequently into the INAS. The pilot then has to turn on the camera equipment well before reaching his target area in order that the camera drums can be rotated to the correct position. As with a strike mission, he then waits for the HUD to change from navigation to attack mode two minutes out from the target, at which point the target is marked for him by an acquisition 'cue' in the HUD. The actual photography takes less than two seconds, and the pilot, having a 'visual' on the target, must decide the best route over or around it to maximize the coverage, hitting the appropriate button on the control column to start 'snapping'. After the run the pilot hits the 'Change Destination' button and his HUD starts displaying the next waypoint.

Cold War Coverage – No.2 (AC) Squadron

During the Cold War, reconnaissance in Central Europe was of prime importance, and to accommodate this No.2 Army Co-operation (AC) Squadron was tasked with operating the Jaguar, the GR.1A, solely in

No.41 Squadron's anniversary jet with a BAe reconnaissance pod, showing two of its camera apertures. BAe

the reconnaissance role in Germany throughout the 1970s to the late 1980s. No.2(AC) Squadron was the last of five former RAF Germany-based Jaguar units to be re-equipped with the Tornado, the squadron finally exchanging its Jaguars for a highly specialized version of the Tornado, also titled the GR.1A, in 1989.

As part of 2 ATAF in NATO's central region, No.2 Squadron's Jaguars were based at RAF Laarbruch, their primary task being to carry out both pre- and post-strike reconnaissance sorties in support of

some fourteen Jaguar GR.1As and a pair of two-seat T.2As, all of which had a superb serviceability rate, well in excess of the minimum requirements laid down by the NATO aircraft availability schedule. Its small size was used to great advantage, down 'amongst the weeds', hoping to 'spoof' orbiting enemy AWACS by being lost in the ground clutter, and remaining below ground-based radar coverage.

Operating at heights well below those of their NATO allies in the same area, the attrition rate for the squadron's Jaguars was

size of the pod was such that it left very little in the way of ground clearance beneath it, a challenge for the pilot and the bane of the groundcrew. Through rigorous training No.2(AC)'s Reconnaissance Intelligence Centre (RIC) also constantly bettered the NATO requirements for the production times for intelligence data.

Unlike No.41(F) Squadron based at RAF Coltishall, No.2(AC) had no definable role within the NATO structure, being committed to any war in the central region. Naturally, if the need arose, the

An 'un-podded' No.2 Squadron Jaguar is prepared 'in the field' for a training sortie. Graham Causer

both the strike/attack Jaguar units based at Brüggen – and latterly the strike/attack Tornado units based at both Brüggen and Laarbruch – along with any further tasking passed to them by other agencies. As a secondary role the 'Recce Cats' also maintained their own attack capability, carrying out armed reconnaissance missions. At its peak No.2(AC) Squadron operated

high, five aircraft being lost in the first twelve years of operations, but this figure does include the pair that collided at Goose Bay in Canada on 16 June 1983 on a pre-*Red Flag* sortie. For its role as the main *in situ* reconnaissance asset for the RAF in Germany, the GR.1A carried the British Aerospace recce pod mounted on its underfuselage centreline pylon. The

unit was able to deploy to any trouble spot as required, and was in fact despatched overseas on a number of occasions, principally in connection with *Red Flag* exercises in America, and the requisite 'pre-*Flag*' training at Goose Bay in Canada. It is also interesting to note, on the subject of deployments, that No.2 (AC)'s pilots were not qualified for in-flight refuelling, due to the lack of a requirement in Germany, and for deployments the aircraft would either 'stage' through various locations, or use tanker-qualified pilots from UK-based squadrons to ferry the aircraft out for them!

The Jaguars used by No.2 Squadron were drawn from two very distinctive batches of

The later incorporation of a pair of AN/ALE-40 flare dispensers under the rear fuselage and a Philips Matra Phimat chaff pod on the starboard outer pylon gave the aircraft some degree of protection against missile threats, and with the addition of an AN/ALQ-101 jammer pod on the port outer wing pylon, this created effective

use of the trusty low-level Hunting BL755 cluster bomb, along with the more standard 'iron bombs' and the internal Aden 30mm cannon. Their skills in this regime were regularly practised on the Nordhorn range, and other flying skills were honed during ACT (air combat training) deployments to Decimonmmanu in Sardinia.

A winter clad-Jaguar GR.1A from No.41(F) Squadron, complete with a BAe recce pod, taxies out onto the snow-packed Bardufoss runway. John Cassidy RAF

aircraft within the serial ranges of XZ101–XZ120 and XZ355–XZ367. This was due to the modifications incorporated in them for the reconnaissance pod's operation, with the first aircraft to be delivered to the Squadron being XZ101, flown on its maiden mission by the unit's 'Boss', Wg Cdr A.F. 'Sandy' Wilson. For self-defence in the perceived hostile environment of an East/West conflict, the Jaguars were capable of carrying a pair of AIM-9 Sidewinder AAMs, but that event would be very rare.

protection for the Jaguar. This 'full fit' did of course have a weight penalty. Carrying the reconnaissance pod, weighing in at 1,200lb (544kg), plus two 264gal (1,200ltr) wing tanks, the jammer and Phimat pods, could cause manoeuvrability problems. However, in the murky skies of central Europe the small size of the Jaguar was considered to be the aircraft's greatest defensive asset.

When resorting to its 'secondary role' of attack, No.2(AC)'s Jaguars relied on the

No.41(F) Squadron – UK Recce Force

'Reconnaissance pilots fly around twenty-five hours a month,' explains Flt Lt Chris Carder of No.41(F) Squadron.

New pilots arrive from the OCU at Lossiemouth, with maybe seventy hours under their belts, thoroughly familiar with the aircraft and weapons techniques, but know next to nothing about recce, and all of the recce training is done here at squadron level. The new pilot's Combat Ready Work Up consists of a short ConVex phase, with seven familiarization trips, followed by an EW phase involving flying, simulators and ground school, and seven gruelling months of recce sorties. Most of the trips will be Vis-Reps, flying at least five targets, capturing them on film and in IR, plus making

his Attack Combat Ready training, and from then on it's a continuous training procedure. We get one slot a year in the NATO Tactical Leadership programme based at Jever in Germany, and it gives the more experienced aircrew the opportunity to train with large packages and gives an insight into other roles, which is then of great benefit to the squadron as a whole.

commanders. 'Despite its superb kit,' continues Chris Carder,

> ... the Jaguar is not an ideal low-level reconnaissance machine. Two seats are the real essentials for a good recce jet, and many pilots would like to have the comfort of an extra pair of eyes – and hands! The recce Jaguar pilot faces quite a challenge, particularly at low-level. He has no

Clad in two-tone grey under the Jaguar '97 upgrade programme, a No.41 Squadron Jaguar is readied for another photo-sortie. f4 Aviation Photobank

a detailed tape recording as he goes. He also writes his findings on a Mission Details Report form, which he scribes whilst in the air. After about five months he's ready for his Limited Combat Ready Check, when one of the senior Bosses, e.g. the CO, his exec. or one of the flight commanders, will fly with him. After seven months he flies with the Boss for his Full Combat Ready Check. This involves a full mission scenario, landing away at an unfamiliar site and working with different ground crew and ATC. He then flies another trip from his land-away site, and if all is OK he gets the 'tick in the box'! Following that he will go through

One of the prime tasks for the Jaguar has been that of defending NATO's northern flank, and, operating some 120 miles (190km) inside the Arctic Circle, Jaguars have been making regular visits to the Royal Norwegian Air Force base of Bardufoss for the past two decades. No.41(F) Squadron is the declared 'Arctic specialists' within the Jaguar Wing, although both Nos 6 and 54(F) Squadrons also make regular trips into the 'cold lands', and reconnaissance in these snowy wastes is of particular importance to both the UK training regime and to NATO

wingman, so keeping a good look out is mandatory, although difficult at times.

Operation *Granby – Desert Storm* Reconnaissance

When the Jaguar force was despatched to the Gulf, they took along with them their own reconnaissance capabilities in the shape of the BAe reconnaissance pod-equipped Jaguar GR1.A. The Jaguars were tasked with pre- and post-strike reconnaissance, and reportedly only two of the

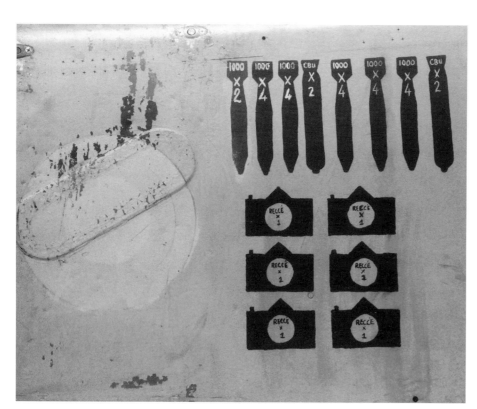

Mission markings applied to XZ358/W 'Diplomatic Service'. Author

(Below) **One of the Vinten supplied LOROP pods, attached to XZ358/W 'Diplomatic Service'.**
Paul Jackson via W. Vinten

twelve jets who saw combat were so configured; however, examination of the reconnaissance mission symbols later applied to the aircraft indicate that three aircraft, XX356/N, XZ358/W and XX962/X, were involved. One aircraft carried the standard BAe reconnaissance pod, but with its vertical linescan unit replaced by an F126 survey camera, and the second was fitted with a new item of kit, the Vinten VICON LOROP pod.

Designed for recce tasks from medium level, the Vinten VICON 18 Srs 600 (lightweight pod) LOROP (LOng Range Oblique Photography) pod, was hurriedly cleared for service as the RAF needed a stand-off reconnaissance capability – and quickly. These compact units contained only a single F.144 Type 690 camera, but with an enormous 900mm, 7-degree field of view lens. Because the LOROP pod was unable to imprint data onto film from its navigation system, as the BAe pod could, these missions were undertaken by a pair of Jaguars, one carrying the LOROP, the other the standard BAe pod, in order to 'track' the imagery. Reportedly, for these particular missions the BAe pod had its vertical linescan unit replaced by an F126 survey camera. A Reconnaissance Interpretation Centre (RIC), provided by No.41(F) Squadron was established with its associated team of photographic interpreters (PIs) to examine the information contained in the pod's sensors, working in the ARTELs in extreme temperatures: the detail and exploitation of the material was exemplary. The recce jets wore the familiar all-over desert sand camouflage scheme as applied to the strike Jaguars (*see* Chapter 3) and wore the same low-vis/no-vis markings.

It was the latter part of January 1991 when the recce-equipped aircraft entered the fray in earnest, although some limited photo trips had already been flown. The aircraft were tasked initially with providing information for the Jaguar force itself and later they were involved in gathering pre-strike information for other agencies: often flying as a pair, they would tag onto an outbound strike for mutual support. The aircraft gathered data on approach routes to future targets and looked at other areas such as already-attacked targets, to see if any further 'work' needed to be undertaken. Despite all the high-tech equipment carried by the recce Jaguars, Sqn Ldr Mike Rondot snapped his own recce photographs with a hand-held 35mm SLR camera to ensure he had a record of 'bombs on target'!

Operation *Warden* – Watching Saddam

Almost as soon as the ceasefire in the Gulf War had been declared and the aircraft returned home, another detachment of desert pink Jaguars were on their way back

XZ364/GJ (in the HAS) and XZ118/FF captured at Incerlik in February 1993, being readied for another Warden sortie. Author

to the Gulf. Eight Jaguars from No.54 Squadron deployed to Incerlik Air Base in Turkey between 4–9 September 1991 to fly armed reconnaissance patrols in conjunction with French Mirage F.1CRs to help police the United Nations' newly-established northern 'no-fly' zone over Iraq. These 'safe havens'; were set up to protect the Iraqi Kurds from Saddam Hussein's post-war retributions.

Jaguars carried the BAe reconnaissance pod, as well as the Vinten VICON LOROP pod with its Type 690 camera. Each sortie was flown as a full combat mission, the crews being fully 'sanitized' and the aircraft armed with overwing Sidewinder AAMs, a full load of chaff and flares, as well as wing-mounted Phimat and ALQ-101 pods. Missions usually lasted some two hours, flown with fighter support usually provided by F-

mer wearer of the 'Mary Rose' paintwork during the Gulf War, received a new caricature. The new nose artwork showed a gun-toting cowboy with a sheriff's badge exclaiming 'Marshall Connelly', in reference to the detachment commander – Group Captain Connelly – whose name was also worn in a blue and red scroll beneath the cockpit. The artwork was applied on 10 November 1991 by Cpl Paul

Carrying the BAe recce pod, XZ364 is prepared for flight from Incerlik as part of Operation Warden.
Note the twin overwing Sidewinders, and Phimat and ALQ-101 pods. Author

The RAF's function, as part of the ongoing UN efforts, came under the aegis of Operation *Warden*. The deployed aircraft would generally operate in pairs, one armed with CBUs, a second configured for reconnaissance. As in the Gulf War, the

16s or F-15s, as well as defence suppression F-4G Phantoms, and ECM-jamming EF-111 'Spark Varks' or EA-6B Prowlers, plus tanker support. Artwork briefly returned to one Jaguar during its *Warden* duties as XZ356, from No.6 Squadron and the for-

Robbins, prior to the unit flying out to Turkey to relieve No.54 Squadron. XZ111 also had a little artwork added, in the shape of the legend 'Wardenbird 1', applied just prior to its return from Turkey to Coltishall.

A pair of RAF Jaguars buzz an HAS at Mosul airfield in Iraq during the summer of 1991 as part of an Operation Warden sortie. Intelligence reports had indicated an Iraqi MiG-23 outside a hangar, and the two Jaguars were despatched to investigate. As can be seen here, the pass was at low level – as witness the posture of the Iraqi figure adopting a 'fingers in the ears' pose. The MiG turned out to be damaged and unusable; such was the commitment of the Coalition to let no stone remain uncovered. Andy Cubin

Operation *Grapple* – Bosnia Hercegovina

During Operation *Grapple*, which was the RAF's contribution to the United Nations-led Operation *Deny Flight* (*see* Chapter 6), the policing of the skies over Bosnia, two Jaguar GR1As, XZ364/GJ and XX720/GB were permanently configured for reconnaissance, one carrying the LOROP system, which was later substituted for the GP-1 pod, the other fitted out with the standard BAe pod, which carried the F126 general survey camera. Based at Gioia del Colle in Italy, a RIC was set up

by No.41(F) Squadron to handle the Jaguars' 'wet film' processing and to provide for its interpretation. The information gathered by the Jaguars was then passed to the 5th ATAF for future mission planning, particularly if CAS were to be called for. The two Jaguars were painted in overall light grey ARTF, designed for medium level operations, and carried as standard a pair of overwing-mounted AIM-9 Sidewinder AAMs, a Phimat chaff dispenser, AN/ALQ-101 jammer pod, Tracor flare launchers and two 264gal wing tanks in what was generally described as the '*Granby* fit'.

The reconnaissance sorties, most of which were flown from medium level, involved two aircraft, one a GR.1A acting as the 'photo-ship', the second aircraft, a standard GR.1A, acting as the 'stinger' to provide vital visual cross-cover for any aerial SAM threats. In response to a UN request, the NATO air raid on Udbina was planned by the Dutch contingent using photos provided by the Jaguar. Although at the time of the attack the target was partially obscured by smoke, the intended targets were all hit, as was evidenced by post-attack recce pictures, again provided by the two Jaguars.

Having just returned from a post-strike reconnaissance sortie, GR1.A XZ364/GJ stands in front of two
of Gioia's sheds. On the centreline station the aircraft carries the Vinten GP-1 LOROP pod as well as
Sidewinder AAMs, and Phimat and ALQ-101 (V) jammer pods. via Gary Madgwick.

Carrying the BAe reconnaissance pod, a Jaguar GR.1A transits out from Gioia del Colle to its assigned area
over Bosnia. BAe

(Above) French two-seater E-02 F-ZWRC was the second Jaguar prototype, first flying on 11 February 1969 from Istres, with Bernard Witt at the controls. The aircraft was subsequently presented at that year's Paris Air Salon, wearing the side number '308'. E-02 made its final flight on 28 February 1979, later moving to the French Technical Training School at Rochfort. BAe.

(Below)
XW563, one of the first production Jaguars, reveals its early non-LRMTS configuration, and three-tone camouflage scheme. BAe

(Top) **A catapult crew prepare the Maritime Jaguar prototype for a launch from the deck of the French aircraft carrier Clemenceau. The Jaguar M was the sole sea-going version to be built, and despite its promise, it was eventually cancelled in favour of the Dassault Super Etendard. The aircraft was later presented to the French Technical Training School at Rochfort.** BAe

(Bottom) **A single-seat Indian Jaguar International, officially known as the Shamsher – an Indian word for a curved assault sword, the literal translation being 'sword of justice'. The Indian Government remain committed to seeing their Jaguar force into the next century, and are, like the RAF and Oman, looking to upgrade their airframes and systems.** BAe

The Omani Air Force selected the option of fitting its aircraft with the RAF-style Ferranti LRMTS nose, as their primary role would be strike/attack. However, the Jaguars were also fitted with air-to-air missiles in keeping with their stated secondary air defence role. The initial batch were fitted with overwing launchers for the French Matra 550 Magic AAMs, while the second batch were also fitted with outboard underwing pylons adapted to carry the American AIM-9P Sidewinder AAM as well as the Magic. BAe

FAE302 with wheels down on approach to Taura. An order from Ecuador for a single squadron's-worth of Jaguar Internationals was placed with SEPECAT in 1974, covering the supply of ten single-seat ES models and a pair of two-seat EB trainers, these aircraft having the distinction of being the first 'true' Jaguar Internationals. BAe

(Above) Wearing the most colourful of Jaguar camouflage schemes is NAF703, a two-seat Jaguar International of the Nigerian Air Force. These aircraft represent the final export success for the Jaguar with the sale of eighteen aircraft in July 1983. These little-used aircraft are now permanently grounded and in a state of disrepair following the Nigerian Government's defence cutbacks in the late 1980s. BAe

(Below) The Gulf War represented something of a watershed for the RAF's Jaguars. Having been already written off in the minds of defence planners, they were in fact the first British strike aircraft deployed to the region. Painted up in a so-called desert sand colour scheme, and receiving a number of 'war modifications', the Jaguars confounded their critics and proved to be one of the major success stories of the conflict. BAe via Tony Thornborough

Tanking from a C135-F, a French Jaguar refuels prior to undertaking a mission into Iraq. The French favoured side-by-side bomb carriers, whereas the RAF used tandem beam carriers. SIRPA Air

(Below) Freshly painted in desert sand, and back at Coltishall, a BAe recce pod-carrying Jaguar GR.1A taxis out for a training mission. To permit the Jaguar to operate low-level reconnaissance missions at speeds approaching Mach 1, the pod incorporated a BAe Dynamics Series 401 Infra-red Linescan System (IRLS) which is carried in the rear of the pod, allowing the Jaguar to make high-speed, very low-level reconnaissance runs. f4 Aviation Photobank

Flt Lt Andy Cubin 'beats up' the runway at Thumrait in a demonstration flight during his time with No.20 Squadron ROAF. This picture amply illustrates the Jaguar's excellent low-level handling abilities – not to mention the consummate skill of the pilot! Andy Cubin

A pair of Jaguars from No.16(R) Squadron, the RAF's Jaguar OCU based at Lossiemouth, pictured against a typical Highland backdrop. Since the arrival of the GR.1B and GR.3, a posting to the Jaguar is a much sought-after prize. Rick Brewell

After a brief three-month respite from their Turkish sojourn manning Operation Warden at Incerlik air force base, Jaguars from Coltishall were again called to support an international operation, this time to help uphold the United Nations Protection Force (UNPROFOR) over Bosnia-Hercegovina. Here we see a superb shot of an Operation Grapple Jaguar, showing the sleek graceful lines of the 'cat'. BAe

(Below) During the early 1990s the RAF found that it was beginning to become more isolated from top-level decision making, due to its lack of an autonomous laser-guided bomb capability. Urgent Operational Requirement 41/94 was raised in June 1994, intended to equip a limited number of Jaguars with the GEC TIALD laser designation pod, giving a precision guided munitions capability that could be employed quickly, especially to the war zone over Bosnia. Here a Jaguar '96 aircraft shows off its new low infra-red two-tone colour scheme and a 1,000lb (454kg) laser-guided bomb on its centreline station.
Rick Brewell

A formation set up to witness the exchange of Bosnia deployment aircraft for Operation Grapple at Gioia del Colle. The outgoing Harrier detachment was relieved by Jaguars making their second tour of duty over the Balkans. Note that two Jaguars retain their light grey ARTF colour, whilst the third carries the two-tone Jaguar '96 colours. John Cassidy RAF

(Below) 'Cubin's Black Cat'. During the 1993–6 airshow seasons, the task of displaying the Jaguar GR.1A to the public was entrusted to Flt Lt Andy Cubin, then of No.16(R) Squadron at Lossiemouth. The striking black and yellow paint job was a true show-stopper, and Andy went on to join the RAF's prestigious Red Arrows display team. Rick Brewell

Wing Commander Chris Harper, OC of No.41 Squadron commented that the Jaguar had performed:

Fabulously well, especially in the light of our more recent exploits over the former Yugoslavia. In our recce role, the imagery we were able to provide for the senior commanders was of an extraordinarily high quality, and using

The Harriers remained on station until they were relieved by the Jaguar force in January 1997; again, two Jaguars were configured for the reconnaissance role, using the Vinten GP-1 and BAe pods, but this time sporting the newer two-tone permanent grey scheme that had been applied to the GR.1B and Jaguar '96 airframes at Coltishall during the Jaguar's 18-month absence from Italy.

system described earlier. When eight Vinten GP-1 Srs 18-601 reconnaissance pods were bought for use by the Harrier and Tornado, a further four were acquired for use by the Jaguar. As with the original BAe pod and the Vinten Vicon LOROP unit used during the Gulf War, the GP-1 can only be carried by the Jaguars of No.41(F) Squadron that are specifically wired for

Flying high over Gorazde, a Vinten GP-1-equipped Jaguar. W. Vinten

our LOROP pod, we were able to confirm the position of military surface-to-air missile systems, troop movements, military vehicles, and any repositioning of forces.

The Jaguars were replaced at Gioia del Colle by a detachment of Harrier GR.7s in July 1995, by which time they had flown over 3,000 operational sorties over Bosnia.

The Vinten Reconnaissance Pod System

The RAF's involvement in operations over Iraq both during and after the Gulf War, together with their monitoring duties over Bosnia, led to the requirement for a dedicated medium-level reconnaissance capability, rather than the traditional

the reconnaissance role. The GP-1 pod has a F144 Type 690 LOROP camera facing forward with a new 18in focal length autofocus lens, which gives a 14-degrees field of view – but remains compatible with optical or electro-optical sensors, and records onto a standard 126mm film – effectively doubling the performance of the earlier lens, thereby allowing the

Jaguar to operate at far greater stand-off ranges. The forward portion of the pod is also fitted with a rotating mirror and lens assembly, allowing the pilot to select any position for true horizon-to-horizon coverage. In the rear is a Type 900 A/B panoramic magazine-loaded camera with a 76mm lens, recording onto a 70mm film, which can be operated at 16fps, and can be used for tracking the LOROP camera and for plotting the location of the LOROP images. With the introduction of the GP-1, the Jaguar force will be able to retire its old BAe system, and by late 1998 a new EO version of the GP-1 will be in service, replacing both the optical, wet film and BAe pods, and will be carried by the upgraded Jaguar GR.3.

In the new EO version of the GP-1, the original Vinten Type 690 LOROP camera will be replaced by a Type 8040 EO sensor, which uses the same optics as the LOROP camera, but records its data in a digital linescan format onto an analogue video tape. This sensor can also be replaced by a pair of Type 8010 EO sensors with a number of configuration options, giving the new pod a 'window'-fitted centre section. The Type 8010 will replace the F.95 cameras. The rear of the pod will house a compact Vinten Integrated Infra-Red Linescan (VIGIL) infra-red linescan unit, some elements of which are derivatives of the Type 4000 unit fitted to the Tornado GR.1A, and will give the Jaguar an unrivalled reconnaissance suite.

Armée de l'Air Jaguar Reconnaissance

French Jaguars have a reconnaissance commitment similar to that of their counterparts in the RAF, and this role is undertaken by EC 4/11 at Bordeaux/Merignac. Early in the Jaguar's service the French developed a podded reconnaissance system by modifying a centreline RP36 264gal (1,200ltr) drop tank which then carried both fuel and cameras, carrying three fixed-position Omera 40 panoramic cameras in the forward section, one facing front and two facing to the rear,

---

Reconnaissance Interpretation Centre

Apart from the 'sharp end', the jets themselves, the other vitally important component for reconnaissance is the processing and exploitation of the films provided by the Jaguar's podded systems, and these are interpreted in the squadrons' Reconnaissance Intelligence Centres (RICs). The RICs are also responsible for recognition and intelligence training for pilots.

For No.2(AC) Squadron, the RIC was made up of a number of Air Portable Reconnaissance Exploitation Laboratories (ARTELS), which were linked together to form a film-processing station and photographic interpretation section. They were considered to be as important as the aircraft themselves, and whilst at Laarbruch they 'lived' within the confines of one of the Hardened Aircraft Shelters. Each ARTEL was completely self-sufficient with its own generators and water supplies, and was designed to be transportable by air in the hold of a Hercules or by land on the back of 4-ton Bedford trucks, and could be uprooted within thirty minutes.

Once the aircraft is down the films are rushed to the RIC, along with the Mission Details Form, the Vis-Rep cassette and the ATM, the requirement being for the film magazines to be unloaded from the aircraft and rushed to the RIC immediately on engine shutdown and made available to commanders within forty-five minutes. Even in full NBC conditions, only six minutes is allowed for the film to be recovered, sealed in a protective bag and rushed to the RIC. Inside the RIC, the process machinery develops the films at a staggering rate of 80ft/min: a whole film in two minutes or the contents of a recce pod, including any IRLS, in six. The RICs can therefore handle eight sorties per hour, or just over seventy sorties per day. The film is then laid onto a light table by a photographic interpreter in consultation with the pilot. Each film is colour coded according to which camera it came from, and they can be motored through quickly to find any relevant point. Close examination then takes place with stereoscopic viewers, and prints are only taken when the target is small or obscured by camouflage. Ten minutes is allowed for interpretation, leaving twenty-five to produce the 'Exrep' (exploitation report). Each target is reported using different categories, such as location, type, modifications, approaches, access, status, activity and defences.

To back-up the photography, in the event of the pilot being immediately re-tasked on arrival back at home base, a visual report is made onto a cassette tape by the pilot while still airborne, and on this he would note areas of importance related to the relevant portion of the film, and this would then be retrieved when the film is unloaded, and used to aid interpretation. Often an HF broadcast in-flight 'IFREP' is needed, when the pilot would relay the mission number, what was seen and a coded report on weather over the target. A pilot may also be re-tasked whilst still returning from his original target: should this happen he would then make his 'Vis-Rep' report via secure radio to whichever agency he was dealing with, so that some verbal data would be available immediately. This information would include what was observed at the target, call sign heading, height, and so on. The system operated by the Jaguar in Germany was similar to that employed by other NATO reconnaissance units, which made deployments and co-operation between bases much more effective.

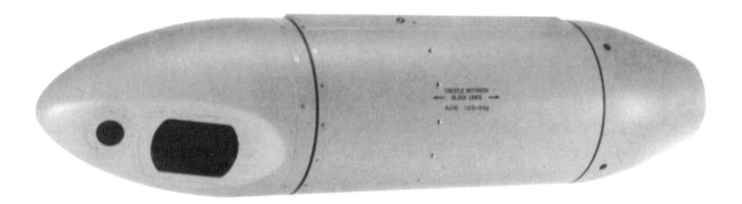

Vicon 18-600 camera pod. Vinten

Vinten Type 690 camera. Vinten

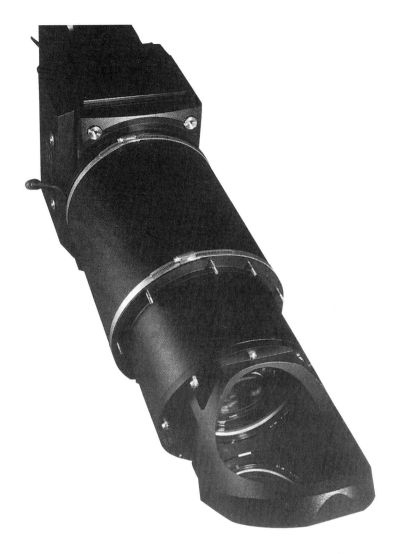

(Below) Jaguar A104 11-EK begins its take-off run during Operation Daguet during the Gulf War. Although armed with 500lb (227kg) 'slick' bombs, it also carries a RP36P recce pod on its centreline, which is in fact a modified fuel tank. Tim Darrah

Armed with 100mm rockets, Sidewinders and a jammer pod, a French Jaguar A takes on fuel from a tanker over Italy before heading into Bosnia on a visual reconnaissance sortie, visually identifying specific targets, as well as using the under-nose mounted Omera 40 strike camera.
via Gary Madgwick

complementing the aircraft's own internal Omera 40, and designating it the RP36P (*reservoir pendulaire*) pod. The French Jaguar's reconnaissance duties were seen as secondary to the aircraft's main attack role, and as a result the final batch of eighty aircraft had their fixed Omera 40 moved further back along the nose (whilst some earlier single-seaters had this retrofitted) and a Thomson-CSF TAV-38 laser rangefinder fitted in its place. During *Desert Storm* operations, however, the Jaguars reportedly carried the RP36P reconnaissance pod on the centreline – of which two slightly different types were available for low- and medium-level work – and for a small number of Jaguar-related missions, moreover, the bulk of the information gathering was left to the specialized Mirage F.1C units.

Operation Aconit – *Iraq*

During April 1991, elements of EC 3/11 arrived at Incerlik Air Force Base in Turkey in order to provide an armed reconnaissance force similar to that provided by the RAF's GR.1As, and to patrol the no-fly zone set up over northern Iraq under the UN-led Operation *Provide Comfort*. Under the Operation *Aconit* banner, five Jaguar As regularly flew both armed and tactical reconnaissance patrols over northern Iraq, with two of the aircraft configured to carry a centreline-mounted RP36P pod, in addition to their internal Omera 40 camera. The Omera 40 produces horizon-to-horizon coverage using 57mm × 249mm negatives on 70mm film, firing at between 2–10fps, with shutter speeds up to

1/10,000th of a second. The Jaguar detachment gave up its reconnaissance duties in March 1994, their tasks being taken over by the specialized Mirage F1.CR aircraft. On return from one mission over Iraq, a C-135F tanker and four Jaguars made a formation flypast over Incerlik to celebrate the 1,000th tanker mission and the 3,000th fighter mission of the *Provide Comfort* operations, during which time one of the aircraft received a special '3,000 Missions' legend on its upper surfaces. From 1992 to date, EC 2/11 have rotated the detachment with EC 3/11, having a mission brief of conventional attack as well as some visual reconnaissance; they put their precision skills at the disposal of the NATO Commanders for Operation *Deliberate Force* in September 1995.

CHAPTER FIVE

Jaguar Export

In the Face of Adversity

Any export deal won by BAC/BAe was always in the face of fierce competition from its SEPECAT partner Dassault, who would stop at nothing to sell their products and rubbish the 'opposition'. From its earliest days the Jaguar was intended to make a huge impact in the export market, and a specially-developed export version, the Jaguar International, was produced to meet the changing face of the world's aviation climate. The International was an excellent machine, built around the RAF's GR.1A with its tried-and-tested avionics and weaponry; it was way ahead of all its contemporaries, offering a variety of mission fits and ordnance options. In the original formula for the Jaguar's production and sales was the premise that SEPECAT would act as main contractor for any export orders; however, in reality SEPECAT had no machinery to handle overseas trade, so if the UK signed a deal, it became a British contract with the French as sub-contractor, and vice-versa (a situation that never arose), which seemed to be a reasonable compromise, giving both parties equal share. However, it must be remembered that one half of SEPECAT, Dassault, was already working hard to sell its own products in the export market, and any Jaguar sales came up against fierce competition from the French side, whose Government added their total support to any export drives. Therefore, it became clear from very early on that the push to export Jaguar was very one-sided, coming only from the UK partner company, constantly fighting a heavy dose of intransigence from Dassault.

BAC (BAe) won a contract to sell the Jaguar to the Indian Air Force, in the face of a challenge from Dassault who were offering their Mirage F.1s in direct competition; for the British sales team it was a fiercely-contested battle – consider how difficult it was to put together a detailed submission to the Indian Government without their partner Dassault knowing about it! Over thirty countries were targeted by the BAC

overseas sales team, and won sales to the Sultanate of Oman, Ecuador and Nigeria. Belgium expressed an interest but in the end brought the Mirage 5 from Dassault, West Germany decided to wait for Tornado, and the Swiss added the Jaguar International to a list of eight other types under consideration for their needs. The Japanese expressed an interest, but decided to produce their own aircraft, the Mitsubishi F-1 (see p.24), which came out looking remarkably similar to the Jaguar! Hopes were high that the navies of Brazil and Argentina would buy the Jaguar M to operate from their aircraft carriers, but that prospect was dashed when the Jaguar M was cancelled.

In 1974 a Jaguar sales team visited Kuwait, and was curiously followed by a team from Dassault, which later, and quite surprisingly, announced a tentative order for fifty Jaguars and sixteen Mirage F.1s; the Mirage order was later confirmed, the Jaguar order not. Turkey considered buying twenty-four Jaguars, but nothing further developed from their early attention. Egypt also looked for around 200 Jaguars, but eventually settled for an armed version of the Dassault-Dornier Alpha Jet. In 1976 Abu Dhabi expressed an interest in buying the Jaguar as an alternative to a second squadron of Mirage IIIs, but the Mirage was eventually selected. Later that year Pakistan considered buying 100 Jaguars if the USA would not supply them A-7 Corsairs, but again the outcome was a contract for Dassault in the shape of the Mirage 5.

During the early 1970s BAC tried hard to sell the now 'in service' Jaguar (offering the International version) to a European consortium of Belgium, the Netherlands, Norway and Denmark, who had formed together to find a successor for their Starfighters. France was again promoting the Mirage F.1, Sweden the Saab Viggen and America the F-16 with BAC offering the Jaguar. With its overwing Magic or Sidewinder AAMs, the Jaguar was now

equipped for the air defence role, as well as being considered superior to the Mirage and F-16 in the ground-attack role; it was offered with 'instant availability', unlike the F-16, and came in at a very favourable price. In an attempt to win the order, a joint strategy was proposed to Dassault: they supply the Mirage F.1 to equip the consortium's interceptor squadrons, and the Jaguar would be supplied to equip the ground-attack squadrons. As the Jaguar was destined for service in a big way with the RAF in Germany, this offered great commonality in terms of European logistics, and as the F.1 had been ordered in quantity by the French Air Force, again logistic support would be readily available.

The proposal failed – due in no small way to M. Dassault, who refused to co-operate with the BAC proposal, despite having a 50 per cent stake in the Jaguar, and a 100 per cent stake in the Mirage. He was adamant that he was going to get the whole four-nation order for the F.1, and was not interested in sharing the cake with anyone, a stance fully supported by the French Government. The other 'fly in the ointment' was the British Government's surprising and unexplained lack of interest in the deal. In the end Dassault and SEPECAT both lost out: through one partner's greed the market was opened up to the USA with the F-16, and a golden opportunity was squandered.

The Jaguar International

The potential for overseas sales of the Jaguar had been realized from the very early stages of its development: clearly it was an excellent aircraft, and one that was endowed with the 'right stuff' in terms of range, power, speed, warload and accuracy. Several foreign countries had expressed an interest in the type even before a dedicated export model had been built. Well before it joined the consortium with Holland, Denmark and Norway, Belgium showed a particular interest in the Jaguar as a replacement for its Lockheed F-104G Starfighters, and went as far as visiting Warton in early 1974 to take a closer look at the aircraft.

Much of the front running for the export Jaguar was undertaken by BAC: although the export version was still a collaborative effort, much of the trials work and weapons clearances were undertaken by BAC using British prototypes based at Warton. The Jaguar International was publicly launched at the Farnborough Air Show in September 1974, a month after the governments of Oman and Ecuador had placed orders for the type(the first custom-built Jaguar International, two-seater G27-266, was destined for Ecuador), and was arrayed in typical 'Farnborough style' with the full complement of weaponry that could be carried. The aircraft chosen to represent latest version of the Jaguar was the first British production aircraft, S-1 XX108, fitted for the occasion with a mock-up of the Agave radar nose. XX108 was BAC's 'Jack of all trades', and rather than entering RAF service it had been retained by BAC and delegated to various proving trials. The aircraft was converted in a three-phase programme into a 'prototype' of the International; also added to the development programme was the second British single-seat prototype, S-07 XW563. XX108, when used as an overseas demonstrator, also carried the civil serial number G-27-213. Originally, the designation 'Jaguar K' was reserved for export models based on the UK version, but it was never applied to any order.

The Jaguar International differs from both the British and French types in a number of key areas, particularly in the powerplant, weapons and the avionics installation. The engines chosen for the aircraft were either the Rolls-Royce Turbomeca Adour Mk804 Dash 26 or the Mk811, the former being similar to the Mk102 fitted to the RAF machines but offering 5,320lb (2,410kg) of dry thrust and 8,040lb (3,645lb) with afterburner, a 27 per cent increase. Power levels attainable from the engine were further increased with the introduction of the Mk811 RT172 Dash 58, which gave 5,520lb (2,505kg) dry and 8,400lb (3,810kg) with afterburner. Take-off performance was enhanced by 10 per cent and there was a 30 per cent increase in the sustained capabilities giving the Jaguar a dogfight or air-superiority capability that was equal, or in some cases better than that of fighters purpose-

built for the role. The uprated engines also improved the Jaguar's performance in 'hot and high conditions', a factor that proved crucial in the sales to both Oman and Ecuador, and that was hoped would also impress other potential customers.

Another of the Jaguar International's selling points was the wide number of options available for avionics and weapons, which could be tailored to the individual customers' needs. A radar nose was mocked-up on XX108 in 1974, and initial air trials were carried out using a French two-seater fitted with a French-built Thomson-CSF Agave radar mounted in the front of a modified 264gal (1,200ltr) (fuel tank carried on the centreline, the radar information being processed in the rear seat where it replaced the moving map display. It was found that, not surprisingly, the Agave considerably extended the versatility of the Jaguar, in air-to-ground, air-to-air and air-to-sea operations, producing detection ranges of 75nm (139km) against medium-sized shipping and 15nm (28km) against fighters. If the radar option were to be required by a customer, the radar display could be either 'heads down', on an MFD or superimposed over the projected map display, or 'heads up' into the pilot's Smiths-Raster HUD by means of a scan conversion unit, thus retaining the moving map display. The Agave radar scanner would be mounted in a standard radome, replacing the LRMTS in the nose of the aircraft. India was later to select a maritime version of the Jaguar fitted with the radar. Customers wishing to retain the laser ranger and marked target seeker – and therefore maintain air-to-ground accuracy – would be offered a smaller version of the Ferranti 105S system mounted in a chin fairing behind the radome. The full 'chisel nosed' LRMTS non-radar version, similar in appearance to the RAF's GR.1 was also available if required. Experiments under the Jaguar International programme were also undertaken to look at low-light television and low visibility sensors.

A wide range of weapons was also cleared for use with the export Jaguar, and this included a full range of 'smart' and 'dumb' bombs, McDonnell Douglas AGM-84 Harpoon, Aerospatiale AM.39 Exocet, MBB Kormoran and the BAe Sea Eagle anti-shipping missiles, as well as items such as Durandal, Belouga and anti-radar missiles already in the inventory of the French and British operators. The aircraft also offered a choice of internal cannon: either the French DEFA or British Aden could be supplied.

A major step forward for the Jaguar came with an air-to-air capability, following the installation of the French Matra 550 Magic infra-red heat-seeking dogfight missiles on the underwing pylons. Although the Jaguar had not been intended specifically to carry such weapons, installation of the comparatively small Magic and the American-made AIM-9 Sidewinder presented no problems. Unique overwing stations were placed on top of the standard wing fence, thus freeing up the underwing pylons for offensive weaponry; the outer wing pylons also carried the necessary wiring to carry and fire Sidewinders. Successful firings from the overwing station were made in 1976 by the British S-07 flying from Warton, the missiles leaving cleanly and their rocket efflux staying clear of the engine intakes. BAC concluded that this was the best position for missile rails, as in many combat situations the aircraft would be pulling round towards its intended target, and the missile seeker heads would be 'looking' upwards from the wing into the turn.

Camouflage and Markings

Jaguar International S-1 XX108 – This aircraft was fitted with a non-LRMTS nose, with the rounded appearance of the French Jaguar A, with its cannon ports faired over and with overwing missile pylons carrying Magic or Sidewinder AAMs. The aircraft did not feature the tail-mounted RWR fairing at this stage. Camouflage was standard RAF dark sea grey and dark green with light aircraft grey undersides, with a black anti-glare panel on the nose and a black fin tip. The aircraft carried a red fin flash near the base of the tail carrying the stylized 'Jaguar' logo in large white lettering, and 'International' in smaller lettering, with red and blue RAF roundels above and below the wings, and below the cockpit. On the port side of the nose the aircraft carried a white circular marking in which was contained a black logo denoting the 'Queens Award For Export Achievement' This aircraft was displayed at the 1974 Paris Air Show fitted with a mock-up of the Agave radar nose, giving the Jaguar a uncharacteristic look. The aircraft retained the RWR RAF markings and camouflage scheme, but the collaborative round logo originally applied to the intakes was rotated through 45 degrees and applied beneath the cockpit.

Jaguar International S-1 XX108, fitted with a non-LRMTS nose, giving the rounded appearance of the French Jaguar A, with its cannon ports faired over and with overwing missile pylons carrying Matra 500 Magic missiles, and sporting the 'Queens Award For Export Achievement' logo.
BAe

Specification – Jaguar International	
Type:	Single-seat tactical support aircraft; reconnaissance capable
Accommodation:	Pilot only, in Martin-Baker E9B (Ecuador), O9B (Oman), IN9B (India), or N9B (Nigeria) ejector seat
Powerplant:	Two Rolls-Royce/Turbomeca Adour Mk811 afterburning turbofans rated at 5,520lb (2,509kg) dry and 9,270lb (4,213kg) with afterburner
Performance:	Max speed 1,056mph (1,690km/h) Climb rate 30,000ft (9,100m) in 90sec Ceiling 45,930ft (13,920m) Range 334 miles (534km) lo-lo-lo, 875 miles (1,400km) hi-lo-hi and 2,190 miles (3,504km) ferry
Weights:	Empty 16,975lb (7,716kg); max 34,612lb (15,700kg)
Dimensions:	Span: 28ft 6in (8.64m); length 55ft 2.5in (16.73m); height: 16ft 0.5in (4.86m)
Armament:	Two 30mm DEFA or Aden cannon with 130/150 rounds of ammunition per gun, plus five external hardpoints for 10,000lb (4,545kg) of stores and two overwing points for Sidewinder or Matra 550 Magic AAMs

Jaguar Prototype S-07 XW563 'International Demonstrator' – two different guises. Initially as the 'demonstrator' the aircraft was fitted with the standard RAF-style chisel nose but with the glass apertures faired over, and the tail-mounted RWR fairing. The aircraft was also fitted with overwing missile launchers. Similar to XX108, XW563 also carried the stylized tail logo, and also a circular intake badge showing the collaborative flags of Britain and France, over which was superimposed a black Jaguar silhouette. This aircraft carried red, white and blue roundels above and below the wings, and beneath the cockpit, with a three-colour fin flash partly obscured by the Jaguar logo. Also of note was the small 'S07' stencilled on the tailfin. Camouflage was again standard RAF dark sea grey, dark green and light aircraft grey.

Specification – Jaguar International Two-seat	
Type:	Two-seat operational conversion trainer
Accommodation:	Pilot (front seat) and instructor (rear seat) in Martin-Baker E9B (Ecuador), O9B (Oman), IN9B (India), or N9B (Nigeria) ejector seats
Powerplant:	Two Rolls-Royce/Turbomeca Adour Mk811 afterburning turbofans rated at 5,520lb (2,509kg) dry and 9,270lb (4,213kg) with afterburner
Performance:	Max speed 1,056mph (1,690km/h) Climb rate 30,000ft (9,100m) in 90sec Ceiling 45,930ft (13,920m) Range 334 miles (534km) lo-lo-lo, 875 miles (1,400km) hi-lo-hi and 2,190 miles (3,504km) ferry
Weights:	Empty 15,432lb (7,000kg); max 34,612lb (15,700kg)
Dimensions:	Span 28ft 6in (8.64m); length 57ft 6.25in (17.43m)
Armament:	One 30mm DEFA or Aden cannon with 130/150 rounds of ammunition per gun, plus five external hardpoints for 10,000lb (4,545kg) of stores and two overwing hardpoints for Sidewinder or Matra 550 Magic AAMs

XW563 fitted with the standard RAF-style chisel nose, but with the glass apertures faired over, and the tail-mounted RWR fairing and Magic AAMs. The logo on the intake was something of a joke, as all of the sales were generated by BAC! BAe

AIM-9L/M Sidewinder Missiles

The third generation of Sidewinder AAMs was introduced in 1976, with the 'Lima' and 'Mike' versions of the world's most successful short-range air-to-air missile. In the 'Lima' variant the warhead was improved with the addition of a sheathing of pre-formed steel rods, triggered by a Hughes DSU-15B active optical proximity fuse, which incorporates a ring of eight gallium arsenide laser diode emitters and a ring of silicon photodiode receivers to provide better warhead detonation and better manoeuvring. The AIM-9M improved on this with a better smokeless motor, better seeker sensitivity and greater resistance to countermeasures. The Sidewinder can be carried on the over-wing launchers fitted to the RAF and International variants of the Jaguar, as well as to the outboard wing pylons.

AIM-9 Sidewinder missile. Author

XX108, now serving with the DERA test fleet at Boscombe Down. GEC/Marconi

Pulling wing vortices, XW563 in its Jaguar International guise. BAe

Indian Jaguars – the *Shamsher*

During the 1970s the Indian Government saw the need to urgently replace its ageing fleet of English Electric Canberras and Hawker Hunters that had been in service since the 1950s. Therefore, they launched their DPSA – 'Deep Penetration Strike Aircraft' – competition in 1978, inviting the world's major aircraft manufacturers to put forward proposals to meet the *Bharatiya Vay Sena*'s (Indian Air Force's) requirement for an aircraft that could penetrate at low level and strike at targets 300 miles inside hostile territory. A further element of this requirement was the need for the aircraft to be readily available and to

be quickly produced in India. The specifications attracted the interest of both Western and Soviet contenders, including Mikoyan-Gurevich with their MiG-23, Sukhoi with their Su-20 and – underlining their attitude to the Jaguar – Dassault-Breguet with export versions of the Mirage F.1. SEPECAT offered the Jaguar International, with the added incentive that India's long tradition of licence-building and further developing foreign types would be a key factor if the aircraft were to be selected.

Eventually, the field was narrowed to three contenders: the Jaguar, the Saab Viggen and the Mirage F.1. The relative merits of each were investigated by the

Indian Government and detailed negotiations entered into with each manufacturer, looking at prices, delivery, transfer of technology and indigenous production. The decision was announced on 6 October 1978, and an extract from it reads thus:

Based on the evaluation and negotiations, it has been decided that the aircraft which will replace the fleet of Canberras and Hunters will be the Jaguar. Firstly, the Jaguar – as do the other two aircraft – adequately meets the requirements of the IAF. Secondly, it is the most economical of the three options. Thirdly, it has the most favourable delivery schedule. Fourthly, the Jaguar has the edge over the other two aircraft in the important characteristic of survival capacity, being the only twin-engined aircraft of the three.

This announcement was followed by the signing of an Intention To Proceed (ITP) document on 21 October, covering an order for 160 aircraft. This document was signed by Sir Frederick W. Page for SEPECAT and Shri S. Banerji, the Indian Defence Secretary, an authority which would subsequently allow the Indian company Hindustan Aeronautics Limited (HAL), to begin establishing a production line for local manufacture of the Jaguar. Under the terms of the agreement, an initial batch of eighteen aircraft would be loaned from RAF stock (a real coup by BAe), forty would be built by SEPECAT at the BAe site at Warton, and the Indians would build a further 120, the deal being worth some £1,000m, the biggest-ever contract of its kind concluded by India at the time. The arrangement had three distinct

phases. Phase 1 involved sixteen single-seat and two two-seat Jaguars as interim aircraft drawn, as already noted, from RAF stocks. Phase 2 was the delivery of thirty-five single-seat and five two-seat direct supply (or 'flyaway') aircraft from BAe at Warton and then Phase 3 was the 120 aircraft to be produced under licence by HAL.

The deal immediately came under fire in the Indian Parliament, but Defence Minister Jagjivan Ram defended the decision to choose the SEPECAT deal over the Mirage F.1, saying the Jaguar was the best value option, as its package included equipment, weapons, spares, modifications, technical assistance and licence and royalty fees. Even at a later stage the French were still trying to scupper the BAe deal in favour of their Mirage: it was reported that the French Ambassador in Delhi had gone to the Indian Defence Ministry the day before the deal was signed with BAe and offered to 'buy out' the contract in favour of supplying the F.1 as

an interim to the Indian Air Force taking the Mirage 2000. This offer was repeated in 1980 by the French President Giscard D'Estaing when he met Prime Minister Indirha Gandhi, reminding her that the original Jaguar supply deal had been struck by her rivals, the Janata party, which had just been succeeded by her new Government, using the 'it was ordered by your rivals, therefore it cannot be any good' contention. The Indian Administration, however, stuck to the BAe deal as the Jaguar actually existed, whereas the Mirage 2000 was not due to go into production until at least 1985.

Twelve IAF officers were chosen for pilot conversion in the UK, and the first four selected to fly the Jaguar arrived at No.226 OCU at RAF Lossiemouth on 26 February 1979; they joined Course 29, with the first Technician/NCO course starting at BAe Warton on the same day. These first four were the Officer Commanding (Designate) of No.14 Squadron IAF, Wg Cdr D.

JI – 'Jaguar Interim' – 004, one of the first Indian Jaguars into service. The first batches of IAF Jaguars were fitted with the RAF-style NAVWASS, which was replaced on the HAL-built examples by the new Smiths Industries DARIN integrated avionics suite. BAe

R. Nadkarni, Sqn Ldrs 'Mike' McMahon and J. S. Sisodia, and Flt Lt S. C. S. Adhikari. After forty-five flying hours on the Jaguar, the Indian pilots were attached to No.54 Squadron at Coltishall for a further twenty hours of tactical flying. As fully integrated members of the unit, they participated in all of its operational procedures such as planning, low-level weapons delivery and strafing. Two more batches of four pilots each trained at Lossiemouth, with the second batch later being attached to an RAF reconnaissance unit.

The first two 'interim' Jaguars were handed over to the IAF at a ceremony at

primary Jaguar operating base of Ambala, some 125 miles (200km) north of Delhi. The two-seater was flown by Tim Ferguson from BAe with Wg Cdr Nadkarni in the back seat, with the single-seat aircraft being flown by Tim Yeo, BAe's project test pilot. A second pair of Jaguars arrived in India on 14 October, once again carrying Wg Cdr Nadkarni, flying this time with Paul Millett, with the Jaguar 'S being flown by IAF pilot Sqn Ldr 'Mike' McMahon. The final UK departure, JI017, left on 14 August 1979.

Eventually all eighteen ex-RAF aircraft were successfully handed over. No.14

and 15 July, and the final aircraft, JS135, leaving the UK on 6 November 1982. A second Jaguar unit, No.5 Squadron (The Tuskers), former operators of the Canberra B(I).58 became operational with these aircraft in the summer of 1981. The 'interim' Jaguars were returned to the UK as promised, after the initial Indian-built production aircraft were issued to Nos 5 and 14 Squadrons at their Ambala base in mid-1981. The first fully HAL-built Jaguars were issued to No.27 Squadron (The Flaming Arrows), former Hunter FGA56A operators, at Bangalore in the summer of 1982, moving to Gorakhpur

JS – 'Jaguar (direct) Supply' – 110, one of the forty aircraft produced by BAe at Warton before production switched to HAL in India. This example is from No.5 Squadron, the 'Tuskers', former operators of the Canberra B(I).58. BAe

Warton on 19 July 1979, with Dr I. P. Singh, the Acting High Commissioner for India in the UK, and Sir Frederick Page from BAe in attendance. These aircraft, a two-seat Jaguar B and a single-seat Jaguar S, were refurbished ex-RAF machines eventually to be returned to the UK, once the HAL-produced aircraft had reached squadron service. They were flown out to India as a pair, arriving on 27 July at the

Squadron (The Bulls, also known as the 'Fighting Fourteenth'), formerly operating the Hunter FGA.56A, was subsequently declared operational in the summer of 1980. Batch 2 of the Indian programme, the forty Warton-built Jaguar Internationals, coded JS101 to JS135 and JT051 to JT055, were officially handed over on 10 February 1981 with JT051 arriving in India on 5 March, JS101 and JS102 on 1

during 1985, with another ex-Canberra unit, No.16 Squadron (The Cobras), also based at Gorakhpur, converting in October 1986. By now the Jaguar was officially known as the *Shamsher*, an Indian word for a curved assault sword, the literal translation being 'Sword of Justice'.

The production line for the HAL-built aircraft got underway – with more than a little help from BAe Warton – although at

Four Shamshers on patrol over the Simala Hills in northern India. BAe

An Indian two-seat Jaguar International formates on a single-seat example. BAe

one time it had seemed that due to political problems, production might need to be switched to the UK. However, BAe came up with the 'CKD' concept; by which production by HAL could be aided with the supply of fuselages and airframe components in 'Completely Knocked Down' kit form, these being freighted out to India in chartered Belfast transports, in progressively less assembled states. The first such sets were flown out on 5 May 1981, with

GR.1s and T.2s. The forty Warton-built Jaguar Internationals were equipped with the overwing pylons for Matra Magic AAMs, the uprated Mk811 engines and the BAe reconnaissance pod. The early batches of IAF Jaguars were fitted with the RAF-style NAVWASS. This was later changed on the HAL-built examples to the new Smiths Industries DARIN (Display, Avionics, Ranging and Inertial Navigation) integrated avionics suite which

Indian Jaguar JI005 was used to trial the Matra Magic missiles at the ASTE (Armament and Systems Testing Establishment) during late 1982, and was also involved in the DARIN development trials. Due to their ground attack/penetration role the aircraft retained the LRMTS nose and tail mounted RWR fairing. Weaponry included BL755 CBUs, Durandal runway cratering munitions, F.1 rocket pods and locally built bombs. A number of the BAe recon-

An impressive line-up of Indian Jaguar Internationals. BAe

the forty-fifth and final airframe to be so supplied being delivered in March 1987; the first Bangalore CKD-assembled aircraft made its maiden flight on 31 March 1982. After the CKD programme, manufacture then switched to HAL's indigenous production. HAL went on to build a further seventy-five Jaguars under licence, the first being delivered in January 1988, and a further order for fifteen Jaguars was placed by the Indian Government in late 1988 but cancelled in 1989 due to the prevailing economic climate.

The ex-RAF aircraft loaned to the IAF were refurbished, Adour Mk804E-powered

included: a French SAGEM Uliss 82 inertial navigation system; a Smiths Industries/GEC-Marconi dual-mode Type 1301 HUDWAS (Head Up Display and Weapons Aiming System) similar to that of the Sea Harrier FRS.1 and showing raster and stroke symbology; a Mil-Std-1553B databus; a Collins UHF/VHF and IFF-400; a GEC-Marconi COMED 2045 combined map and electronic display akin to that of the F-18 Hornet; and a HAL IFF 400AM. The cockpits were fitted with the Martin-Baker IN9B Mk2 zero-zero ejector seat, and the aircraft were powered by the license-built HAL Adour Mk811.

naissance pods were also supplied, along with the necessary photographic exploitation systems. A previously denied maritime strike version of the Jaguar has also been developed by HAL, and is fully described later in this section.

The eighteen 'on loan' Jaguars drawn from RAF reserve stocks were from various units, but in the main were provided by No.6 Squadron, with BAe Warton carrying out the necessary refurbishment and repainting to the interim standard. The first two aircraft so treated were the two-seaters: XX138 (RAF code) to B3 (BAe code) which became JI001(IAF code, for 'Jaguar

Interim') and XX720/B8/JI002. The forty direct-supply aircraft carried the JS designation (Jaguar (direct) Supply), coded JS136 onward, with HAL-produced aircraft carrying the JT code and the maritime version, JM. Two of the 'borrowed' aircraft, JI006 and JI011, were lost in Indian service and JI001 was sold to Oman, with the remainder returning to the UK beginning with JI012, JI015 and JI018 on 7 June 1982, and concluding with JI008 and JI017 on 19 October 1984. Ten of the batch were returned to RAF service and the others were scrapped.

RAF-Loaned Aircraft

Single-seat: XX720, XX117, XX115, XX116, XX728, XX725, XX111, XX729, XX736, XX734, XX737, XX738, XX740 and XX118.

Two-seat: XX138, XX143.

These airframes carried the test registrations G-27-319, -321, -320, -317, -315, -322, -323, -316, -324, -325, -326, -327, -328, -329, -331 and -318, respectively.

XZ397 and XZ398 (both single-seaters) remained in storage at BAe Warton.

The Indian Government remains committed to seeing their Jaguar force into the next century, and are, like the RAF and Oman, looking to upgrade their airframes and systems. One of the items currently on India's 'shopping list' is the order placed with Israeli Aircraft Industries for the *Litening* laser designator pod, a direct competitor to the British TIALD system.

Camouflage and Markings

The 'interim' and 'flyaway' Jaguars were all supplied carrying standard RAF dark sea grey and dark green camouflage, which was subsequently retained on the HAL-built models, with a black fin tip and anti-glare panel. Saffron, white and green Indian roundels are carried above and below the wings and on the forward fuselage with a three-colour flash at the base of the tailfin. These flashes were considerably larger on the 'interim' Jaguars than on the 'flyaway' batch. Codes resemble the RAF style of two letters and three numbers, usually in black.

No.5 Squadron carries its elephant insignia on the extreme nose of its aircraft, and this consists of a green arrowhead outlined in yellow with the unit's logo contained in a white circle, which replaces its previous version, of a black logo on an orange circular background. No.14 Squadron carries its rampaging bull flanked by red and yellow chequers on the engine intakes. No.16 has a coiled Cobra insignia on the intakes. No.27 carries a yellow

JS121 from No.14 Squadron, the 'Bulls', equipped with the uprated Adour Mk811 engines and a Martin-Baker IN9B MkII zero-zero ejector seat. BAe

flaming arrow shot through a red '27' in a white disc, outlined in blue, also flanked by red and yellow chequers.

Maritime Shamsher

Although at one time having its existence denied by the IAF, the maritime version of the Jaguar is unique to the Indian Air Force (although Nigeria was reported to have been interested in acquiring six such aircraft at one time), and incorporates a nose-mounted Thomson-CSF Agave radar installation that was an 'unadopted' option for the original Jaguar International con-

sharp nose radome, of a similar style (but not size) to that of the F-4 Phantom, having been tested previously in a modified RAE Canberra. The Agave radar, which has dramatically altered the Jaguar's profile, necessitating the relocation of the nose-mounted pitot tube, has a range of around 70nm (130km) against a typical ship target and around 15nm (28km) against a typical fighter-sized target, and gives an idea of what the Jaguar M might finally have looked like. The dual-mode (air-to-air and air-to-surface) Agave, interfaced with the DARIN nav/attack system and the SAGEM COMED, has been complemented by the

aircraft have been so converted by HAL and one of their number was lost due to handling difficulties during development trials for the system. The first of the new variant flew in 1985 and was handed over to the IAF in the January 1986, with six being delivered by December 1992, and a further two in mid-1993, all of which were converted from the CKD-production batch. The maritime version forms 'A' Flight within No.6 Squadron (The Dragons), which is a composite unit based at Poona; the Jaguar element is assigned to strike duties, whilst 'B' Flight operates the elderly Canberra B(I)12 in the maritime reconnaissance role. Camouflage

Maritime Jaguar JM255 in the colours of No.6 Squadron, the Agave radar nose adding a new dimension to the Shamsher's operations. BAe

cept. As has been discussed earlier the Agave (as is now fitted to the French Super Etendard carrier-based strike aircraft) was originally trialled as an underfuselage podded accessory; however, the Indian Air Force had other plans for the stores station, and the radar was therefore fitted into a

addition of a underfuselage mounting for a single BAe Sea Eagle anti-shipping missile, with two 264gal (1,200ltr) fuel tanks on the inner wing pylons; the aircraft is also reported to be capable of carrying a pair of Sea Eagle missiles on the inner wing pylons with a single tank on the centreline. Only eight

for the maritime variant is a very smart 'over water' scheme of a disruptive wraparound light blue-grey and dark blue-grey with a black anti-glare panel and fin tip, and black codes with the last three digits being repeated in saffron red on the nosewheel door. The aircraft are coded JM250–JM258.

BAe Sea Eagle Missile

Sea Eagle has its basis in the Martel ASM; however, the new missile has considerably greater range and was specifically designed for the anti-ship role. Powered by the Microturbo TR1 80-1 air breathing engine, the Sea Eagle has state-of-the-art systems and a modern INS and microprocessor into which the launch aircraft can feed the target's position, bearing, course and speed just prior to launch. The missile then cruises at low level to reduce the chance of being spotted by radar or visual means, and in the terminal phase is guided by its Marconi active radar. The 500lb (227kg) impact/delay blast fragmentation warhead is effective against most naval targets.

BAe Sea Eagle missile. BAe

Arabian Flights – Omani Jaguars

During the early 1970s Oman, like many other of its Middle Eastern neighbours, was seeking to modernize its air defence systems. In August 1974, following an excellent sales pitch from the BAC team, the *Al Quwwat al Jawwiya al Sultanat Oman* or Sultanate of Oman's Air Force (SOAF, referred to after 1990 as the Royal Air Force of Oman) ordered a batch of twelve Jaguar Internationals: ten single-seaters designated Jaguar S(0).1 and a pair of two-seat aircraft designated Jaguar

A Jaguar B(O).2 taxies out from Thumrait. This particular two-seater is one of the original order, indicated by the lack of the nose-mounted IFR probe. BAe

SOAF Jaguars in the 'finishing shop' at BAe Warton. BAe

B(0).2. At the same time as this, a similar order was being placed by Ecuador. Along with Oman's purchase of the twelve Jaguars came a further contract for British Aerospace Dynamics to supply the Rapier SAM system, along with other orders for ground radar and communications equipment. This was something of a coup for the British Aerospace team, and a remarkable achievement for the Jaguar International. For the 1977 Paris Air Show, BAe displayed aircraft 202 and 204 in civilian codes – G-BEET and G-BETB.

Initial deliveries of the aircraft were made to the SOAF commencing on 4 March 1977, when one two-seater and one single-seater were handed over at Warton; the aircraft left for Oman on the 7th, with the full order being completed by spring 1978. The first unit to equip with the new aircraft was No.8 Squadron based at Thumrait, from where they moved to Al Masirah, a former RAF base in 1979. The unit performed strike and air defence duties, a role that up to that time had been fulfilled by aircraft borrowed from the Imperial Iranian Air Force; the arrival of the 'Desert Cats' now allowed the Omani Air Force to undertake these duties itself. It had been originally planned to replace the BAC Strikemasters of No.5 Squadron with the Jaguar, but an upsurge in rebel activity in their area caused the Strike-masters' retention.

The Jaguar Internationals were an outstanding success, and the SOAF were exceptionally pleased with their new aircraft, so much so that a re-order was received in the middle of 1980 for an additional twelve, again ten single-seaters and a pair of two-seat trainers, with one further two-seater being acquired from the RAF via India as an attrition replacement. As with the previous order in 1974, the Jaguar was part of a larger deal between the UK and Oman covering other defence equipment, including an order for the improved Rapier system together with its associated hardware. With this latest batch of aircraft the SOAF formed No.20 Squadron, also based at Al Masirah, who had their full complement of Jaguars on strength by late 1983, the last three aircraft being handed over at Warton on 23 November. During the late 1980s the Jaguars returned to

were visited during a hectic six-week spell. Despite great interest being shown in the aircraft, flown on these occasions by BAC Military Aircraft Divisions chief test pilot Peter Ginger, with navigator Roy Kenward in the back seat, no further orders were forthcoming from the area. The engines,

the processing power of the original MCS 920M computer fitted to the RAF machines. The SOAF Jaguars are also reported to be able to fire the Aerospatiale AM-39 Exocet sea-skimming missile, in part reviving another maritime connection – pioneered by the Indian Air Force –

The second purchase of Jaguars by the SOAF is readied for flyout to Oman. Nearest the camera is G27-376/214, a 'T-Bird' with the unique (to the International version) nose-mounted IFR probe, and tail-mounted RWR.
BAe

Thumrait, with the ROAF BAe Hawks taking up residence at Al Masirah.

The first twelve SOAF Jaguars were fitted with the Adour Mk804 engine, whereas the second batch were fitted with the improved Mk811-26, the Batch 2 two-seaters being fitted with the Dash-26 series engines. One of their number G-27-376, the first 'custom built' Jaguar International, was used by BAC as a sales tool around the Middle East during an intensive tour in 1975, when Abu Dhabi, Dubai, Saudi Arabia, Qatar, Kuwait, Iran and Turkey

cause of some debate as to their hot weather performance, proved to have no major problems in the harsh desert environment, where operating temperatures exceeded 125°F (52°C) in the hot season with up to 95 per cent relative humidity.

The SOAF selected the option of fitting its aircraft with the RAF-style Ferranti LRMTS nose, as their primary role would be strike/attack. All of the SOAF Jaguars have the Marconi 920ATC NAVWASS computer, a unit also fitted to the Ecuadorian Internationals, which gives double

that had been broken with the cancellation of the Jaguar M in 1973. Two unusual features grace the final two SOAF Jaguar trainers: firstly they have a fin-mounted ARI 18233 RWR similar to that found on the single-seat aircraft; and secondly, they have a fixed forward IFR probe in place of the nose pitot tube usually found on the French training aircraft.

The Jaguars were also configured to carry air-to-air missiles in keeping with their stated secondary air defence role. The initial batch was fitted with overwing

Four Jaguars on patrol over the Omani coastline. Of note is the underwing carriage of the Matra 550 Magic AAM. BAe launchers for the French Matra 550 Magic AAMs, while the second batch were also fitted with their outboard underwing pylons adapted to carry the American AIM-9P Sidewinder. The Jaguar's duties in the primary air defence role have now all but disappeared, following the introduction of the Panavia Tornado F.3 into service, the Jaguars concentrating on their mission of close support and strike.

fleet, and include the new systems on its aircraft proposed in the RAF's 'Jaguar 96 and 97' programme. In September 1997 the UK Defence Secretary, George Robertson, signed an agreement with His Excellency Sayyid Badr bin Saud bin Harab Al Busaidi, the Sultanate of Oman's Defence Minister, to upgrade Oman's surviving Jaguar fleet of sixteen single-seat and three two-seat aircraft to

Camouflage and Markings

All of Oman's Jaguar Internationals are painted in a wraparound desert colour scheme of dark earth BS381C/450 and middle stone BS381C/638, with a black anti-glare panel in front of the windshield. The top of the tailfin above the RWR is very dark brown, with the leading edges of the tailfin, the tailplanes and the wings being painted

A brace of ROAF Jaguar Internationals. The Jaguars are also reported to be able to fire the Aerospatiale AM-39 Exocet sea-skimming missile. BAe

Omani Jaguar '86 Upgrade

Early in 1986 Ferranti was contracted by the SOAF to supply their FIN1064 nav/attack systems to upgrade the Omani Jaguars to a similar standard as their RAF counterparts. The work was undertaken at BAe Warton, where the last of the 21-aircraft upgrade was completed in October 1989.

Omani Jaguar '97 Upgrade

Having been impressed by the upgrade in capability given to the RAF Jaguars, Oman decided that it too would update its

the latest RAF '97 standard. The deal, reported to be worth around £40 million, included upgraded avionics, new internal navigation system and the GEC Marconi TIALD system. This would keep the Omani Air Force's Jaguars viable well into the 21st century, and was the first export sale of the upgrade, developed jointly by the DERA and RAF. One of the Omani Jaguars was sent to Boscombe Down during autumn 1997, and was then flown on to BAe Warton, where it was reportedly painted medium grey with RAF insignia, but carrying an Omani identification number on the top of its tailfin.

black, as are the front edges of the engine intakes, and the underfuselage stabilizers. A small Omani crest is applied to both sides of the tailfin which, on the aircraft assigned to No.6 Squadron, features a red shield with a white detailed design applied to it, whereas the aircraft assigned to No.20 carry a blue shield with a gold design. The aircraft's individual ID code is applied to the upper rear fuselage, notated in Arabic script. Of note is a white 'rescue' instruction panel applied just ahead of the intakes. Aircraft codes are allocated in the sequences 200–210 and 213–222 for the single seaters, and 211–212 and 223–224 for the two-seaters.

Definitely 'getting the low down'! A superb demonstration of low flying by then Flt Lt Andy Cubin during his time in Oman – straight between the hangars! Andy Cubin

Jaguars for Ecuador

In the north-western corner of South America lies Ecuador, one of the smallest countries in the region, and one that for decades suffered considerable territorial losses to neighbouring Peru. The determined Ecuadorians had struggled to strengthen their weak armed forces, but were constantly inhibited by the scarce economic resources of the country and the low value of their currency on the international markets. However, the situation was totally transformed in 1971 with the discovery of oil, since when the Ecuadorian forces have been re-armed and hugely improved. This new force was amply demonstrated in early 1981 when Peruvian troops were outfought during thirteen days of border hostilities.

Ecuadorian military aviation was born as a branch of the Army, the *Ejercito Ecuatoriana*, which at that time also included the country's naval forces. The formal creation of the *Escuela Militar de Aviacion* took place at Guayaquil on 27 October 1920, and this became an independent service during 1945, as the *Fuerza Area Ecuatoriana* (FAE).

The air force's flying equipment is distributed between: *Comando de Operaciones* (Operations Command), which is divided into two strike-fighter wings; the *Grupo de Transportes Aeros Militares* (Air Transport Group); and the *Escuela Superior Militar de Aviacion* (Air School). *Ala de Combate 21* (the 21st Fighter Wing) is the main strike element of the FAE, and operates three squadrons from *Base Aerea Miltar* Taura near Quito, some 180 miles (290km) from the capital Guayaquil. The most senior combat unit of the FAE is the *Escuadron de Combate 2111 'Aguilas'* ('Eagles') which dates back to 1954, when the Gloster Meteor FR.9 was introduced into service. The Meteor was the first jet to fly with the FAE, and remained in service until as late as 1977 when it was retired following the introduction of the Jaguar International.

Following the close examination of the Jaguar by the commander-in-chief of the Ecuadorian Air Force, an order for a single squadron's worth of Jaguar Internationals was placed with SEPECAT in 1974, covering the supply of twelve aircraft: ten single-seat ES models and a pair of two-seat EB trainers, with these aircraft having the distinction of being the first 'true' export Jaguar Internationals. The first Jaguar of this order carried the 'B'-condition (civil) serial number G-27-266 before its delivery, first flying on 19 August 1976, and was the first International to take to the air. Interestingly, G-27-266 was in fact used by BAe as an export sales tool for a brief period before delivery to Ecuador. Six FAE pilots received Jaguar conversion training with No.226 OCU at Lossiemouth before the first of the new aircraft (283 and 289) were delivered on 4 January 1977, the order being completed by 24 October. Ecuador opted to retain the aircraft's accurate strike capabilities and so kept the LRMTS nose and the Marconi-Elliott NAVWASS along with its associated sub-systems, together with the tail-mounted ARI 18223 RWR. The aircraft were also fitted with the overwing missile launchers, for

It was perhaps the export-rated Adour Mk811 engines which were the greatest cause for concern, as the aircraft would need to operate in extreme conditions, in terms not only of temperature, but also of humidity. Apart from the humidity itself, the aircraft would also need to be able to operate from airfields at high altitude such as Latacunga, 9,100ft (2,760m) above sea level in the Andes. BAe took an aircraft and a flight team out to Ecuador to trial the Jaguar at Latacunga, which experiences

rather than shipping the aircraft out in knocked-down form. The Jaguars staged out in pairs without any engineering support *en-route*, travelling via West Africa, Ascension Island and Brazil. The merits of the inertial navigation system were proven on the long Atlantic leg of 1,224nm (2,267km) from Ascension to Recife without update fixes, the pilots noting only a minor system error on arrival in Ecuador.

By the middle of 1991, only seven single-seat and one two-seat aircraft from the

A pair of Ecuadorian Jaguar Internationals get airborne from Warton at the start of their long delivery flight to Taura. BAe

carrying the Matra 550 Magic AAM, in common with the FAE Mirage F.1As and IAI Kfirs. The Jaguars provide the FAE with a formidable strike capability for the first time in many years, and with the introduction of their new mount, the *Aguilas* changed their name to the *Jaguares* in 1981 – for very obvious reasons!

temperature as high as ISA+68°F (20°C). The aircraft and its systems operated superbly and was able to lift an impressive warload, and even demonstrated its ability to recover on one engine. The capability of the aircraft and its systems was amply demonstrated by the aircrew's decision to carry out direct flight deliveries to Ecuador,

original order remained in service, and to balance the attrition, three further ex-RAF GR.1s were purchased in August that year, these being XX121, XX722 and XX744, with Ecuador holding an option on a further three. The aircraft underwent refurbishment by BAe before delivery. Because the FAE have no Jaguar simulator, the

FAE302, the second Jaguar International to be delivered to the FAE in 1977. Six FAE pilots received Jaguar conversion training with No.226 OCU at Lossiemouth before the first of the new aircraft were delivered on 4 January 1977. BAe

FAE312, one of a pair of Jaguar EB trainers ordered by the FAE. BAe

Ecuadorian Jaguar pilots are required to attend a special course at Lossiemouth every eighteen months to receive an emergency procedures checkout by OCU staff.

Camouflage and Markings

The Ecuador Jaguar Internationals were delivered in the standard RAF camouflage scheme of dark sea grey and dark green

Ecuador serials follow a pattern based on the aircraft's production numbers. The single-seaters carry the code numbers FAE300 to FAE310/G-27-266, -267, -289, -305, -309, -318, -327, -329, -340, -348 and -349, while the two-seaters carry the codes FAE311 and FAE312/G-27-283 and -302. To date three of the single seat aircraft, FAE303, FAE308 and FAE310 have been lost in accidents.

This order consisted of thirteen single-seat 'NS' and five two-seat 'NB'. The batch was ordered in July 1983 and deliveries began in early 1984 to the sole Nigerian Jaguar operating base at Makurdi. Around the same time came expressions of interest from Chile, which looked at purchasing eighteen ex-RAF Jaguars to be armed with Exocet anti-shipping missiles; these plans were abandoned in 1984 due to funding

The Jaguares logo on the side of FAE311; also of note is the Peligro lettering on the ejector seat warning triangles. With the introduction of their new mount, the Aguilas changed their name to the Jaguares in 1981 – for very obvious reasons! BAe

disruptive upper surfaces and light aircraft grey undersides. The aircraft carry black identification markings on their tailfins, along with small yellow, blue and red national flags, with full-colour roundels and FAE lettering on the upper and lower sides of the wings. The fin top is black and the aircraft feature an anti-glare panel on the nose.

'Cats in Africa' – Nigerian Exports

Following nearly five years of on-off negotiations, the most recent export success for the Jaguar was the sale of eighteen Internationals, with an option for eighteen more (with at least six to be fitted with the Agave radar) to the Nigerian Air Force.

problems. In Nigeria, a military coup ended civilian rule at the end of December 1983, creating questions over the Jaguars' future within the Nigerian armed forces. However, the military government decided to continue with the contract, seeing the Jaguar as a valuable asset to their air force, and the deliveries were completed in 1985. During the late 1980s, however, the

Nigerian government announced the withdrawal of the Jaguar from service as an economy measure. The last flight of a Nigerian Jaguar was made in early 1990, by which time four of their number – one single-seater and three two-seaters – had been lost in flying accidents.

The Nigerian Jaguars were fitted to the same standards as the other export models and carried the overwing Sidewinder missile launchers and the more powerful Adour Mk811-58 engines. As with the

during the late 1980s there was only enough money to buy two tanker loads of fuel per year to service the entire fleet. Currently, although externally the aircraft seem in pristine condition, internally they are in a very poor state of repair, with the fuel cells' sealant having perished, the hydraulic lines needing replacement and the engines corroding badly due to neglect and having spent the last eight years entirely on outside store. These aircraft have incredibly low airframe lives with the

This is a sad predicament for these aircraft, which are still the most up-to-date Jaguar Internationals to have been produced. British Aerospace had at one point during the early 1990s considered recovering the aircraft, and 'buying' them back at a knock-down price – £0.00 – before refurbishing them either for the aforementioned possible sale to Chile or for use by the RAF. The 'bargain price' was a real bone of contention for BAe, who were still owed some £19 million by Nigeria, a figure

Immaculate two-seater NAF703; it is hard to believe that the Nigerian Jaguars are now grounded and in a state of disrepair. Bae

other export customers, Nigeria's requirements for the aircraft were in the ground attack/close support role, and they therefore opted to retain the accuracy bestowed upon the aircraft by the LRMTS nose.

At the time of writing, the remaining Nigerian Jaguar Internationals languish at their Makurdi base, permanently grounded, through lack of spares and an acute shortage of aviation fuel; apparently,

'youngest' having only thirty hours 'on the clock' and the 'oldest' only 300 hours, with at least six others under the 200 hours' mark. Reports indicate that the Nigerian Air Force could not even afford the tow tractors to handle the jets, and that they were aligning the aircraft's compasses (compass swings) by tying ropes to the nose wheels and having anyone available pull the aircraft into position.

which has since been written off as a bad debt, with Rolls-Royce also having a figure in excess of £20 million remaining unpaid. Since corruption remains rife within the Nigerian Government, with many fingers in the military budget, its hardly surprising the money was outstanding. The Chile plan also reportedly fell foul of the anticipated pay-offs by BAe to the 'right people' in the Nigerian Government, plus the

With its Adour Mk811s in full afterburner, the first Nigerian two-seater gets airborne from BAe Warton on a pre-delivery flight. BAe

A superb view of the underside of a Nigerian Jaguar, resplendent in its three tone wraparound camouflage colours. BAe

higher-than-expected repair costs, which would have resulted in an even greater financial loss for BAe, which had totally withdrawn their technical support from the country in the late 1980s. The later RAF plan was also no longer an option due to the RAF's own Jaguar refurbishment programme, which got underway in 1993, so its seems these aircraft will simply be left to rot.

Camouflage and Markings

Apart from the high visibility 'raspberry ripple' paint scheme applied to the British test and evaluation aircraft based at Boscombe Down, the Nigerian aircraft carried the most colourful wraparound operational camouflage scheme, of mid stone, sage green and dark grass green. The Nigerian Jaguars carry the codes NF701–NF705 (two-seaters) and NF706–NF718 (single-seaters).

'Copy' Cats

The Jaguar has had its share of competition, not only from Dassault and his Mirage family, but also from aircraft such as the F-16 Fighting Falcon, F-18 Hornet, A-7 Corsair, A-4 Skyhawk, the Soviet MiG-23 and MiG-27, and so on. However, it is often said that imitation is the sincerest form of flattery, and this is true of two aircraft which have used the SEPECAT product as a baseline for their own design.

Closely based on the Jaguar is the Mitsubishi F-1, which has the same slender, high wing, drooped tailplanes and rough-field landing gear. Plus, its is powered by two Ishikawjima-Harima TF40-801A engines – otherwise known as licence-built Rolls Royce/Turbomeca Adour Mk102 two-shaft augmented turbofans! The Japanese had at one time expressed an interest in buying the Jaguar, but instead went on to build the indigenous Mitsubishi T-2 supersonic trainer, ordered in 1967, from which was derived the F-1 single-seat close support fighter in 1972.

As with the T-2/F-1, the Jaguar's influence filtered into Yugoslavia and Romania with their collaborative SOKO/CNIAR-93 Orao. A far less ambitious aircraft than the Jaguar or F-1, it uses two Rolls-Royce Viper turbojet engines for lower cost at the expense of higher fuel consumption. Once again the high wing and robust twin-wheel undercarriage give it a 'Jaguar-like' appearance, and the Orao is fitted with a Martin-Baker Mk10 ejector seat. Interestingly enough, it was an attack by two Bosnian Serb Orao aircraft based at Udbina airfield in the Krajina region, within a UN 'Safe Haven' in Bihac, to the north-west of Bosnia on 19 November 1995, that sparked off Operation *Deliberate Force*, and the retaliatory strike by NATO forces included a bombing raid by RAF Jaguars.

The 'Jaguar-esque' Mitsubishi T-2. via Author

CHAPTER SIX

War and Keeping the Peace

Jaguars in the 1990s

Operation *Granby*

Barely a week after the invasion of Kuwait by Iraq, and a scant forty-eight hours after the announcement by the then UK Defence Secretary, Tom King, that fighting units were to be deployed to the Gulf Region, the RAF's Jaguar wing at Coltishall deployed the first British strike aircraft into the conflict area. Under the codename Operation *Granby*, aircraft were drawn from each of the three squadrons on the base, together with their associated pilots, groundcrew and reconnaissance interpretation personnel. Supported by additional crews from No.226 OCU at RAF Lossiemouth, they were despatched to Thumrait in the Sultanate of Oman to join the growing number of Coalition aircraft participating in the US-led Operation *Desert Shield*. It came as something of a surprise to many observers that the first British strike aircraft to be sent into the area was the Jaguar, as a growing number had been inclined to write off the ageing 'cats' as a means of keeping flying personnel occupied until the arrival of the Eurofighter.

Well trained for the 'rapid reaction' role, the Jaguar force was hastily prepared at Coltishall for immediate service on arrival in the Gulf. Most visible was their camouflage scheme, an overwash of a colour described as 'Desert Sand ARTF'

XX970, resplendent in its new 'desert sand' colour scheme gets airborne in the second wave, bound for the Gulf. RAF Coltishall

(Alkaline Removable Temporary Finish), reportedly designed for low-level operations by Philip Barley at the Royal Aircraft Establishment; despite its 'sand' title, the colour had a definite pink hue! Thirteen aircraft were so treated, devoid of any squadron markings and carrying pale pink and pale blue roundels below the cockpit, and black serial numbers on the rear fuselage. Each aircraft carried a Westinghouse ALQ-101(V) jammer pod and a Phimat chaff dispenser on the outer wing pylons, together with two Tracor AN/ALE-40 flare dispensers scabbed onto the underside engine access panels. Nine of the thirteen Jaguars were standard GR.1As and carried three external fuel tanks, one on each inner wing pylon and one on the centreline, whilst the remaining four GR1As were fitted with a BAe recce pod on their centreline stations. These thirteen aircraft were not ideally suited to the desert style of operations, and were seen as an interim measure whilst a second batch, destined to be brought up to a higher modification state were being prepared for deployment.

Under the leadership of Wing Commander Jerry Connoly, OC No.6 Squadron, twelve of the thirteen aircraft left Coltishall on the morning of 11 August 1990, taking off in four waves; the first aircraft to taxi out being XZ263, piloted by Sqn Ldr Alex Muskett. The thirteenth aircraft, XX766, remained at Coltishall as a spare.

On arrival in Thumrait the detachment set about a period of intense training and acquainting themselves with the rigours of desert flying, thereby making a statement of intent to Iraq, should they not withdraw from Kuwait as directed by the United Nations, or indeed threaten Saudi Arabia and its neighbours. In order to make way for the growing number of RAF Tornado GR.1s arriving from Germany, the Jaguars deployed from Thumrait to Muharraq International Airport in Bahrain from early October, the crews being billeted in the Diplomat Hotel – luxury living, and a far cry from the spartan accommodation at Thumrait! The Connoly-led detachment were soon relieved of their duties by the fresh batch of 'desert modified' Jaguars from the UK and the first of their aircraft arrived back at Coltishall on 27 October.

The replacement aircraft formed up under the banner of No.41 (Composite) Squadron, and were led by Wg Cdr Bill Pixton, who had some twenty-two pilots drawn from all of the Jaguar units under his command. Seven of these aircraft –

XX725, XX733, XZ119, XZ358, XZ364, XZ367 and XZ375 – arrived at Muharraq on 23 October and a further five – XX748, XX754, XX962, XZ118 and XZ356 – arrived on 2 November.

These aircraft carried what became known as the 'Granby Stage 3 Upgrades', which made them the most effective Jaguars in the RAF's inventory. In the process of applying these much-needed modifications, the RAF generously assailed the STF (Special Trials Fit) procedure in order to get upgrades and vital items of kit cleared for use (in a similar manner to that expended on the Harriers during the Falklands War nearly a decade earlier). The Adour Mk104 engines were given greater thrust and better hot weather performance, 'tweaking' them for higher turbine temperatures, going from 700° to 725°C; the ARI-18223 RHWR was upgraded to 'Sky Guardian 200-13PD' standard, giving an improved capability to detect and identify scanning pulse doppler radars at long range; and a Vinten colour HUD video recording facility added, replacing the mono wet film arrangement.

The aircraft were also fitted with overwing Sidewinder missile pylons, directly above their inner wing stations, allowing them to carry the all-aspect AIM-9L. These items were fitted as standard on the Jaguar International variant, but not taken up by the RAF; however, it was reported that the overwing pylons mounted on the twelve Jaguars were bought by the MoD from the Sultan of Oman's Air Force; they gave the aircraft a very comforting self-defence capability without reducing their offensive abilities. The AAM modification had been trialled aboard XZ385/GM of No.54 Squadron at the A&AEE, Boscombe Down, in September 1990 and was quickly (within a week) approved for use by the Jaguars in the Gulf. The aircraft also carried the revised AN/ALQ-101(V)-10 noise/deception jammer which uses a ventral gondola to increase the pod's capacity and detection frequency coverage. Also carried were the trusty Phimat chaff pod and twin Tracor AN/ALE-40 flare dispensers. The AN/ALE-40s were modified to fire the Type 118 and M206 flares, which burn hotter and for longer, and the firing configuration modified to allow flares to be released with the aircraft's wheels down. The Jaguars were also fitted with a MkXII Mode 4 IFF, and a Magnavox AN/ARC-164 Have Quick frequency-hopping UHF replacing the little-

used stand-by UHF outfit, complementing the standard ARI 23315/4 set. To better aid communications the usual twin homing VHF aerial arrangement mounted behind the canopy was traded in for a larger single UHF T-shaped blade aerial. The Jaguars were also treated with SWAM (surface wave radar absorbent material) on their leading edges and RAM (radar absorbent material) tiles on their engine intakes to help reduce their radar cross-section. In a similar vein to the SWAM layer, the Jaguar's windscreens were also treated with a coating of gold film. The pilots' forward vision was also improved by the removal of the forward warning panels and the annoying g meter which hung from the windshield's bracing strip.

Markings on the aircraft were also changed, the major alteration being the switch in colour of the serial numbers from black to white, with the aircrafts' single letter code being reduced in size and placed on the nosewheel door. In order to confuse the enemy, most of the aircraft sported a black 'false canopy' under the nose, using the lines of the nosewheel doors as their basis, with at least four variations in style noted. Pale pink and pale blue roundels were carried, and white 'Danger' triangles appeared beneath the canopy rails. The desert sand paint scheme extended to all areas of the airframe except the engine exhausts and the dull metallic red of the twin cannon ports.

During their work-up period the Jaguars routinely carried a pair of 264gal (1,200ltr) wing tanks, which limited their offensive load to two 1,000lb (454kg) bombs with retard tails or a pair of BL755 CBUs. The Jaguar force's only casualty occurred in this period. Whilst flying XX754, a GR.1A from No.54 Squadron, Flt Lt Keith Collister was killed during a low-flying exercise on 13 November. This served to galvanize thinking about the Jaguars' low-level operations over the desert, and their tactics were subsequently examined and changed, before the conflict began, switching to a higher operating altitude. This took them out of the range of AAA and shoulder-launched SAMs, and gave them the maximum benefit from working with the Coalition's specialized defence suppression, ECM jamming and fighter support assets.

The change in operating height led to some changes to the Jaguar's weapons, which were tailored to low-level use. The retard tails on the bombs were replaced by free-fall fins and the CBUs were replaced by a new item of kit, the Bristol Aerospace (Canada) CRV-7 2.75in (7cm) high-velocity rocket, of which nineteen were carried in the American-made LAU-500B/A pod. The CRV-7 has a speed of around Mach 4 with an excellent accuracy and range, making it ideally suited for the new operating height. The Paveway II laser guided bombs were also trialled for use by the Jaguar, but

interdiction (BAI), mainly in Kuwait, the Jaguars were assigned to day operations, their work constrained only by bad weather. The crews were organized into two eight-ship cells, required to carry out two missions per day. Their first strike was, however, only a four-ship when Sqn Ldr Mike Gordon, Flt Lt Steve Thomas, Flt Lt Roger Crowden and Fg Off Malcolm Rainer

crews was their wish to take along something useful to get them out of the desert – like a foldaway pocket camel! After the initial rush of missions it soon became apparent that the Jaguars' stores configuration could be altered, and the amount of ordnance carried could be effectively doubled. As a consequence the wing tanks were replaced by tandem-beam bomb carriers

Preparing to strike, RAF Jaguar GR.1A XZ106/O, armed with four 1,000lb freefall bombs on tandem beam carriers, twin Sidewinder AAMs, Phimat and ALQ-101(V) jammer pod. RAF via Tony Thornborough

were not carried during the conflict. Most of the pilots had the opportunity to fire off a few training rounds on the King Fahd Weapons Range in Saudi Arabia during the last few days before the UN Deadline.

In the early hours of 17 January 1991 *Desert Shield* became *Desert Storm* as the Coalition forces began the process of forcibly ejecting the Iraqi invaders from Kuwait. Tasked with battlefield air

attacked an army barracks in occupied Kuwait. The pilots were organized into 'constituted fours' and operated together throughout the war. Each was fully 'sanitized' of squadron insignia and personal items. They carried with them some gold sovereigns, a copy of the relevant part of the Geneva Convention, a strobe light, a far-from-useful map and a 9mm pistol. The favourite joke amongst the detachment

each capable of holding two 1,000lb (454kg) bombs and a single fuel tank was carried on the centreline. The CRV-7 was used from the very outset, but the hastily prepared integration with the weapons aiming computer caused disappointing and inaccurate delivery. It was therefore temporarily withdrawn whilst technicians at Ferranti reconfigured the software, and within two weeks it was back in action.

Bristol Aerospace CRV-7 Rocket

Designed and built by the Bristol Aerospace Company of Canada, the CRV-7 has been designed to offer a considerably higher velocity and a flatter, more accurate and therefore a more 'aimable' trajectory than the traditional FFAR types. Less susceptible to the effects of gravity and crosswinds, the CRV-7 has three times the kinetic energy on impact of its rivals, and can be carried by both fixed- and rotary-winged aircraft. The rockets are spin-stabilized by a fluted exhaust nozzle and have three wrap-around tail fins which are spring-actuated immediately after launch for maximum stability. The CRV-7 is also noted for its warhead options, its considerable range and low angular dispersion. Powered by either an RLU-5002(B) C-14 solid propellant rocket for use by fixed-wing aircraft or an RLU-5002(B) C-15 for use by helicopters, the CRV-7 has a range of some 7,100yd (6,450m),

speed varying between 2,798–3,351mph (4,500–5,400km/h), depending on warhead, and is launched from the American-built LAU-5003A/A pod, each carrying nineteen rounds.

CRV-7 has a number of warhead options: the M151 HE blast/fragmentation type designed for use against soft targets; the M156 white phosphorus/incendiary type for target-marking; the M229 HE blast/fragmentation for soft-skinned vehicles; the M257 flare for night illumination; the M247 HDEP shaped charge for light armoured vehicles; the WDU-4A/A and WDU-13/A varieties armed with flechettes for area saturation; the WAU-5001/B plastic-cased, tungsten rod penetrator for use against heavy tanks; the BAH-002 for light tanks; and the RA-79 anti-ship warhead with a kinetic penetrator combined with delay-action fuzing.

XZ118 'Buster Gonad' gets airborne carrying two CRV-7 pods (just visible behind the ALQ-101 jammer).
RAF via Tony Thornborough

However effective the BL755 CBU was at low-level, it was not designed for medium-altitude work, and the Jaguar initially had no alternative. The answer came in the shape of the American CBU-87 Rockeye II, which was effective in medium-altitude use. The CBU-87 went into operation on 28 January, and rapidly gained admiration from its users; only eight BL755s were eventually used, and these during the first days of the

war. Flt Lt Max Emtage described the CBU-87 as '... a really nasty piece of equipment – really quite vicious ... it's excellent against troops, excellent against soft-skinned vehicles and against ammo and petrol stores'.

Like the Tornados by night, the Jaguars ran the gauntlet of Iraqi AAA, as Flt Lt Mike Sears recounts: 'It's the first time many of us had seen the stuff coming at us, it certainly concentrates the mind, and

those times were the longest moments of my life.'

The Jaguars' forays took them mainly to the southern parts of Kuwait, although sorties were made to the north and into Iraq itself. The better weather of 19 January saw the first full day's operations for the Jaguars, flying some nineteen trips to attack SAM and artillery sites; later their tasks widened to include fuel and ammunition dumps and command centres, as well attacks on coastal SY-1 'Silkworm' batteries to help 'spoof' the Iraqis into believing that an amphibious landing was on the cards. In these attacks, the Jaguars clearly demonstrated their ability to make precision attacks without the help of radar.

With the CRV-7 now in the inventory, one interesting and well-televised demonstration was given when two Jaguars, one flown by Wg Cdr Pixton, destroyed a 1,120-ton *Polnochny-C*-class landing craft.

four passes using 30mm cannon fire, something that would never have been normally attempted in a high-threat environment. As Pixton later explained, 'We almost set up an academic range pattern on the ship. I know this sounds terrible, and my counterparts at home will probably have a fit!'

Pixton himself had the total respect of the officers under him. It was his stated aim to bring home the same number of people he started out with, and he

Whenever feasible, the formation would be as tightly packed as possible, rolling in with little interval between the jets, so all the bombs were delivered, and the aircraft outbound, before any defenders could begin shooting.

3 February saw the Jaguars involved in the re-taking of Faylakah Island off the coast of Kuwait, using 1,000lb (454kg) air-burst bombs against Iraqi gun emplacements. With the Jaguars, Tornados and, to a lesser extent, Buccaneers using up

XX962 flying low over the desert, armed with a 1,000lb LGB and two very comforting Sidewinder AAMs.
via Gary Madgwick

The tactics used by the two aircraft broke virtually every standard operating procedure, but such was the curious operating environment that the Coalition forces found themselves in that it was practicable. With total air supremacy, and an orbiting AWACS informing them that 'the picture was clear' the situation was uniquely benign. Pixton and his wingman made two passes ripple-firing CRV-7 rockets, and

involved his pilots in all the mission planning stages. He remained adamant that the judgement on any attack was left to the detachment, and his formation leaders knew he would back their decisions all the way to the top. The strike formation would always carry the same type of weapon: sometimes the lead pair would have instantaneous fuzing, the second pair air-burst fuzing, for 'daisy cutting' the area.

ordnance from the British stockpiles, the 'quality' bomb fuzes became scarce, so the Jaguars switched to using air-burst fuzes and late in the conflict even began to use up old pistol fuzes that had been declared obsolete after World War II!

The bombing campaign against the Iraqi Republican Guard intensified in early February, and sorties against Iraqi communications posts were undertaken, as well as a re-attack on a pontoon bridge hit by LGBs dropped from Tornados a few days earlier. As a precursor to the ground war – Operation *Desert Sabre* – the Jaguars targeted individual artillery pieces, and notable hits included a ZSU/23-4 four-barrel AAA system, the aircraft also successfully destroying

information for the Jaguar force itself, and later for pre-strike information for other agencies. Often flying in pairs, they would 'tag onto' an outbound strike for mutual support. The aircraft gathered data on approach routes to future targets and looked for other areas such as already

Patrol). Sortie lengths for these particular missions were around four hours, with aerial tanking, and on one of these patrols the Jaguars almost made a unique air-to-air engagement. A pair of aircraft were on SARCAP, waiting for any call for assistance, when a misunderstanding about the

A pair of thirsty Jaguars take on fuel from a No.101 Squadron VC-10 tanker, during a familiarization sortie during August 1990. RAF

five Astros multi-ramp rocket launchers in the process.

Late January was the cue for the reconnaissance Jaguars to enter the fray in earnest, although some limited recce sorties had already been flown. The aircraft were initially tasked with providing

attacked targets to see if any further work needed to be undertaken.

The Jaguars also had a secondary role of providing a so-called 'cab rank' service, being airborne and available for SuCAP (Support Combat Air Patrol) and SAR-CAP (Search And Rescue Combat Air

type of aircraft they were with a ground controller saw them vectored to intercept three Iraqi jets coming out of the south. The controller, who had just been working with US Marine Corps F/A-18 Hornets thought the Jaguars were air defence-capable, and although the pilots tried to make

A pair of CRV-7-armed 'cats' head out to their targets. RAF via Tony Thornborough

A pilot climbs aboard his Jaguar, which is laden with four 1,000lb (454kg) bombs on tandem beam carriers, for a raid into occupied Kuwait. via Gary Madgwick

(Above) '**Welcome Home Desert Cats**'. Author

Happy to be home safely. Author

it clear they were not interceptors, they were pulled from their station to go after the contacts. Thankfully for the Jaguars the aircraft, which turned out to be Iraqi Mirages, were shot down by Saudi F-15s, although the pilots felt confident that if they had got within visual range of the targets, they would have been well able to handle them!

When the ground war ended and hostilities ceased, the Jaguars were quickly returned home, arriving back at Coltishall on 12–13 March 1991 to a rapturous welcome from wives, families, colleagues and well-wishers. The banner above the No.6 Squadron headquarters said it all – 'Welcome Home Desert Cats'.

Gulf Graffiti – The Jaguars' Desert Artwork

As the war progressed, ground crews began to add mission symbols on the forward fuselage side, and all of the aircraft bar XX748/U gained some kind of 'nose art'

with names such as 'Katrina Jane' and 'Debbie' added for good measure. These caricatures did not meet with universal approval of the pilots and senior officers, who claimed that by historical precedent it was up to them what appeared on their aircraft; nevertheless, they added a new dimension to the conflict, and sent aircraft spotters into a frenzy of activity! These 'works' ranged from the artistic to the outrageous, and amongst others featured ladies in various states of undress and over-the-top characters from the popular 'adult comic' Viz, including 'Buster Gonad' with his wheelbarrow full of appendages, the formidable 'Fat Slags' and the very windy 'Johnny Fartpants'. The artwork was in general applied to the port side of the nose, the exception being XX962, which sported the 'Fat Slags' on its starboard side and an Arabian lady on the port side. XX748 carried no artwork at all, whilst XZ367 changed its nose art during the conflict from a scantily-clad maiden called 'Debbie' to the more sedate picture of a 'Yorkshire Rose'.

Mission symbols were also applied in the form of black silhouettes depicting the type of ordnance dropped or equipment employed with, in some cases, the amount 'disposed of' being written in white onto the symbol. Some markings took the shape of bombs, others CBUs or CRV-7 rocket pods. The CRV-7s were marked in two ways: either a plan view of the LAU pod, or a circular cross-section with white rockets inside. Reconnaissance missions were denoted by black 'SLR camera' silhouettes, with the number of missions undertaken painted in black in the 'lens' area. Although Sidewinder AAMs were never fired in anger, at least three of the Jaguars show a 'winder launch' as part of their mission symbols. Officially, the missiles were launched in error, one reportedly due to a wiring malfunction on the overwing pylon – 'some spare wiggely amps', to quote a ground crewman. XZ106/O had the word 'Truck' written on its Sidewinder symbol, and it must be left to the imagination as to the possible use of that particular missile; XX748 carried the

XZ119/Z Katrina Jane. Author

XZ364/Q Sadman. Author

XZ367/P Yorkshire Rose (previously Debbie). Author

XZ375/S The avid Guardian Reader. Author

XX725/T Johnny Fartpants. Author

XX962/X Fat Slags/Arabian Lady. Author

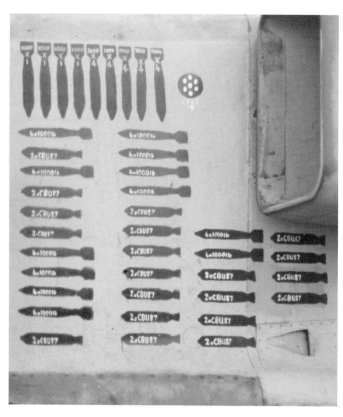

XZ725/T Mission Symbols. Author

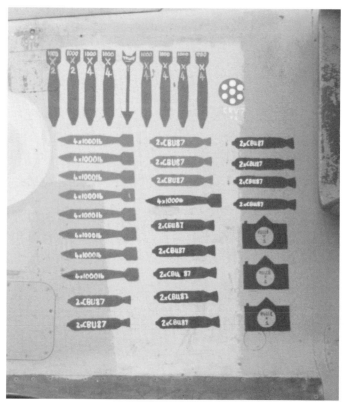

XZ106/O Mission Symbols. Author

word 'Oops' on its missile marking; and XZ118 just quoted 'SWM x 1'. Wg Cdr Pixton's personal mount, XX356/N. carried his pennant beneath the windshield, and featured one of the more aesthetic artworks , 'Mary Rose'. One of the more amiable caricatures was a pink Spitfire featuring a moustachioed pilot complete with World War II goggles and flying helmet. The artwork was generously named 'Baggers' after the oldest member of the Jaguar detachment, 54-year-old Sqn Ldr David Bagshaw, who undertook both bombing and reconnaissance missions during the war and who clocked up over 4,000 hours on type, on 8 January 1991, a feat unlikely to be repeated.

XX733/R Baggers. Author

Preserving the 'Art'

Post-Gulf War, most of the *Granby* aircraft had their desert sand scheme removed, the squadrons' groundcrew getting to work with the scrubbing brush! A few aircraft received a new coat of sand and were re-deployed in Operation *Warden*, but the engineers tried to preserve as many of the artworks for as long as possible, and 'worked around' the caricatures, allowing them to appear, albeit for a brief period, over the standard grey/green scheme. The 'desert sand' colour did prove a challenge to remove from around some of the panels, though!

The remains of 'Johnny Fartpants' after a good scrubbing! Author

RAF desert sand camouflage. BAe

Top surface view of the RAF Jaguars' desert camouflage. BAe

Mission Facts

Sorties and Combat Missions Flown

Type	Sorties Flown	Combat Missions
SuCAP/SARCAP	48	23
Reconnaissance	31	21
BAI	538	114

Ordnance Delivered	
1,000lb free-fall bomb	750
CBU-87 Rockeye II	385
BL755 CBU	8
CRV-7 rockets	608 (32 × 19-round pods)
30mm rounds	9,600

Combat Flight Hours	921hrs 50mins

Armée de l'Air in *Desert Storm* – Operation *Daguet*

The second European, and largest, user of the Jaguar in the Gulf War was the French *Armée de l'Air*, which deployed some twenty-eight (*see below*) Jaguar As as part of Operation *Daguet*, the French contribution to *Desert Storm*. Toul-Rosieres-based *11ᵉ Escadre de Chasse* was placed on a standby footing for Gulf duties on 16 September 1990, but it was not until 18 October that its first eight aircraft were despatched to the area under the command of Colonel Marc Amberg; these were followed by a further eight on the 21st. Their destination was the remote air base of Al Ahsa near Hufuf, some 80 miles to the south-west of Dhrahran, a site reportedly requested by the then pro-Iraqi French Defence Minister, Jean-Pierre Chevenement, in order that the aircraft might keep a fairly low-profile yet still be seen to be part of the overall Coalition strategy. A further detachment of twelve Jaguars arrived in early January, the aircraft now representing all three of the Toul units; EC 1/11 'Roussillon', EC 2/11 'Vosages' and EC 3/11 'Corse', plus elements of EC 4/11 'Jura' from Bordeaux; the new arrivals also included pilots from the *7ᵉᵐᵉ Escadre* at St Dizier.

Although the 'official' figures state that only twenty-eight aircraft were deployed, it can be assumed, with reference not only to photographic coverage and television pictures, but also the number of aircraft painted in desert colours, that some thirty-five aircraft were actually deployed to the region, with only twenty-eight being *operational* at any one time. A further three aircraft were painted-up for service in the

An AS.30L/ATLIS II-armed Jaguar from EC 4/11 'Jura'. Note the ATLIS centreline pylon shape.
SIRPA/Air

Aerospatiale AS.30 Missile

The AS.30 is manufactured by *Division Engins Taqtiques de Aerospatiale* (now Euromissile France), and was first introduced in 1960, as the Nord 5401, to provide the Dassault Mirage III attack fighter with an air-launched weapon with a modest stand-off capability. The original design for the AS.30 was essentially a scaled-up AS.20, an earlier ASM now retired from service, powered by a two-stage SNPE/Aerospatiale solid-propellant rocket motor. The missile has four delta wings in a cruciform pattern mid-way along its body, and allowed the carrier aircraft to come no closer than 3,280yd (3,000m) from its target, the operator then using a radio command to steer the missile into the visual line of sight with a CEP (Circular Error Probable, or error distance from a chosen impact point) of less than 32.8ft (10m). The weapon was 12ft 7in (3.84m) long with an X12 warhead, or 12ft 11in (3.94m) long with an X35 warhead. The AS.30TCA came into service in 1964, and was a development of the basic AS.30, now using TCA semi-automatic command to line of sight and infra-red tracking, and introduced flick-open fins indexed to the wings to replace the system of control spoilers in the two exhaust nozzles.

The AS.30L – L for Laser – was introduced in 1985, and has been in service with the *Armée de l'Air* since 1986. This much improved model was designed to work with the Thomson-CSF/Martin-Marietta ATLIS II laser designator pod, allowing the aircraft to launch the missile and break away while the laser pod continues to designate the locked-in target for the missile. Guidance is provided by a strapdown inertial axial gyro-scope platform for the midcourse phase, and a Thomson-CSF Ariel semi-active laser for the terminal phase, which produces a CEP of 6.5ft (2.2m). The warhead has a hardened steel case, and in combination with an impact speed of some 875kt (1,620km/h), provides the missile with the ability to penetrate 2m-thick concrete before the 529lb (240kg) warhead is detonated. It can be launched from a range of up to 6 miles (10km) from its intended target. The missile has a length of just under 12ft (3.7m), and a diameter of 13in (33cm), weighs 1,146lb (520kg). Ironically, Iraq had acquired some 300 of these weapons, but had expended all but a few in the long war with Iran. Around sixty AS.30Ls were fired by the Jaguar As during the Gulf War, and reports indicate an approximate kill rate of 80 per cent. The French had some 180 in stock at the outbreak of the conflict, and a further fifty-five were ordered just prior to the beginning of the air war.

Aerospatiale AS.30L missile. Aerospatiale

AS.30L missile en route **to its target**…

…Impact! Aerospatiale

Gulf, but remained in France throughout the conflict.

Lacking sophisticated equipment such as the FIN 1064 and LRMTS fitted to the RAF's Jaguar GR.1s, the French Jaguars had only a simple Thomson-CSF CILAS TAV-38 laser rangefinder under the nose, and they also lacked the ability to carry the overwing Sidewinder missile launchers.

One new item of kit did emerge, albeit as a last minute navigational addition, when the pilots were each given a hand-held GPS system which they attached inside the cockpits of their Jaguars, using strips of Velcro. They could, though, fit the excellent Thomson-CSF ATLIS (Automatic Tracking Laser Illumination System) laser-designator pod to their centreline station,

providing them with a self-contained precision weapon delivery system, this being used most successfully with the Aerospatiale AS 30L missile.

For self-defence, the Jaguars used a combination of a single Matra 550 AAM, or a Matra Phimat or Bofors BOZ-103 chaff/flare pod mounted on the starboard outer wing pylon, balanced by a Dassault

Jaguar A armed with *(l–r)* Matra 550 Magic, AS.30L, Alkan chaff and flare dispenser, ATLIS II, 264gal (1,200ltr) fuel tank and Barax jammer pod. SIRPA/Air

Electronique Barracudaor, Barem or Remora wide-band ECM detector/jammer pod on the port outer wing pylon. Also fitted was a 56-cartridge Alkan 5020/5021 conformal chaff and flare launcher beneath each wing root, and occasionally an 18-cartridge Lacroix flare dispenser was carried in the tailcone in place of the dragchute; the suite was completed by the

(226kg) bombs, each of the latter able to be carried on twin side-by-side carriers fitted on the inner wing pylons. The Jaguars also, of course, had their internal DEFA 553 cannon, with 300 rounds of ammunition, ideal for strafing. Other items of kit employed on occasions were centreline-mounted Thomson Brandt BAP100 anti-runway bombs, a Jaguar being capable of

by the French political climate. The Jaguar As first mission took place on 17 January 1991, Day 1 of the war, and consisted of twelve aircraft, launched at 0530 local for a raid on a 'Scud' missile facility at the Ahmed Al Jaber air base in Kuwait. The Jaguars laid down a number of Belouga aerial grenade cannisters from a height of just 100ft (30m), and launched a number of

An AS.30L-armed Jaguar taxies out in the cool of the desert morning, en route **for another attack mission.**
via Gary Madgwick

aircraft's own internal Thomson-CSF TH RWR on the tailfin. For EW support, the Thomson-CSF Caiman or Basilisk pods were carried. When not employed in the designator role with the ATLIS pod, the centreline station was used to carry a 264gal (1,200ltr) RP36 fuel tank.

On the offensive side of things, weaponry included the aforementioned AS 30L missile, Matra/Thomson Brandt Belouga 640lb (290kg) grenade dispenser weapon, and 'slick' 250lb (113kg) and 500lb

carrying two clusters of nine weapons each in a 14-3-M2 launcher; the Thomson Brandt BAP 120 anti-armour bombs, similar in employment to the BAP-100; LR-F1 non-reloading launchers containing 68mm rockets each; and, towards the final phase of the war, twin SAMP BLG 450 laser-guided bombs.

Like the RAF Jaguars the *Armée de l'Air*'s aircraft were assigned only to daylight operations; however, they were constrained not only by the weather, but also

AS.30L missiles. One French pilot was reported to have commented that the aircraft were subjected to some intense defensive fire from ZSU radar-tracked cannon, shoulder launched SAMs and AAA as they streaked in at low level:

'We were flying so low that the countermeasures (flares) that we launched – we could see bouncing up off the ground. As soon as the weapons were released, we cleared the target and headed out – no time to enjoy the fireworks or the spectacle'.

Thomson-CSF/Marin-Marietta ATLIS II Pod

Using the experience that had been gained by the American forces in the employment of their Bullpup air-to-surface missile, France had begun to explore the technology of an air-launched weapon with 'plenty of clout' that could be fired from a stand-off range and locked onto a target by means of a laser-equipped pod which would continue to illuminate the precise strike zone while the aircraft was moving away from the target.

To work with the proposed system, Aerospatiale produced the AS.30L laser-guided missile, and flight tests got underway at Cazaux, France's weapons development centre just south of Bordeaux near the *Basin d'Arcachon* during 1971. Laser 'sparkle' was provided by a Cilas ITAY-71 'gun' which was contained in a Thomson-CSF/Martin-Marietta ATLIS II pod carried on the aircraft's centreline station. This combination represented the world's first autonomous laser missile/designator package to be employed by a single-seat aircraft. Operational deliveries to the *Armée de l'Air* began in 1983, and the combination continues to be the weapon of choice for stand-off precision attack. First tested in 1976–77, the original MkI pod was supplanted by the MkII which was both shorter and lighter than its predecessor. AS.30L launch trials were successfully undertaken in early 1980 over the Landes test range, culminating in a full firing on 4 April.

The ATLIS pod itself consists of a laser designator and a wide-angle television camera, the field of view being a narrow beam slaved to the line of the laser beam. The assembly is gimballed so that the unit is held steady, regardless of the attitude of the aircraft. The second part of the aircraft's laser system is a modular guidance unit called ARIEL which is fitted into the nose of the AS.30L missile, and to laser-guided bombs.

Using the ATLIS system, the pilot of the carrier aircraft would usually visually acquire the target, taking a rough line of sight through his HUD. He then switches his eyeline 'heads down' to his TV tab, and with a hand controller makes an accurate 'fix'. He then fires a laser burst to determine target distance, and the system switches to automatic track. As soon as the missile is within range of the target a cue comes up and he presses the 'pickle' button to launch the missile. No matter how violent his manoeuvring is off the target, the laser always stays locked on until impact. A safety feature incorporated in the system is a 'pitch and roll and dangerous height' indicator which are displayed onto the TV tab to warn the pilot of the aircraft's positioning when he is 'heads down'. In bad weather or in poor visibility, the navigation computer is relied on to put the aircraft into the target area, and then the pilot relies on his TV camera, which has an operating capability in the near infra-red electromagnetic spectrum, and an enlarged picture is supplied on the monitor screen. ATLIS also allows for one Jaguar to illuminate targets for other aircraft to drop laser-guided bombs, and during large-scale attacks, confusion is lessened by coding each laser with a different pulse rate, to which the associated receiver in the munition is also tuned.

ATLIS II targeting pod. John Blackman

Scene through the ATLIS designation pod as it illuminates a vessel for an **AS.30L** missile ...

...the impact of the missile is precise and deadly, and punches a huge hole in the vessel's side *(below)*.
SIRPA/Air

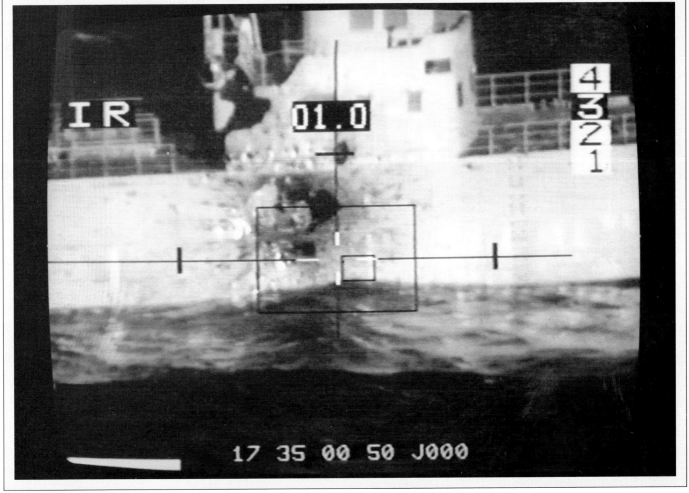

The murderous AAA the aircraft encountered resulted in damage to four of their number. One took a shell directly in the starboard engine, but the most severe damage was inflicted on a Jaguar which was hit adjacent to the port engine exhaust by a shoulder-launched SA-7 missile, which set fire to the engine. The pilot was able to retain control of the aircraft and made an emergency diversion to the US base at Jubail, with the rear of the aircraft badly holed; it was later crated and

Having learned the same hard lesson as the RAF about low-level operations, a further twelve Jaguars, in three groups of four, raided a munitions dump at Ras Al Quilayah on Kuwait's coast, some 19 miles (30km) from Kuwait City, during the morning of 18 January, this time flying at medium level. Operating without 'top cover' and profiting from the earlier destruction of the Iraqi radars and SAM tracking systems, four of them once more carried laser-guided AS.30L missiles, which were released against storage

Jaguar pilot. 'As we used it against some very highly defended targets, the difficulties we faced were made more so by the Jaguar being only single-seat – in which we also serve as the weapons officer. We usually started viewing the targets through our ATLIS pods at distances as far as 10–12 miles [16–20km] out, using the × magnification feature, and then firing the missile from around 10km out.

Some details of the Ras Al Quilayah raid were later broadcast on TV, to show the

Armed with four 500lb (226kg) bombs, a single centreline fuel tank, a Matra 550 Magic and a Barax jammer pod. via Gary Madgwick

returned to France. Of the other three, one of the pilots was extremely fortunate, having an AAA shell pass right through his canopy and his flying helmet, grazing his scalp and requiring him to take urgent medical attention whilst still in his cockpit back on the ground at Al Ahasa. The raid itself had taken only six minutes.

hangers in the dive from 4,000ft (1,220m) and at a stand-off range of 7.5 miles (10km). The AS.30Ls were primarily designed for low-level attacks, but were reconfigured for medium altitude delivery:

The 10km stand-off range of the AS.30L was particularly important to us,' explained one

world's media the precision of the Allied bombing campaign. Viewed through an ATLIS pod, an ammunition shed is targeted by the system's laser, the pilot, in contact with an orbiting AWACS, confirming his visual acquisition. There is a brief flash as the missile enters the frame from the left, and destroys the building, blowing one of the doors away completely, the pilot confidently announcing, 'Bravo Victor, Bravo Victor', as he banks away.

Meanwhile, the other eight Jaguars dropped 250lb (113kg) bombs onto their targets from 15,000ft (4,570m). The Ras Al Quilayah site was reportedly 1,000yd (900m) long and 750yd (685m) wide and consisted of hangars surrounded by concrete blast revetments, some of which had been designed to house MM-39 Exocet sea-skimming missiles captured from the

vessels, and on the 23rd eight more hit artillery positions with 250lb bombs. With the switch to a higher operating altitude, the efficiency of the Belouga system was seriously degraded, as it was principally a low-level weapon, and thereafter saw limited use. Some accounts also indicate that the Jaguars launched a number of Matra R-3 100mm unguided rockets. The Jaguars were seen to be carrying a centreline RP36P reconnaissance pod for a small number of 'in-house' missions, though the

stepping up the momentum of operations to two missions per day; the first such raid took place on 24 January when attacks were made against mechanized units of the elite Republican Guard, and their entrenched gun emplacements. The change of direction also led to the lifting of the grounding imposed on the French Mirage F.1CRs of the 33rd *Escadre de Reconnaissance*, also based at Al Ahsa (the embargo having been sensibly imposed to avoid possible confusion with Iraqi F.1s),

Bomb rack empty, 11-MV from EC 2/11 taxies back into Al Ahsa, canopy opened to get a little fresh air and relieve the tension. Tim Darrah

Kuwaiti Navy during the August invasion. The same facility was re-attacked on the 19th, and was due for more attention on the 20th, but this mission was called back due to severe thunderstorms in the area. The weather again grounded the Jaguars on the 21st, but the following day, six aircraft launched their AS.30Ls against Iraqi

bulk of the information gathering was left to the specialized Mirage units.

With the resignation of the French Defence Minister Chevenement, after his pro-Iraqi stance was overruled by President Mitterand, his successor, Pierre Joxe, took a more positive line and allowed strike missions to be flown into Iraq,

and they began 'flying shotgun' with the Jaguar raids. The first such combined operation took place on the 26th, when two Mirage F.1CRs used their Cyrano IVMR radars and Uliss-47 INS to provide six Jaguars with accurate navigational data for a raid on a divisional command post and artillery positions in southern

A153 from 3/11 'Corse'. Note the dark (usually green) camouflage paintwork on the rear fuselage engine access panels, the sand colour having blistered off. Author

Jaguar A-107 taxies out from Al Ahsa en route into Iraq, armed with four 1,000lb (454kg) bombs, Matra 550 Magic AAM and Barax jammer pod. SIRPA Air

Kuwait. The Jaguars subsequently began attack sorties against sites at Tallil, Shaiba and Jalibah.

In the campaign to sever Iraqi communications lines the Jaguars used their AS30Ls against a number of bridges on 10 February, but thereafter attention turned to battlefield targets as the deadline for the ground war approached, and the aircraft remained active until 27 February. By the end of the war the Jaguars had flown 615 sorties in 1,088 flying hours, and made 185 'contacts' with Boeing C-135FR tankers from 93ᵉ *Escadre* from Riyadh. There are indications from other publications that at least one two-seat Jaguar E from EC 4/11 operated in the Gulf, and indeed was photographed over the desert; however, one must remain sceptical as to whether these non-combat capable aircraft would have been so deployed. The Jaguars started to return to France on 5 March.

Operation *Daguet* Jaguars
Aircraft code letter/numbers were carried on the engine intake sides or beneath the cockpit thus: A104 11-EK (beneath cockpit) and A100 11-ER (intake sides)

EC1/11 'Roussillon': aircraft from flights GC111/6-6e and GC111/6-5e

A12 11-EB	A127 11-EH	A99 11-EI
A137 11-EJ	A104 11-EK	A130 11-EN
A122 11-EQ	A100 11-ER*	A94 1-ES
A139 11EV		

A101 11-ED, A133 11-EF and A140 11-EL painted but not deployed to the Gulf

Chad colour scheme

EC 2/11 'Vosages': aircraft from flights SPA91 and SPA97

A103 11-MA	A90 11-MB	A123 11-MG
A117 11-MH	A89 11-MM	A112 11-MO
A108 11-MP	A98 11-MT	A107 11-MV

EC 3/11 'Corse': aircraft from flights SPA88 and SPA69

A153 11-RA	A38 11-RE	A97 11-RG*
A58 11-RH	A135 11-RJ	A149 11-RK
A115 11-RL	A158 11RM#	A119 11-RO
A153 11-RV	A1 11-RW	A87 11-RX

*No ID codes carried
#Chad colour scheme

EC 4/11 'Jura': aircraft from flights SPA158 and SPA161

A148 11-YD	A91 11-YG	A150 11-YK#
A123 11-YN	A157 11-YS	

Most of the EC 4/11 aircraft deployed carried the 'Chad' scheme of chocolate and sand

colour scheme wrapped around undersides

Camouflage and Markings

As in their operations in Chad, the French Jaguars received a desert camouflage scheme, with three distinct styles being used. The paint scheme itself had five versions, each consisting of three basic colours, either chocolate/dark tan and sand/desert pink, applied in a disruptive pattern to the upper surfaces, with aluminium applied to the lower surfaces and wing pylons, or cream/beige and sand/stone disruptive upper surfaces,

A158/11-EM from EC11, looking rather weary post-war – obviously the ravages of the desert in Daguet **and** Crécerelle **have taken their toll.** via Gary Madgwick

again with aluminium undersides and wing pylons. Unconfirmed reports indicate that a few of the Jaguars may have received a pale blue or turquoise colour on their undersides. Individual aircraft codes were of the stencilled variety, usually in black, but again a couple of variations were noted. One aircraft, A103/11-MA, was also pictured wearing fourteen bomb silhouette mission symbols. Full-colour national insignia could be found on the rear fuselage sides and wings, with unit emblems applied on the tailfins. As the Jaguars were worked hard, their colour schemes began to reflect the situation, with heavy exhaust staining, touched-up panels, and bleached paintwork. A few aircraft, such as A123/11-YN, retained their unit's tail emblem.

Balkans Policing – Bosnia-Hercegovina

RAF Jaguars – Operation Grapple

After a brief three-month respite from their Turkish sojourn, manning Operation *Warden* at Incerlik, the Jaguars from Coltishall were again called to support an internation-

al operation, this time to help maintain the United Nations Protection Force (UNPROFOR) over Bosnia-Hercegovina, in an airborne policing operation entitled *Deny Flight*, for which the UK's participation was known as Operation *Grapple*. No.6 Squadron was the first to depart for the Italian air base of Gioia del Colle, taking out twelve Jaguars on 22 February 1993, and from then on sharing the manning of the detachment with Nos 54 and 41 Squadrons. For their duties over Bosnia, the aircraft were painted in an all-over light grey ARTF colour scheme, retaining the '*Warden/Granby* fit' of overwing Sidewinder launchers, Tracor flare dispensers, Phimat chaff dispenser and ALQ-101 ECM pod, and 'tweaked' engines, with the only addition being an extra radio to allow for communications with in-theatre command and control agencies. Also worth noting was, that unlike in the Gulf, the Bosnia aircraft carried two 264gal (1,200ltr) tanks on their

Armed with two 1,000lb (454kg) bombs on the centreline, XZ362/GC awaits its pilot for another Balkans patrol. via author

wing stations and two 1,000lb (454kg) bombs on the centreline, rather than the opposite, as over Iraq.

By the middle of 1994 the detachment strength had fallen slightly, but each squadron rotated nine pilots for up to five-week stints in Italy. Working patterns involved a 'six-days on and two days off' roster, with the aircraft flying almost every

Serb Army had launched a rocket attack. *Deny Flight* became *Deliberate Force* and RAF Jaguars were tasked, as part of a NATO package, to carry out a retaliatory strike, hitting a static T-55 tank near the village of Osijek, within the Sarajevo exclusion zone, each aircraft dropping a pair of 1,000lb bombs. On 19 November two Bosnian Serb Orao light attack aircraft,

the target area. However, the following day, a strike involving units from the UK, USA, Holland and France attacked the airfield. Because of their lack of of an autonomous laser designation capability, and therefore unable to carry PGMs, the Jaguars were relegated to a fairly minor role. Two aircraft from No.54 Squadron were involved in the strike, (one of which

XZ112/GA caught in transit to the Bosnia area with two 1,000lb bombs on the centreline. Also of note is the as yet un-greyed Phimat pod. John Cassidy RAF

day, and typically each pilot logging over twenty sorties during a 'tour'. With tensions running high during 1994, the Jaguar detachment was called into action on two occasions. The first event was on 22 September 1994, when French UN personnel called for air support after the Bosnian

based at Udbina airfield in the Krajina region, attacked the 'Safe Haven' in Bihac to the north-west of Bosnia. In response a raid was planned on the airfield using Jaguar reconnaissance photos. The foray was originally destined for 20 November, but cancelled due to bad weather over

was flown by the unit's OC, Wg Cdr Tim Keress) and both dropped 1,000lb bombs onto the airfield's perimeter track from an altitude of some 8,000ft (2,440m), both jets successfully hitting their targets. This was undoubtedly the largest air raid in NATO's history.

'Veggie One'

In a scene reminiscent of the Gulf War nose art, one of the aircraft that took part in the Udbina raid carried a special marking for a short while. XZ375/GR had a very smart bright orange carrot applied to its nose, with the legend 'Veggie One' at its side. The reason cited was that the aircraft's pilot was a vegetarian, a fact seized upon by the Jaguar groundcrew, who presented the jet for his approval in its latest livery! Also applied was a small black bomb silhouette, denoting the more serious nature of the aircraft's work, carrying the script, 21st Nov '94.

(Above) **Close up of the 'carrot-art'.** Author

'Veggie One's mission marking. Author

Missions over Bosnia were generally flown as pairs, so there was always mutual support. As a general rule these pairs were configured for the close support role. After leaving Gioia and crossing the Adriatic, the Jaguars would enter Bosnian airspace at medium level, the formation leader making contact with the ground Forward Air Control agency, or with airborne FACs such as F-18D Hornets or OA-10 'Warthogs'. The FAC's job was to locate the target and allocate it to the Jaguars, who had to make certain of the correct identification before any attack was made. The wingman played the role of 'shotgun', watching his leader's 'six' and also dealt with the orbiting AWACS. Once the lead was happy with the target, he briefed his wingman on its exact location, and the pair prepared to attack. This often entailed a climb to higher level, before rolling in for a dive-bombing pass, thus avoiding radar-directed AAA, missiles and small arms fire. Only one aircraft was lost during the Jaguars' time in Bosnia, a No.54 Squadron aircraft flown by a Danish exchange pilot who was forced to eject over the Adriatic following an engine failure on 21 June 1995, subsequently being picked up

unhurt by a Royal Navy Sea King helicopter scrambled from Split.

The Harrier GR.7 replaced the Jaguar on 1 August 1995. When UNPROFOR changed its role to become the United Nations Implementation Force (IFOR), Operation *Deny Flight* became Operation *Decisive Endeavour*, and in December 1996 IFOR's role changed again to become the United Nations Stabilization Force (SFOR), and Operation *Decisive Edge* then became Operation *Deliberate Guard*.

The Jaguars' Bosnia reconnaissance missions are dealt with on pp.95–7.

Armée de l'Air *Jaguar – Operation* Crécerelle

The *Armée de l'Air* has had similar commitments in Bosnia to the RAF under UN Resolution 781, taking part in the setting up of the air exclusion zone. For the Jaguar, this began on 6 April 1993, with Jaguar As from the EC11 at Toul-Rosieres deploying to Trevise Istrania air base in Italy under Operation *Crécerelle*, with other elements of EC 3/11 and EC 3/7 also basing at Rivolto during January and July, rotating the commitments between the *Force d'Action*

Exterieure players. The main task of the Jaguar in theatre was to provide a stand-off precision capability with their AS.30L missiles, precision bombing using both guided and un-guided weapons, and reconnaissance over Bosnia-Hercegovina. Capitane J. Berring of EC 3/7 recounts a typical Rivolto assignment:

The weather over Bosnia-Hercegovina is always very changeable, and on occasions our missions were cancelled due to the low cloudbase, however, the climate is favourable for the aircraft, and allows us to carry a full complement of weapons and deco's. Once en route to a patrol, we usually rendezvous with one of our C-135F tankers before entering the special corridor through the heart of Bosnia that takes us to our allotted task area, where we add our protection to the ethnic minorities. We then drop down to a medium level, which as we enter our zone almost always sends a shiver down your back. The first feeling is one of amazement, when flying above the countryside: all looks very calm. However, when reaching the populated areas you can see devastated buildings and many vehicles scurrying on the roads. On our patrols we are required to linger for a while over the inhabited areas, where we can see many

XZ357/FK on patrol over Bosnia-Hercegovina. BAe

hundreds of derelict houses, which meant countless broken lives. On the subject of vehicles, the all-white UN motors are easy to spot – except when it snows! We are usually under the control of a ground-based FAC, and he organizes our tasks, right up until we call 'Bingo Fuel', when we climb out to a higher altitude and re-track the air corridor and head back to base.

Lt Col Blanc spoke of the Jaguar detachment at Istrania:

ambiguities, which were were able to discuss with the commanders. Whilst our aircraft were on the ramp at Istrania, the mechanics were able to carry out any maintenance, repairs, or reconfigure them for another mission. For one scenario we departed Istrania at 0500 hours local with the mechanics having to work all night to re-role the aircraft and ensure we had the correct weaponry loaded for the mission. On this occasion my aircraft was armed with eight 100mm rockets in two pods for a close air support sortie

Jaguars' wings, and could be guided to their target by our ATLIS pods. This particular weapon was tested for the first time at Cazaux fifteen days before we got it, and our ground crews rose to the occasion to fit the aircraft out quickly. This proves the high degree of training in the French Air Force, the way both the air and ground crews were quickly able to adapt to a new weapon. The work over Bosnia and our other out-of-area commitments also proves that the Jaguar is equal to anything asked of it. At Istrania our detachment

Armed with two AIM-9M Sidewinder AAMs, XZ360/FN is a former Granby aircraft – denoted by the single blade aerial behind the canopy. RAF

During our visual reconnaissance missions from Istrania, we were effective in giving our 'If Reps' (In-Flight Reports) and accounting immediately on the state of any objective with which we were tasked. We usually take two C-135F refuelling slots for our missions, and on return we were able to debrief and confirm our reports from the aircrafts' cameras and our video cassettes, which over some sites were not without certain

when we were to cover ground troops, whilst others in the formation carried 500lb [226kg] slick bombs and 1,000lb [452kg] LGBs with ATLIS, and each of us carried a full load of decoys.

We also flew with the American GBU-12 LGBs for the first time over Bosnia, using a standard Mk82 bomb fitted with a Paveway II kit. Two GBU-12 were carried beneath each of the

of nine pilots and thirty-five ground crew worked extremely well, as did our logistics chain back to our home base; however, I must also pay tribute to our Italian hosts who gave us excellent support. The emphasis we place on realistic training has paid handsomely for the pilots, especially in such exercises as *Central Enterprise* and *Cold Fire*, and also practising aerial refuelling under the control of AWACS.

CHAPTER SEVEN

Towards the Millennium and Beyond

The Jaguar forces' success in the Gulf War was astonishing, and in operations over the Balkans it had once again proved the flexibility of the aircraft; with its new-found recognition as a formidable weapons and reconnaissance platform, the Jaguar was therefore a system that merited a little more 'inward investment'. During the early 1990s, the British MoD had become acutely aware of the RAF's poor ability to self-designate laser-guided bombs, and the then Chief of the Defence Staff, Sir Peter Harding, initiated an urgent examination of the provision of designation equipment for all RAF offensive aircraft such as Tornado, Harrier and Jaguar. The project was given high priority, as the RAF was beginning to become more isolated from top-level decision-making due to its lack of an autonomous LGB capability. The studies revealed that while the Tornado was becoming laser-equipped, the Harrier had more than enough operational commitments and was bringing into service its own new items of kit, and so, almost by default, the Jaguar was the logical choice to receive the most attention; after all, it had already proved it was a more-than-capable 'old timer'! Harding therefore prompted the raising of an Urgent Operational Requirement – UOR 41/94 – in June 1994 to give a limited number of Jaguars a laser designation ability that could be employed quickly, especially to the war zone over Bosnia.

Consequently, in autumn 1994 it was announced, as a result of the MOD's 'Frontline First' initiative, that all of the RAF's surviving sixty-three Jaguars would eventually undergo a comprehensive avionics and weapons upgrade that would ensure the aircraft's future until at the very least the year 2008. The most immediate of the proposals for these upgrades concerned ten GR.1As and two T.2As which would be modified to carry the GEC Ferranti 'Thermal Imaging Airborne Laser Designation' system, or 'TIALD', the new laser-equipped versions to be known 'unofficially' as the Jaguar GR.1B and T.2B respectively. This upgrade, developed jointly by the Defence Evaluation and

Research Agency (previously the DRA, which had become an independent agency in April 1995) and the RAF would make these twelve aircraft capable of self-designation at medium level of all current and future PGMs, and confer on them a stand-off designation capability for PGMs dropped by other Jaguars, Harriers or Tornados. Thus the Jaguar wing would be more suited to the 'self-contained rapid reaction role' it had been employed on during the early part of the decade. This would then endow the aircraft with a comparable, yet far more flexible system than that already established with the French Jaguars and their ALTIS II /AS-30L system.

Jaguar GR.1B – 'Laser Cats'

TIALD was first brought into RAF service with the Tornado during the Gulf War, though it had in fact initially been trialled for the Tornado aboard a Jaguar, the DRA's so-called 'NightCat', Jaguar T.2A XX833. The NightCat was one of a number of aircraft used by the DRA for passive night attack studies, using TV, IR and electro-optical sensors rather than radar, paving the way for programmes on the Harrier GR.7 and Tornado GR.4. XX833 had been originally delivered to the RAE at Farnborough on 8 April 1988 for laser modifications, which included a new HUD, the MIL STD 1553B databus, and a new head-down display (HDD). The aircraft then flew with an underwing GEC-Marconi podded ATLANTIC (Airborne Targeting Low Altitude Thermal Imaging and Cueing) Type 1010 FLIR system, to test procedures, and monitor the aircraft's other arrangements, such as presenting an image onto the HUD and HDD. The NightCat later flew with an 'A-Model' TIALD pod, which was subsequently removed and rushed out to the Middle East for urgent service in the Gulf War.

Despite the sterling work by the RAE, at the time the TIALD trials were not directly aimed at the Jaguar – more towards

Harrier and the Eurofighter 2000 – but they proved that TIALD could be operated in a single-seat aircraft by reducing the cockpit workload to 'one task at a time', refining the display formats by fine-tuning the TIALD system for ease of operation. XX833 then acted as a technology demonstrator during a one-year programme that ran from August 1992 until August 1993, and following the 1994 UOR, the aircraft was again involved in the dedicated Jaguar/TIALD installation when it was transferred to the SAOEU for them to lay down the operating procedures for its release to service.

The Jaguar's TIALD pod was fully integrated into the aircraft's avionics systems and harmonized with the INS, and was externally mounted on the centreline station of the aircraft, where there are fewer obstructions to the field of view for the articulated sensor head. In its 'designator' role the Jaguar would also carry a Phimat, ALQ-101(V)-10 jammer pod and a pair of 264gal (1,200ltr) fuel tanks. To accommodate TIALD operations, the aircraft have been fitted with a new high resolution/high brightness Marconi FD 4500 A4 wide angle HUD, capable of displaying raster FLIR imagery to actual (1:1) size, with a 24-degree field of view. Also included is a new HDD in the shape of a Marconi PMD with a GEC symbol generator and a GEC digital map generator, (both taken from the Tornado GR.4 upgrade programme) which can display either the synthetic moving map, or the TIALD television or thermal images; the unit later being referred to as an MPCD (Multi Purpose Colour Display). With the pilot having to 'tell' the TIALD pod where to look, the addition of a Rockwell-Collins GPS linked to a modified version of the FIN 1065, the FIN 1065C, and the powerful Mil Std 1553B databus was also essential to the system's success. The FIN 1064C has improved navigational accuracy, and allowed automatic target acquisition by the TIALD tracker. The unit was also only half the cost of the Plessy system 'borrowed'

Specification – Jaguar GR.1B/GR.3

Type:	Single-seat tactical strike and ground attack fighter/bomber with secondary reconnaissance capability. Capable of self/stand-off laser designation of PGMs. New avionics fit
Accommodation:	Pilot only, in Martin-Baker Mk9 zero-zero ejector seat
Powerplant:	Two Rolls Royce Turbomeca Adour Mk104 afterburning turbofans rated at 5,320lb (2,418kg) dry and 8,040lb (3,655kg) with afterburner – Mk106 in projected upgrade
Performance:	Max speed 1,056mph (1,690km/h) Climb rate 30,000ft (9,100m) in 90sec Ceiling 45,930ft (13,920m) Range 334 miles (534km) lo-lo-lo, 875 miles (1,400km) hi-lo-hi and 2,190 miles (3,504km) ferry
Weights:	Empty 15,432lb (7,000kg); normal 24,149lb (11,000kg); max 34,612lb (15,700kg)
Dimensions:	Length 55ft 2.5in (16.73m); span 28ft 6in (8.64m); height 16ft 10.5in (5.11m)
Armament:	Twin 30mm Aden cannon with 150 rounds per gun, plus five external hardpoints for a total of 10,000lb (4,545kg) of stores, including CRV-7 air-to-surface rockets, over/under wing Sidewinder AAMs, CBUs, and standard and laser-guided bombs, non-nuclear

from Tornado/Harrier stocks, and fitted in the first few aircraft and the NightCat XX833. The TIALD modification is a major one, and has effectively trebled the amount of software in each aircraft; however, the computing capacity of the Jaguar has been progressively increased over the years, from the 27K memory of the original NAVWASS, to 64K memory in the FIN 1064 and the greater capacity employed in the FIN 1064C of the GR.1B.

The need to be able to record TIALD imagery also necessitated the installation of dual video recorders. The Vinten video camera and recorder originally installed in the *Granby* Jaguars and incorporated into the earlier Smiths Industries HUD, was now adapted to work with the newly-installed GEC/Marconi HUD; however, it was decided that, in order to capture the TIALD images, a separate second Vinten recorder was needed. Incorporation of the 1553B has also allowed for the use of a strengthened SIAC laptop personal computer, for built-in tests of critical systems at

Before the TIALD handover was completed the single-seat fit was tested by one of Boscombe Down's fully instrumented trials Jaguars, XX108, which unlike the front-line aircraft carried the pod on one of its inner wing pylons. GEC/Marconi

squadron level, and as the digital databus was now also linked to all seven weapons pylons, it allowed for a wider range of ordnance to be considered.

To be able to control TIALD in a single-seat cockpit, a HOTAS (Hands On Throttle And Stick) set-up was required. To accommodate this, stick tops from stored Tornado F.2s were added, as were hand controllers recovered from scrapped Harrier GR.3s. The already uprated RWR was again modified, this time to the revised Sky Guardian 200-15PD standard, which is now considered as the production version of the STF fit applied to the *Granby* aircraft. The GR.1B's cockpits are also NVG-compatible, and plans are in hand to fit NVG-covert external lighting, invisible to the naked eye, which can also be flashed in a pre-determined pattern to give accurate night formation references. An undernose GEC-Marconi 1010 FLIR system is also under consideration for the GR.1B/GR.3 if funds permit, with the DRA having already successfully flown the NightCat Jaguar with a suitable (although pod-mounted) FLIR system fitted.

Before the actual production programme began, the DRA flew a further three-month trial using the NightCat Jaguar to convert the software and systems from research to operational standards. In many respects therefore, the UOR 41/94 standard was a 'productionized' version of the NightCat's trials configuration, made suitable for front-line use. TIALD was first flown as a full trial installation on a DERA-converted production Jaguar, XX748(TI) on 11 January 1995, and handed over to the RAF at Boscombe Down on 24 February. Before the handover was completed, however, the single-seat fit was tested by one of Boscombe Down's fully instrumented trials Jaguars, XX108, which unlike the front-line aircraft carried the pod on one of its inner wing pylons, balanced by a 1,000lb (454kg) LGB on the opposite side, and a centreline fuel tank.

The next two aircraft to be modified for TIALD, XZ381 and XX962, acted as Proof Installations (PI-1 and PI-2), being converted at Boscombe Down by engineering teams from RAF St Athan, leaving seven other GR.1Bs and two T.2Bs to be modified at St Athan, each conversion taking around forty-two days. DERA delivered all twelve aircraft within twelve months, the last arriving at Coltishall in the spring of 1997, at an overall cost of just under £12 million. The final aircraft was delivered in the Jaguar '96

configuration, described on pp.162–5. As the Jaguar had been already declared a 'mature' aircraft in 1990, and therefore in its declining years, so the conversion was managed directly from Whitehall; consequently, these quite major improvements to the aircraft could be undertaken using Service Engineering Modifications (SEMs), which effectively took the manufacturers and the MoD's own Procurement Executive department 'out of the loop', allowing the RAF itself to determine who would undertake the modification programme. Therefore the improvement package was designed by the 'in-house' DERA at Farnborough, and carried out by technicians at RAF St Athan, at a fraction of the cost and time that may have been quoted by commercial companies had they been invited to tender for the work.

To accommodate this new role for the aircraft, a small cadre of pilots was initially formed to operate the TIALD Jaguar and train other aircrew on its employment, with around five training sorties being necessary to qualify the pilots in its use. Although the addition of the new system has increased the pilots' workload, Wg Cdr Chris Harper, OC No.41(F) Squadron, and a fervent supporter of the TIALD-configured Jaguar, is adamant that the expansion in cockpit duties should be 'well within the capacity of any Jaguar flyer', a situation which has already been borne out in operational use.

Video Games?

As there was a need for the TIALD pilot to practice his 'switchology' and finger movements in the HOTAS-equipped cockpit, DID, a computer games manufacturer, produced a simple PC-based 'game simulation' which presented TIALD symbology on a representative picture, which was connected in real time to a stick top and hand controller; and has proved very popular since its delivery in August 1994.

According to Sqn Ldr Peter Birch, OC STANEVAL at RAF Coltishall and the TIALD Project Officer, the introduction of the new system has been, 'History in the making for the Jaguar. It has made the aircraft the only single-seater in the RAF's inventory capable of supersonic speed, able to designate its own weaponry and also provide the same service to others'. Wg Cdr Harper described the aircraft as, 'Hugely successful, well up to the expectations that drove on the initial Urgent Operational Requirement to install TIALD on the Jaguar.'

TIALD over Bosnia – Deliberate Force Designators

The Jaguar/TIALD combination was soon used operationally, when it when it saw service over Bosnia, designating PGMs dropped by the resident Harrier GR.7s in order to minimize 'collateral damage' during *Deliberate Force* operations. No.6 Squadron had already left Gioia del Colle in Italy on 31 January 1995, having handed over the manning of Operation *Grapple*, the UK's contribution to *Deny Flight* to the Harrier force; however, the Jaguar force continued to maintain two TIALD-equipped aircraft at RAF Coltishall on forty-eight hours' notice to deploy, manned on a rotational basis by crews from the three operational units. The first TIALD Jaguars over Bosnia were XX962 and XZ725, on 27 May 1995, which had been configured to trial the self-designation of PGMs, and were almost called into action for a strike against Bosnian Serb guns on this first trip!

No.6 Squadron took over the standby commitment on 24 August 1995, and shortly after this date an artillery shell exploded in a Sarajevo market square, and Operation *Deliberate Force* commenced. The squadron received 'notice to deploy' its two aircraft on the morning of 29 August, and as a result Sqn Ldr Alex Muskett left Coltishall at 1700hrs, flying XX725/GU and arriving at Gioia later that evening, followed by Sqn Ldr Simon Blake in the early morning of 30 August flying XX962/EK, both pilots being supported by VC-10 tanker. RAF operations commenced on the afternoon of 30 August when the two Jaguars and four Harrier GR.7s attacked an ammunition storage depot in the vicinity of Sarajevo, each GR.7 carrying a pair of 1,000lb Paveway II LGBs. The Jaguars 'buddy-lased' the targets, and were able to use the TIALDs' video imagery as evidence of the weapons' accuracy and lack of collateral damage. Because of the urgent requirement to have the TIALD system operating over the Balkans, the two Jaguars still retained their original Operation *Warden* light grey ARTF, though with the TIALD pod itself being dark green with yellow warning symbols. The Jaguars' markings were pale blue and pale pink, with white serial numbers and tailcodes, the latter being repeated on the nosewheel door. Again because of the imperative need to get TIALD into operation, the two Jaguars arrived at Gioia using one pod owned by GEC Marconi and

The TIALD System

The GEC Ferranti-designed TIALD system is primarily a day/night/adverse weather laser designator pod which can pinpoint targets for PGMs, the accuracy of which is wholly dependent on the laser 'spot' being skilfully directed onto the target. As the PGM does not recognize the target, only the laser spot, it is vital that the targeting pod is pointed with precision, and remains locked onto the target until the weapon hits. To accommodate this the TIALD pod has a TV wavelength at 0.7–1.0 microns, a 1.06 micron laser and a thermal imager at 8–12 microns, which allows the system to have a compact size, with optics that ensure the sensors are boresighted precisely with the aiming mark, affording unmatched precision, which allows TIALD to pick off targets well beyond normal visual range.

cockpit MFD; this allows the pilot to select the best option either prior to or during an attack. The image from both of these sensors can be recorded simultaneously and continuously, thus making it a useful reconnaissance tool as well. TIALD was initially developed for the Tornado force, destined eventually to equip a 'pathfinder' unit; however, events in the Middle East during 1991 saw the system hastily passed through its final development stages, with GEC Ferranti making two pods available to the RAF for the Gulf War, culminating in the first Tornado/TIALD strike on 10 February against hardened aircraft shelters at the H3 Airfield complex in south-west Iraq.

In order to make the TIALD pod work successfully on the Jaguar, minor software changes were made within the erasable programmable read-only memories (EPROMS)

XX729, a TIALD-equipped Jaguar GR.1B from No.6 Squadron, showing a typical designation fit. RAF

TIALD's large sightline, or 'field of view regard', allows maximum scope for manoeuvre on approach, which is coupled with an auto-tracking facility that enables the aircraft to adopt evasive tactics if under fire during the terminal phase of its attack. During target acquisition, the pod is set to 'field of view' mode, either 'narrow' for target identification and designation, or 'wide' for acquisition. The 'narrow' field is further enhanced by an electronic zoom facility. Once the target has been overlaid by the cross hairs, the system can be switched to auto-track, which maintains the target aspect without the pilot needing to make any further inputs. To enable maximum coverage in differing weather conditions, TIALD carries both thermal imaging and TV sensors, both of which operate simultaneously, either image being displayed at the flick of a switch onto the

in a single line replaceable unit (LRU) which makes the pod type-specific. The TIALD pods used by the Jaguar are the -200 series, its structure being designed and manufactured by Vinten and incorporating the British Aerospace Systems and Equipment (BASE) VITS 1000 Vectoring Imaging Tracker System. They do not have the -400 series' more powerful electric supply to the ball motor. Because the pilots have to go 'heads-down' during target designation, a symbol generator has been provided to present the aircraft's attitude, altitude and speed, superimposed onto the TIALD video picture in the HDD. The system is also capable of automatically predicting the target's position, and slaving the seeker head onto it and locking the sightline, even if the target is obscured until the Jaguar has pulled up to loft an LGB onto it.

The TIALD System *(continued)*

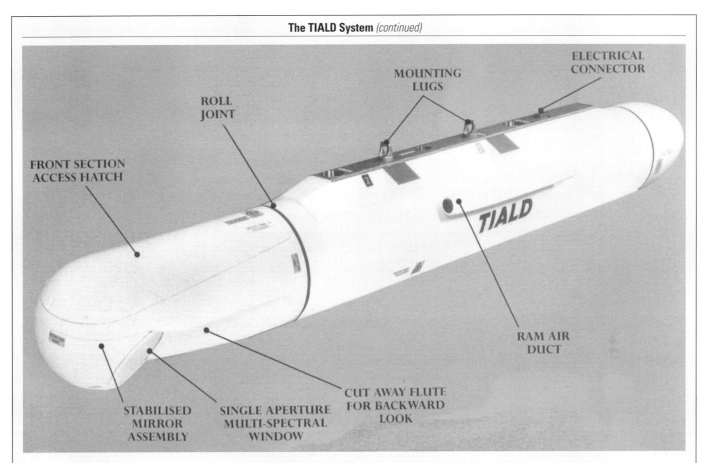

ROLL
JOINT

MOUNTING
LUGS

ELECTRICAL
CONNECTOR

FRONT SECTION
ACCESS HATCH

TIALD

RAM AIR
DUCT

STABILISED
MIRROR
ASSEMBLY

SINGLE APERTURE
MULTI-SPECTRAL
WINDOW

CUT AWAY FLUTE
FOR BACKWARD
LOOK

The GEC/Marconi TIALD pod. GEC/Marconi

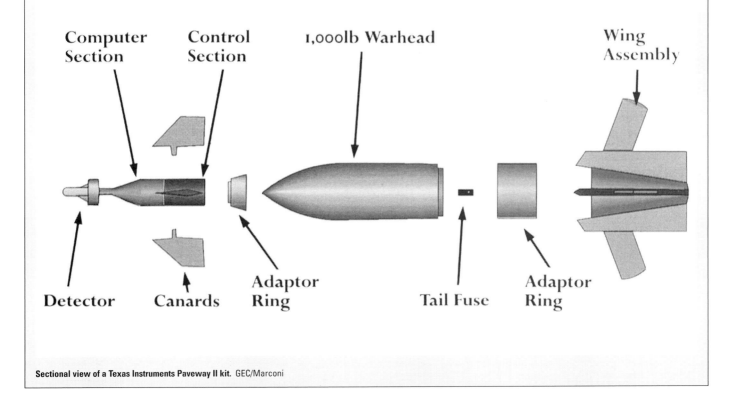

Computer
Section

Control
Section

1,000lb Warhead

Wing
Assembly

Detector

Canards

Adaptor
Ring

Tail Fuse

Adaptor
Ring

Sectional view of a Texas Instruments Paveway II kit. GEC/Marconi

The **TIALD System** *(continued)*

View of a power station seen by the pod's thermal imager. GEC/Marconi.

(Below) **The same view, but by selecting the TV sensor, this dramatically reveals further detail, highlighting the presence of boats, not readily apparent using the thermal image.** GEC/Marconi

Differing TIALD positions were tried during the Jaguars' stay at Gioia; here we see the TIALD pod positioned on the inner wing pylon. via Sqn Ldr Alex Muskett

another 'borrowed' from the Tornado wing at RAF Brüggen in Germany.

During the *Deliberate Force* operations, Muskett and Blake flew twenty-five combat sorties, guiding a total of forty-eight PGMs onto target, and acquiring further targets for a number of 1,000lb freefall bombs. Some of the targets proved to be quite testing, being less easy to pick up than those attacked in the flat wide open terrain of the desert; however, the duo achieved an enviable strike rate, and fully

justified the work undertaken by the DERA and GEC in integrating the TIALD pod and its associated avionics fitted to Jaguar. Whilst based at Gioia del Colle, the Jaguar duo also took the opportunity to carry out a few 'self-designated' trial missions with both TIALD and PGMs fitted to their aircraft, though it must be stressed that no weapons were actually dropped. Varying fits were tested, from the 'standard' configuration of TIALD on the centreline and PGMs on the wing pylons, to TIALD

on the starboard inner wing pylon, 264gal tank on the centreline and a single 1,000lb LGB on the port inner wing pylon.

During February 1997, the Jaguars returned to Gioia del Colle to retake the *Grapple* detachment from the Harriers. The in-theatre aircraft carried the latest two-tone grey scheme, and brought with them their TIALD capability, and laser-guided munitions, with five of the first Jaguar '96 standard aircraft deploying to Bosnia in March.

The seeker head of a 1,000lb (454kg) Paveway II kit, which responds to the laser energy reflected from a target, having been directed by designation systems such as TIALD. Author

Jaguar T.2B

The Jaguar T.2B is externally identical to the T.2A, the differences lying in the internal fit. The role of the T.2B is two-fold. Firstly, it serves as a flying classroom to instruct pilots on the use of TIALD, and to carry out continuation training and check rides. Secondly, as it has the same capabilities as the GR.1B, in time of war it could also serve as a laser designator, and because of the 'extra set of eyes' in the back seat, would provide useful reconnaissance and forward air control expertise, although the aircraft's lack of an RWR would need rectifying before a true combat role could be considered. The two production T.2Bs are both based at RAF Coltishall, XX835 being on strength with

No.6 Squadron and XX146 with No.54 Squadron. All TIALD-related training is undertaken at squadron level, and is overseen by a small TIALD management team operating between the two units. As with the single-seaters, the Jaguar's TIALD pod is fully integrated into the aircraft's avionics systems and harmonized to the INS, and is externally mounted on the centreline station of the aircraft. The T.2B has been fitted with dual high resolution/high brightness Marconi FD 4500 A4 wide angle HUDs, a pair of Ferranti moving map displays with symbol generators, a Rockwell-Collins GPS linked to the FIN 1065C INS, and a 1553B databus. Again, similarly to the single seat aircraft, the T.2Bs have received the latest two-tone permanent grey colour scheme.

Further Upgrades

During 1995, further delays with the Eurofighter 2000 programme led to Jaguar being slated to remain in service for longer than the original UOR plan had envisaged, and under a process known as 'Alternative Assumptions', the RAF re-allocated funds to maintain the aircraft for an extended period. This would form a schedule of staged upgrades, with annual phases known as Jaguar '96, '97, and possibly '98.

Jaguar '96 (Jaguar GR.3)

The Jaguar '96 upgrade phase incorporated all the full Stage 3 *Granby* modifications and many of the elements of the

No.41(F)'s Jaguar T.2B is prepared for a training sortie from outside a HAS at RAF Honington in mid-1997. The Jaguar force deployed to Honington from June to December of that year whilst improvements were made to Coltishall's runways. f4 Aviation Photobank

Captured on its return from a training trip, No.41(F)'s two-seat Jaguar GR.1B on finals. The high-visibility squadron markings provide a pleasing contrast to the two-tone grey camouflage. f4 Aviation Photobank

The original Jaguar cockpit was described as 'an ergonomic slum', but with the GR.1B and GR.3 the layout is much more 'user-friendly'. Of note in this GR.1B cockpit shot is the centre MPD replacing the old moving map, the new HUD and the ex-Tornado F.2 sticktop. BAe

UOR 41/94 programme, and was managed directly by the Jaguar Support Authority within the headquarters of RAF Logistics Command, with a senior Jaguar pilot being appointed as the Jaguar Upgrade Project Officer (JUPO), based at Coltishall. For the Jaguar '96 improvements, all of the RAF's remaining sixty-four GR.1As and eighteen T.2As were to be brought up to the GR.1B/T.2B standard, but with additional improvements on the already upgraded baseline. The old systems were replaced by new items on a 'spend to save' basis, these pieces of kit being more maintainable, cheaper to support and again

increasing the aircrafts' operational capabilities. These modifications were incorporated under a series of SEMs, being permanent modifications supported by full clearance procedures, unlike the temporary STFs used for the *Granby* modifications. 'New' (onward from the GR.1B standard) changes included the addition of the Mil-Std-1553B digital databus, the Rockwell-Collins GPS which is integrated with a new Terrain Reference Navigation System (TRNS) embedded in a further-modified FIN 1064C. The aircrafts' original HUD and its electronics box, digital map generator and the symbol generator

have also been replaced by a new wide-angle HUD unit, which also displays the g the aircraft is pulling, thus making up for the removal of the original 'g-meter' on the cockpit coaming. The symbol generator and digital map processors built onto one computer card (acquired from the C-130J Hercules programme) and the aircraft were also given an intelligent, predictive ground proximity warning arrangement using the BASE TERPROM (Terrain Profile Matching) system.

The TERPROM system aids low-level flight without using external aids or radar, by comparing the terrain encountered with stored digital terrain and obstacle data, and provides the pilot with a female voice warning (the AVAD – the British equivalent to the American 'Bitchin' Betty') to 'pull up' or be aware of any obstruction. TERPROM also operates in association with a new PC-based Mission Planning System (MPS) which uses the same data cartridge, and can produce a three-dimensional terrain map, even using reconnaissance imagery to display a very realistic picture. The new system will eventually replace the PODS 'Brick', allowing all the data from the MPS to be input into the aircraft's computer system. TERPROM will also aid the reconnaissance mission by being able to 'programme in' a particular sensor to automatically cue up to 'shoot' a particular target. The Jaguar '96s also have a custom-built stick top and hand

controller, produced to a 'pilot's requirement' by Ultra Ltd, rather than using items recovered from obsolete aircraft.

At the time of writing, not all Jaguar '96 aircraft have the full TIALD capability, but the wiring is *in situ* when funding becomes available for the complete fit, with only the original ten UOR 41/94 aircraft having the full TIALD facilities. The first aircraft to the Jaguar '96 configuration, XX738, was in fact the final aircraft of the UOR batch, which flew in January 1996, and was delivered to Coltishall in March 1997 and its initial sortie was flown by Flt Lt Jez Milne, who commented that it took very little time to get used to the new cockpit facilities. With full clearance being gained for the Jaguar '96 in February 1998 the type were redesignated Jaguar GR.3 and T.4 respectively.

Jaguar '97 (Jaguar GR.5)

Further improvements came under the Jaguar '97 programme, using the same SEMs as Jaguar '96, with DERA designating the modifications and St Athan incorporating them into the aircraft. The Jaguar '97 configuration was applied to all Jaguar '96 and UOR 41/94 aircraft, providing a common fleet-wide standard. These 'further improved' Jaguar GR.3s will be able to carry LGBs and TIALD as a self-designation 'cell', and will also be able to carry the various types of reconnaissance pod. The cockpit MPCD was replaced by a GEC-Marconi 6 × 8in active matrix liquid crystal display in portrait format, which is better able to show the moving map and the TIALD imagery. Another major Jaguar '97 element is the GEC-Marconi/Honeywell

The future looks bright for the Jaguar: with its upgrade programme, all of the RAF's fleet will have a superior and effective avionics suite, much of which is the envy of many modern 'mud-movers'. Here a TIALD-equipped Jaguar from No.6 Squadron formates with a No.54 Squadron aircraft armed with a 1,000lb (454kg) laser-guided bomb and a No.41 Squadron machine carrying a 1,000lb freefall bomb. Rick Brewell

Helmet Mounted Sighting System (HMSS) fitted to a standard HISL Alpha lightweight flying helmet, incorporating a tiny projector that projects symbology directly onto the inside of the visor. Its initial operation is that of pointing the TIALD's seeker head onto potential targets, slewing to wherever the pilot looks, but it could be used for other purposes such as targeting ASRAMM missiles. A further self-protection enhancement will be the addition of the Common Rail Launcher (CRL) on the overwing Sidewinder pylon, which will allow for the carriage of the nose-mounted Vinten VICON Type 90 or Type 1010 FLIR, and the installation of the Ariel Towed Radar Decoy, either in the body of the ALQ-101 jammer pod (interior space being provided by replacing the unit's older travelling wave tubes with newer integrated circuits), or by replacing the tail-mounted brake parachute. Further advanced weaponry is also being considered, such as ASRAMM, the Brimstone advanced anti-armour weapon, the MCDW (Minimum Collateral Damage Weapon), and BAe's ALARM anti-radar missile. The final element of the aircraft's their 'Warden Colours' of 'temporary' light grey ARTF and pale pink/pale blue insignia. This was subsequently replaced by a new 'permanent' camouflage scheme which was applied to the Jaguar '96/'97 upgrade aircraft. This colour scheme features fresh-looking two-tone Low Infra-Red (LIR) grey colour, identical to that carried by the Harrier GR.7 and Tornado GR.1/A/B fleets; these colours being dark sea grey uppersurfaces and around the cockpit, and dark camouflage grey on the fuselage sides, tailfin and undersurfaces, with the two-tone colour also being split

Full-colour squadron markings brighten up the drab grey of XZ362/GC, a GR.1B from No.54 Squadron.
Rick Brewell

Swedish BOL chaff adaptor and, if funding allows, ASRAMM missiles. The NVG-compatible cockpit is also a major feature of the Jaguar '97, and includes new filters, electro-luminescent floodlights and replacement panel illumination.

Jaguar Towards 2000

The future prospect for further upgrades is carried in the so-called Jaguar '98 proposals, and include such items as an under-improvement programme will be the upgrade of the Adour engines from Mk104 to Mk106 standard. This would involve using elements from the US Navy's Goshawk Adour 871 powerplant and the improved afterburner unit from the Adour Mk811 export version.

Camouflage and Markings

To suit the aircraft's medium-level operating altitude, the aircraft initially retained 60-40 on the underwing fuel tanks. Wartime markings are, as can be expected, almost non-existent. Small black code letters are applied to the fin, and reduced-size serial numbers applied to the rear fuselage, with full-colour reduced-size red and blue roundels on the wings and below the cockpit, and a small red and blue flash at the base of the tailfin. For peacetime operations, larger, more flamboyant full-colour squadron insignia are carried on the tails and on the intakes.

Individual Aircraft Histories

Royal Air Force Jaguars

NUMBER	TYPE	NOTES
XW560	S	A&AEE Crashed 14.8.72 at Boscombe Down and burnt out in ground fire
XW563	S	Chosen to promote Jaguar International
XW566	B	DRA Avionics & Sensors Farnborough
XX108	GR.1	DRA Boscombe Down
XX109	GR.1	Ground instruction at Coltishall as 8918M
XX110	GR.1	To RAF Cosford for ground instruction as 8955M
XX111	GR.1	First Jaguar delivered to the RAF (without chisel nose). Later to Indian Air Force. Now stored RAF Shawbury
XX112	GR.1/A	Part of the initial deployment to Oman, 12.8.91. Non-combatant. Painted desert sand
XX113	GR.1	No.226 OCU. Crashed 17.7.81
XX114	GR.1	No.226 OCU. Crashed 19.9.83
XX115	GR.1	Part of the initial deployment to Oman, 12.8.91. Non-combatant. Painted desert sand. To No.1 SoTT Cosford as 8821M, ex Indian AF loan
XX116	GR.1/A	RAF St Athan, ex Indian AF loan
XX117	GR.1/A	DTEO DRA Boscombe Down, ex Indian AF loan
XX118	GR.1	Ex Indian AF loan
XX119	GR.1	Ground instruction with No.16(R) Squadron Lossiemouth as 8898M. Passed to FJTS DTEO as GR.1B GD
XX120	GR.1	No.54 Squadron. Crashed 17.9.76 at Samsoe Island Denmark during exercise Teamwork 76
XX121	GR.1	No.1 SoTT Cosford as 8892M. Refurbished and sold to Ecuador 1991
XX122	GR.1	No.54 Squadron. Crashed 2.4.82
XX136	T.2	A&AEE. Flew at 1974 Farnborough Show. Crashed 22.11.74 near Wimborne St Giles
XX137	T.2	No.226 OCU. Crashed 6.2.76 at RAF Lossiemouth, flew into Moray Firth after running out of fuel due to a pressure leak
XX138	T.2A	To Omani Air Force
XX139	T.2A	No.16(R) Squadron Lossiemouth
XX140	T.2	No.1 SoTT Cosford as 9008M
XX141	T.2A	No.6 Squadron Coltishall
XX142	T.2	No.226 OCU. Crashed 22.6.79 into Moray Firth 10 miles (16km) from RAF Lossiemouth

NUMBER	TYPE	NOTES
XX143	T.2B	RAF Lossiemouth
XX144	T.2A	No.16(R) Squadron Lossiemouth coded 'U'
XX145	T.2	Empire Test Pilots School Boscombe Down
XX146	T.2B	No.54 Squadron Coltishall
XX147	T.2	No.17 Squadron. Crashed 26.3.79 following a bird strike. Crew ejected safely
XX148	T.2	No.226 OCU. Crashed 29.7.77 at Whittingham, both crew killed
XX149	T.2	No.226 OCU. Crashed 27.4.78 flying into a mountain at Cullen Banff
XX150	T.2	No.16(R) Squadron Lossiemouth
XX719	GR.1/A	Part of the initial deployment to Oman, 12.8.91. Non-combatant. Painted desert sand
XX720	GR.1/A(T)	No.54 Squadron Coltishall, ex Indian AF loan
XX721	GR.1	No54 Squadron. Crashed 22.6.83
XX722	GR.1	Refurbished and sold to Ecuador 1991
XX723	GR.1B	No.54 Squadron Coltishall
XX724	GR.1/A	Stored Shawbury
XX725	GR.1/A	*Desert Storm* coded 'T', with 'Johnny Fartpants' nose art and desert sand scheme. To SAOEU Boscombe Down September 1997
XX726	GR.1	First aircraft to carry the production 'chisel nose'. No.1 SoTT Cosford as 8947M
XX727	GR.1	To RAF Cosford for ground instruction as 8951M
XX728	GR.1	No.6 Squadron, ex Indian AF loan. Crashed 7.10.85
XX729	GR.1/A(T)	No.6 Squadron Coltishall, ex Indian AF loan
XX730	GR.1	To RAF Cosford for ground instruction as 8952M
XX731	GR.1/A	No.6 Squadron. Crashed 7.10.85
XX732	GR.1/A	No.226 OCU. Crashed 27.11.86
XX733	GR.1/A	Desert Storm coded 'R', with 'Baggers' nose art and desert sand scheme. Crashed 23.1.96 at Coltishall
XX734	GR.1	Ex Indian AF loan
XX735	GR.1	No.6 Squadron. Crashed 15.9.76 at Eggbeck Germany during Exercise *Teamwork 76*

NUMBER	TYPE	NOTES
XX736	GR.1	Ex Indian AF loan. Forward fuselage to BAe Brough as 9110M. Now at Coltishall BDRT
XX737	GR.1/A	No.6 Squadron Coltishall, ex Indian AF loan
XX738	GR.1B(T)	FJTS Boscombe Down, ex Indian AF loan
XX739	GR.1	No.1 SoTT Cosford
XX740	GR.1	To Omani Air Force, ex Indian AF loan
XX741	GR.1/A	Part of the initial deployment to Oman, 12.8.91. Non-combatant. Painted desert sand. Stored Shawbury
XX742	GR.1	No.6 Squadron. Crashed 19.4.83
XX743	GR.1	No.1 SoTT Cosford as 8949M
XX744	GR.1	No.1 SoTT Cosford as 8892M. Refurbished and sold to Ecuador 1991
XX745	GR.1/A	No.16(R) Squadron Lossiemouth
XX746	GR.1A	No.1 SoTT Cosford as 8895M
XX747	GR.1	RAFC Cranwell AMIF as 8903M
XX748	GR.1B	*Desert Storm* coded 'U'. No nose art. Desert sand scheme. No.54 Squadron Coltishall
XX749	GR.1	No.226 OCU. Crashed 10.12.79, Lumsden, Aberdeenshire, colliding with XX755 on low level training exercise. Pilot killed
XX750	GR.1	No.14 Squadron. Crashed 7.2.84
XX751	GR.1	To RAF Cosford for ground instruction as 8937M
XX752	GR.1/A	No.6 Squadron Coltishall
XX753	GR.1	RAF EP&TU St Athan as 9087M
XX754	GR.1/A	No.54 Squadron. Crashed 13.11.90 over Qatar. Flt Lt Keith Collister killed
XX755	GR.1	No.226 OCU. Crashed 10.12.79, Lumsden, Aberdeenshire, colliding with XX749
XX756	GR.1	No.1 SoTT Cosford as 8899M
XX757	GR.1	No.1 SoTT Cosford as 8948M
XX758	GR.1	No.226 OCU Crashed 18.11.81
XX759	GR.1	No.226 OCU. Crashed 1.11.78, Selkirk. Ecuadorian trainee pilot killed
XX760	GR.1	No.14 Squadron. Crashed 13.9.82
XX761	GR.1	No.226 OCU Crashed 6.6.78 after ground fire. Cockpit salvaged for ground instruction as 8600M
XX762	GR.1	No.226 OCU. Crashed into mountains 23.11.79, near Dalmally, Argyll
XX763	GR.1	RAF CTTS St Athan as 9009M
XX764	GR.1	RAF CTTS St Athan as 9010M
XX765	GR.1	Converted to ACT. Now on display Cosford Aerospace Museum
XX766	GR.1/A	No.6 Squadron Coltishall
XX767	GR.1/A	No.54 Squadron Coltishall
XX768	GR.1	No.17 Squadron. Crashed 29.9.82
XX817	GR.1	No.17 Squadron. Crashed 17.7.80 at München-Gladbach, Germany. Pilot ejected
XX818	GR.1	No.1 SoTT Cosford as 8923M
XX819	GR.1	No.1 SoTT Cosford as 8923M

NUMBER	TYPE	NOTES
XX820	GR.1	No.31 Squadron. Crashed 11.6.82
XX821	GR.1	AMIF RAF Cranwell as 8896M
XX822	GR.1	No.14 Squadron. Crashed 2.7.76 15 miles (24km) west of Alhorn Germany. Pilot killed – the first Jaguar fatality
XX823	GR.1	No.17 Squadron. Crashed 25.7.78, Cagliari, Sardinia, flying into a hill during an APC sortie from Decimomannu
XX824	GR.1	No.1 SoTT Cosford as 9019M coded 'AD'
XX825	GR.1	No.1 SoTT Cosford as 9020M coded 'BN'
XX826	GR.1	No.1 SoTT Cosford as 9021M
XX827	GR.1	No.17 Squadron. Crashed 12.2.81 on the Nellis Ranges USA during a *Red Flag* exercise
XX828	T.2	No.226 OCU. Crashed 1.6.81
XX829	T.2A	No.16(R) Squadron Lossiemouth
XX830	T.2	Empire Test Pilots School
XX831	T.2	No.226 OCU. Crashed 12.2.81, Lossiemouth
XX832	T.2	No.16(R) Squadron Lossiemouth
XX833	T.2B	SAOEU Boscombe Down
XX834	T.2A	
XX835	T.2B	No.41 Squadron Coltishall
XX836	T.2	Stored Shawbury
XX837	T.2	No.1 SoTT Cosford 8978M
XX838	T.2A	Stored Shawbury
XX839	T.2A	To RAF CTTS St Athan as 9255M
XX840	T.2A	Stored Shawbury
XX841	T.2A	No.6 Squadron Coltishall
XX842	T.2A(T)	No.41 Squadron Coltishall
XX843	T.2A	
XX844	T.2	St Athan as 9023M
XX845	T.2A	No.6 Squadron Coltishall
XX846	T.2A	No.54 Squadron Coltishall
XX847	T.2A	Stored St Athan
XX915	T.2	Empire Test Pilots School. Crashed 17.1.84
XX916	T.2	Empire Test Pilots School. Crashed 24.7.81
XX955	GR.1A	Stored Shawbury
XX956	GR.1	No.1 SoTT Cosford at 8950M
XX957	GR.1	
XX958	GR.1	No.1 SoTT Cosford as 9022M
XX959	GR.1	To RAF Cosford for Ground Instruction as 8953M
XX960	GR.1	No.14 Squadron. Crashed 18.7.89, Islehorn, Germany. Pilot ejected safely
XX961	GR.1	No.17 Squadron. Crashed 25.5.80 after colliding with XX964 over RAF Brüggen during overhead break for landing. Pilot killed
XX962	GR.1B	*Desert Storm* coded 'X', with 'Fat Slags'/'St Georgina' nose art and desert sand scheme. AMIF Cranwell
XX963	GR.1	
XX964	GR.1	No.17 Squadron. Crashed at RAF Brüggen 28.5.80 after colliding with XX961

NUMBER	TYPE	NOTES
XX965	GR.1A	Damaged Coltishall 11.96. AMIF Cranwell
XX966	GR.1A	No.1 SoTT Cosford as 8904M
XX967	GR.1A	No.1 SoTT Cosford as 9006M
XX968	GR.1A	Formerly No.31 Squadron now at No.1 SoTT Cosford as 9007M
XX969	GR.1A	No.1 SoTT Cosford as 8897M
XX970	GR.1/A/B	Part of the initial deployment to Oman 12.8.91, first Jaguar to leave UK. Non-combatant. Painted desert sand
XX971	GR.1	No.31 Squadron. Crashed during take-off 21.3.78, Lahr, Germany
XX972	GR.1	No.31 Squadron. Crashed 6.8.81
XX973	GR.1	No.31 Squadron. Crashed 14.4.81 4 miles (6.5km) north west of Gütersloh, Germany
XX974	GR.1A	Part of the initial deployment to Oman 12.8.91. Non-combatant. Painted desert sand. No.54 Squadron Coltishall
XX975	GR.1	No.1 SoTT Cosford as 8905M
XX976	GR.1	No.1 SoTT Cosford as 8906M
XX977	GR.1	St Athan BDRT as 9132M
XX978	GR.1	No.31 Squadron. Crashed 14.4.77, Verden, Germany. Hit house, pilot killed
XX979	GR.1A	FJTS Boscombe Down
XZ101	GR.1A	First reconnaissance Jaguar issued to No.2 (AC) Squadron. Stored Coltishall
XZ102	GR.1	No.2 Squadron. Crashed 14.12.76 10 miles (16km) north-east of Laarbruch
XZ103	GR.1A	No.41 Squadron Coltishall
XZ104	GR.1A	No.41 Squadron Coltishall
XZ105	GR.1	No.2 Squadron. Crashed 16.6.83
XZ106	GR.1B	Desert Storm coded 'O', with 'Rule Britannia' nose art and desert sand scheme. No.41 Squadron Coltishall
XZ107	GR.1A	No.41 Squadron Coltishall
XZ108	GR.1A	No.54 Squadron Coltishall
XZ109	GR.1A	No.2 Squadron. Now No.54 Squadron Coltishall
XZ110	GR.1	No.2 Squadron. Crashed 16.6.93
XZ111	GR.1A	Stored St Athan, returned to Coltishall 9.97
XZ112	GR.1B	No.54 Squadron Coltishall
XZ113	GR.1A	Stored Coltishall
XZ114	GR.1A	Stored Shawbury
XZ115	GR.1B	Stored Coltishall
XZ116	GR.1	No.41 Squadron. Crashed 17.6.87
XZ117	GR.1A	St Athan
XZ118	GR.1A	Desert Storm coded 'Y', with 'Buster Gonad' nose art and desert sand scheme. Stored Coltishall
XZ119	GR.1A	Desert Storm coded 'Z', 'Katrina Jane' nose art and desert sand scheme. AMIF Cranwell
XZ120	GR.1	No.41 Squadron. Crashed into sea 25.2.77, Nordholm, Denmark
XZ355	GR.1	SAOEU Boscombe Down
XZ356	GR.1A	No.6 Squadron Coltishall. Nose art 'White Rose' and desert sand scheme. In Operation Warden carried 'Marshall Connelly' nose art

NUMBER	TYPE	NOTES
XZ357	GR.1A	Part of the initial deployment to Oman, 12.8.91. Non-combatant. Painted desert sand. No.41 Squadron Coltishall
XZ358	GR.1A	Desert Storm coded 'W', with 'Diplomatic Service' nose art and desert sand scheme. AMIF Cranwell
XZ359	GR.1A	Crashed off St Abbs Head 13.4.89
XZ360	GR.1A	No.41 Squadron Coltishall
XZ361	GR.1A	No.41 Squadron Coltishall
XZ362	GR.1B	No.6 Squadron. Crashed in Alaska 24.6.96
XZ363	GR.1B	Part of the initial deployment to Oman, 12.8.91. Non-combatant. Painted desert sand. Stored RAF St Athan
XZ364	GR.1A	Desert Storm coded 'Q', with 'Sadman' nose art and desert sand scheme. No.54 Squadron Coltishall
XZ365	GR.1A	No.2 Squadron. Crashed 10.7.85
XZ366	GR.1A	No.41 Squadron Coltishall
XZ367	GR.1B	Desert Storm coded 'P' with 'Debbie' nose art, later changed to 'White Rose' and desert sand scheme. No.54 Squadron Coltishall
XZ368	GR.1	No.1 SoTT Cosford as 8900M
XZ369	GR.1B	Part of the initial deployment to Oman, 12.8.91. Non-combatant. Painted desert sand. No.6 Squadron Coltishall
XZ370	GR.1	No.2 SoTT RAF Cosford as 9004M
XZ371	GR.1	RAF Cosford for ground instruction
XZ372	GR.1A/B	Part of the initial deployment to Oman, 12.8.91. Non-combatant. FJTS Boscombe Down. To St Athan for conversion 9.97
XZ373	GR.1A	No.54 Squadron. Crashed in the Adriatic 21.6.95
XZ374	GR.1	No.1 SoTT Cosford as 9005M
XZ375	GR.1B	Desert Storm coded 'S' with 'The Avid Guardian Reader' nose art and desert sand scheme. To CTTS St Athan as 9255M
XZ376	GR.1	No.17 Squadron. Crashed 7.3.83
XZ377	GR.1A	No.6 Squadron Coltishall
XZ378	GR.1A	Stored Shawbury
XZ381	GR.1B	No.6 Squadron Coltishall coded 'EC'
XZ382	GR.1	BDRT Coltishall
XZ383	GR.1	No.1 SoTT Cosford as 8901M
XZ384	GR.1	RAF Cosford for ground instruction as 8954M
XZ385	GR.1A	No.16(R) Squadron Lossiemouth
XZ386	GR.1A	No.226 OCU. Crashed 24.6.87
XZ387	GR.1A	
XZ388	GR.1	No.14 Squadron. Crashed 2.4.85
XZ389	GR.1	No.1 SoTT Cosford as 8946M coded 'BL'
XZ390	GR.1	No.1 SoTT Cosford as 90003M
XZ391	GR.1A	No.16(R) Squadron Lossiemouth
XZ392	GR.1A	Stored Shawbury
XZ393	GR.1A	No.54 Squadron. Crashed 12.7.84
XZ394	GR.1	No.54 Squadron Coltishall
XZ395	GR.1A	No. 54 Squadron. Crashed 22.8.84

NUMBER	TYPE	NOTES
XZ396	GR.1A	Part of the initial deployment to Oman, 12.8.91. Non-combatant. Painted desert sand. AMF Coltishall
XZ397	GR.1	To Indian Air Force
XZ398	GR.1A	No.41 Squadron Coltishall, ex Indian AF loan

NUMBER	TYPE	NOTES
XZ399	GR.1B	No.6 Squadron as 'EJ'
XZ400	GR.1A	Stored Shawbury
ZB615	T.2	Fast Jet Test Squadron Boscombe Down

French Air Force Jaguars

NUMBER	TYPE	DELIVERY	NOTES
A1	Jaguar A		
A2	Jaguar A	11-RA	
A3	Jaguar A		
A4	Jaguar A		
A5	Jaguar A		
A6	Jaguar A	7-HB	
A7	Jaguar A		WFU
A8	Jaguar A		
A9	Jaguar A		
A10	Jaguar A		
A11	Jaguar A		
A12	Jaguar A		
A13	Jaguar A		
A14	Jaguar A	7-PO	
A15	Jaguar A	7-HG	
A16	Jaguar A		
A17	Jaguar A		
A18	Jaguar A		Written off 27.7.81
A19	Jaguar A		
A20	Jaguar A		Written off 30.1.81
A21	Jaguar A		
A22	Jaguar A	7-H	EC 1/7
A23	Jaguar A	7-HH	
A24	Jaguar A		
A25	Jaguar A	7-PU	
A26	Jaguar A	11-MH	
A27	Jaguar A		
A28	Jaguar A	7-HB	
A29	Jaguar A	7-PE	
A30	Jaguar A		Written off 26.4.82
A31	Jaguar A		
A32	Jaguar A		
A33	Jaguar A		
A34	Jaguar A	7-ID	
A35	Jaguar A	7-IH	
A36	Jaguar A		
A37	Jaguar A	11-RB	
A38	Jaguar A	7-PV	
A39	Jaguar A	7-HI	
A40	Jaguar A	7-H0	
A41	Jaguar A		
A42	Jaguar A		Written off 1.7.82
A43	Jaguar A	7-HF	
A44	Jaguar A		
A45	Jaguar A	7-1B	Written off 12.7.79
A46	Jaguar A	7-HP	
A47	Jaguar A	7-HJ	
A48	Jaguar A		
A49	Jaguar A	II-RD	
A50	Jaguar A	7-IE	
A51	Jaguar A		Written off 16.6.81
A52	Jaguar A	11-RQ	Written off 1978
A53	Jaguar A	7-HD	
A54	Jaguar A	11-MN	
A55	Jaguar A	7-PA	
A56	Jaguar A		
A57	Jaguar A	7-NB	Written off 11.5.84
A58	Jaguar A	7-HL	
A59	Jaguar A		
A60	Jaguar A		
A61	Jaguar A	11-RG	
A62	Jaguar A	3XI	
A63	Jaguar A		Written off 20.6.79
A64	Jaguar A	7-IS	Written off 18.3.81
A65	Jaguar A		
A66	Jaguar A	7-IB	
A67	Jaguar A		
A68	Jaguar A	3-XG	Written off 5.2.81
A69	Jaguar A	7-IN	Written off 20.5.84
A70	Jaguar A		
A71	Jaguar A		Written off 14.11.77
A72	Jaguar A		
A73	Jaguar A		
A74	Jaguar A	7-IJ	
A75	Jaguar A		
A76	Jaguar A		
A77	Jaguar A		Written off 7.7.82
A78	Jaguar A	7-HM	Written off 28.3.84
A79	Jaguar A		
A80	Jaguar A		
A81	Jaguar A	11-MA	Written off 24.1.84
A82	Jaguar A	7-HM	
A83	Jaguar A		
A84	Jaguar A	7-HA	
A85	Jaguar A	11-MG	Written off 3.1.86
A86	Jaguar A	7-IQ	
A87	Jaguar A	7-HN	
A88	Jaguar A	7-II	
A89	Jaguar A	11-RE	
A90	Jaguar A	11-MI	
A91	Jaguar A		
A92	Jaguar A	7-HC	
A93	Jaguar A		
A94	Jaguar A		
A95	Jaguar A		
A96	Jaguar A	7-ID	

NUMBER	TYPE	DELIVERY	NOTES	NUMBER	TYPE	DELIVERY	NOTES
A97	Jaguar A	11-RH		A150	Jaguar A		
A98	Jaguar A			A151	Jaguar A	11-RS	
A99	Jaguar A	11-RJ		A152	Jaguar A		
A100	Jaguar A	7-HK		A153	Jaguar A	11-RO	
A101	Jaguar A			A154	Jaguar A	7-IN	
A102	Jaguar A	11-YK	Written off 16.8.83	A155	Jaguar A		Written off 14.9.82
A103	Jaguar A	II-RI		A156	Jaguar A		Written off 1985
A104	Jaguar A			A157	Jaguar A	11-MW	
A105	Jaguar A	7-IT		A158	Jaguar A	11-RM	
A106	Jaguar A	11-ES	Written off 14.10.78	A159	Jaguar A	11-RV	
A107	Jaguar A	7IG		A160	Jaguar A	7-IV	
A108	Jaguar A	11-RF		E1	Jaguar E	CEV	
A109	Jaguar A		Written off 1980	E2	Jaguar E	7-PG	
A110	Jaguar A			E3	Jaguar E	339-WF	
A111	Jaguar A		Written off 1979	E4	Jaguar E		
A112	Jaguar A	11-MA		E5	Jaguar E	11-RY	
A113	Jaguar A	7-IR		E6	Jaguar E	7-PD	
A114	Jaguar A	11-YB	Written off 10.3.82	E7	Jaguar E		
A115	Jaguar A			E8	Jaguar E	339-WG	
A116	Jaguar A	11-MW	Written off 30.6.86	E9	Jaguar E	7-PL	
A117	Jaguar A			E10	Jaguar E	7-IC	
A118	Jaguar A			E11	Jaguar E	339-WH	
A119	Jaguar A			E12	Jaguar E	7-PI	
A120	Jaguar A	11-MR		E13	Jaguar E	7-PF	
A121	Jaguar A			E14	Jaguar E	7-PN	Written off 21.7.79
A122	Jaguar A	11-RL		E15	Jaguar E		
A123	Jaguar A	11-RQ		E16	Jaguar E		
A124	Jaguar A	7-IM		E17	Jaguar E		
A125	Jaguar A			E18	Jaguar E	11-RN	
A126	Jaguar A			E19	Jaguar E	7-PN	
A127	Jaguar A	7-PC		E20	Jaguar E	7-PR	
A128	Jaguar A	7-IU		E21	Jaguar E	7-PB	
A129	Jaguar A	11-RP		E22	Jaguar E	339-WK	
A130	Jaguar A			E23	Jaguar E		
A131	Jaguar A	7-IC		E24	Jaguar E	7-PH	
A132	Jaguar A	11-EA	Written off 13.2.82	E25	Jaguar E		
A133	Jaguar A	11-MT		E26	Jaguar E		Written off 26.3.75
A134	Jaguar A		Written off 25.6.82	E27	Jaguar E		
A135	Jaguar A	II-RU		E28	Jaguar E	7-PS	
A136	Jaguar A			E29	Jaguar E	339-WJ	
A137	Jaguar A			E30	Jaguar E	7-PK	Formerly 11-RC
A138	Jaguar A			E31	Jaguar E		
A139	Jaguar A	11-RC		E32	Jaguar E		
A140	Jaguar A			E33	Jaguar E		
A141	Jaguar A	11-RT		E34	Jaguar E		Written off 2.7.75
A142	Jaguar A			E35	Jaguar E	7-PJ	
A143	Jaguar A	11-MH	Written off 10.1.84	E36	Jaguar E	339-WI	
A144	Jaguar A	7-IF		E37	Jaguar E	7-PQ	
A145	Jaguar A	7-1Q		E38	Jaguar E		
A146	Jaguar A	11-RQ	Written off 4.88	E39	Jaguar E		
A147	Jaguar A	1-EB	Written off 5.12.84	E40	Jaguar E		
A148	Jaguar A	7-IL		M-05	Jaguar M		Rochfort for ground instruction
A149	Jaguar A	11-RK					

Glossary

A&AEE	Aeroplane and Armament Evaluation Establishment	DPSA	Deep Penetration Strike Aircraft
AAA	Anti-Aircraft Artillery	DRA	Defence Research Agency
AAM	Air-to-Air Missile	DTEO	Defence Test and Evaluation Organization
ACMI	Air Combat Manoeuvring Instrumentation	ECM	Electronic Countermeasures
ACT	Active Control Technology	EFA	European Fighter Aircraft
AI	Area Interdiction	ETPS	Empire Test Pilots School
AMU	Aircraft Maintenance Unit	FAC	Forward Air Control
ARTEL	Air Portable Reconnaissance Exploitation Laboratory	FAE	*Fuerza Aerea Ecuatoriana*
		FATac	*Force Aériennie Tactique*
ARTF	Alkaline Removable Temporary Finish	FBW	Fly-By-Wire
		FFAR	Folding-fin Aerial Rocket
ASTE	Armament and Systems Testing Establishment	FJTS	Fast Jet Test Squadron
ATAF	Allied Tactical Air Force	FLIR	Forward-Looking Infra-Red
ATLANTIC	Airborne Targeting Low Altitude Thermal Imaging and Cueing	FOD	Foreign Object Damage
		FRA	First Run Attack
ATLIS	Automatic Tracking Laser Illuminating System	GPF	General Purpose Fragmentation
		GPS	Global Positioning System
ATM	Air Task Message	HAL	Hindustan Aeronautics Limited
AWACS	Airbourne Warning and Control System	HAS	Hardened Aircraft Shelter
CAS	Close Air Support	HDD	Head-Down Display
CATac	*Commandement Aérien Tactique*	HEAT	High Explosive Anti-Tank
CBLS	Carrier Bomb Light Stores	HMSS	Helmet Mounted Sighting System
CBU	Cluster Bomb Unit	HOTAS	Hands On Throttle And Stick
CEAM	*Centre d'Experiences Aériennes Militaires*	HSI	Heading Speed Indicator
CEP	Circular Error Probable	HUD	Head Up Display
CEV	*Centre d'Essais en Vol*	HUDWAS	Head-Up Display and Weapons Aiming System
CFS	Central Flying School		
CITAC 339	*Centre d'Instruction Tactique 339*	IAF	Indian Air Force
CKD	Completely Knocked-Down	IAM	Institute of Aviation Medicine
CRL	Common Rail Launcher	IFF	Identification Friend or Foe
DARIN	Display, Avionics, Ranging and Inertial Navigation	IFR	In-Flight Refuelling
DERA	Defence Evaluation and Research Agency	IFREP	In-Flight Report

ILS	Instrument Landing System		
INAS	Inertial Navigation and Attack System		
IP	Initial Point		
IRLS	Infra-Red Linescan System		
JCT	Jaguar Conversion Team		
JMU	Jaguar Maintenance Unit		
JOCU	Jaguar Operational Conversion Unit		
JUPO	Jaguar Upgrade Project Officer		
LIR	Low Infra-Red		
LOROP	Long Range Oblique Photography		
LRMTS	Laser Rangefinder and Marked Target Seeker		
MCDW	Minimum Collateral Damage Weapon		
MFD	Multi-Function Display		
MILES	Multiple Laser Engagement System		
MPCD	Multi-Purpose Colour Display		
MPS	Mission Planning System		
MU	Maintenance Unit		
NAVWASS	Navigation and Weapons Aiming Sub-System		
NBC	Nuclear, Biological and Chemical		
NVG	Night Vision Goggles		
OCU	Operational Conversion Unit		
PBF	Pilot Briefing Facility		
PGM	Precision Guided Munition		
PI	Photographic Interpreter		
PMD	Precision Munitions Delivery		
PODS	Portable Data Store		
RAE	Royal Aircraft Establishment		
RAF	Royal Air Force		
RAFG	Royal Air Force Germany		
RAM	Radar Absorbent Material		
RFMDS	*Red Flag* Measurement and Debriefing System		

RHWR	Radar Homing and Warning Receiver	SEP	Specific Excess Power	TACAN	Tactical Air Navigation
RIC	Reconnaissance Intelligence Centre	SEPECAT	*Société Européenne de Production de l'Avion d'Ecole Combat et*	TERPROM	Terrain Profile Matching
RNorAF	Royal Norwegian Air Force		*d'Appui Tactique*	TIALD	Thermal Imaging Airborne Laser Designation
RWR	Radar Warning Receiver	SOAF	Sultan of Oman's Air Force	TRNS	Terrain Reference Navigation System
SACEUR	Supreme Allied Commander Europe	SOP	Standard Operating Procedure	UOR	Urgent Operational Requirement
SAM	Surface-to-Air Missile	SoTT	School of Technical Training	VIGIL	Vinten Integrated Infra-Red Linescan
SAOEU	Strike/Attack Operational Evaluation Unit	STANEVAL	Standards Evaluation	VOR	VHF Omni-directional Radio Range
SAP	Simulated Attack Profile	SuCAP	Support Combat Air Patrol	WAMS	Weapons Aiming Mode Selector
SARCAP	Search And Rescue Combat Air Patrol	SWAM	Surface Wave Radar Absorbent Material		
SEM	Service Engineering Modifications	TABS	Total Avionics Briefing System		

Index